GO FASTER WORKBOOKS

WITH MICROSOFT EXCEL 2016 A COMPONENT OF OFFICE 365

A guide on how to improve workbook performance in Microsoft Excel 2016

Simon A. Towell

GO FASTER WORKBOOKS

Copyright © 2018 Simon A. Towell

Note: The example workbooks and attached project code modules used throughout this document are available from the www.prodatauk.com website.

First Edition

From the author:

My love of computing began in 1976. At Grammar School I studied BASIC (in an ICL mainframe environment) for an A/S level in Computer Programming and was made prefect in charge of the computer link to the local college. I went on to learn ALGOL, COBOL and FORTRAN as part of my University degree course in Business Operation and Control – which included Cost and Management Accountancy, Operational Research Mathematics and many other business-related subjects.

My degree course also included a year out in industry, working at the T&N Group on IT projects for Turner Brothers (waste control for this poly V belt manufacturer in DMARS), British Industrial Plastics (raw material requirements planning in BASIC), Ferodo (brake lining loading system in DMARS) and at HQ (Stock Control in COBOL) in an IBM mainframe/DEC mini environment.

I was fortunate in my first role post University to be Technical Director of a start-up based near Manchester. Our financial backer paid for us to spend one month in the USA sourcing products; visiting corporations in New York and California (including the Silicon Valley area). I managed to get my first look at the CP/M operating system, UCSD Pascal, the IBM PC being demonstrated at the World Trade Centre and a timely visit to the 7th West Coast Computer Faire in San Francisco.

At the start of my career I also had a spell as a computing teacher/trainer on the UK government Youth Training Scheme at Medway Itec during which time I gained a City & Guilds Teaching in Higher Education Certificate and became a part-time teacher of Adult Education classes in Information Technology.

After the Itec I became Data Processing Manager for a Telemarketing firm using CP/M, Concurrent DOS, dBASE II and FoxBase.

I was also Software Director for a well-established Systems House before going into business with a friend and colleague. During this time, I gained exposure to many xBase languages running on DOS, XENIX and UNIX and was involved in many high-profile projects including work for the MOD, ITN, GEC Avionics and many other household names.

For the next twelve years I was co-owner of a Distributor (selling Fox Software and Advanced Digital Networks ranges of products) supporting a large dealer network (prior to Microsoft purchasing Fox Software). We supplied complete network infrastructures transitioning from Novell to Microsoft Windows Server, when Windows NT was launched. We also became Pegasus Accredited Developers and Resellers, as well as dealers for a number of other products. One of our memory enhancing products for DOS resulted in me being asked to be a guest speaker for Compaq (now part of Hewlett Packard) and as distributors for Fox Software I was asked to speak at the Users Group meetings.

Since 1990 I have specialized in business applications for Chartered Accountants such as the Time Recording/Fees Ledger system (Visual FoxPro and Excel VBA) and Final Accounts Production/iXBRL Tagging solution (Excel VBA). Some of my legacy systems from the early nineties are still in use today.

I have an extensive knowledge of the Microsoft range of products including Office (and its various components), Windows, Windows Server, Exchange & SQL Servers plus Visual Studio (Visual Basic & C#).

From time to time I develop apps for mobile devices in the Windows, IOS and Android marketplaces using Typescript (Javascript) in conjunction with the Ionic Framework (Angular based) and the PouchDB (NoSQL) database.

More recently I have worked on a number of corporate projects including migrations to Office 365 where my knowledge of Excel and VBA was in high demand.

This guide is the culmination of my experiences starting with Microsoft Excel 97 and then developing for all versions up to and including the current release.

DOCUMENT CONVENTIONS

The following are the common typographical conventions used within this document:

Choosing a menu type item from an input device i.e. left-click (mouse), one finger tap (trackpad), press (tablet).

- o Format: Italic text as shown.
- o Example: *click*

Activate a context sensitive pop-up menu.

- o Format: Italic text as shown.
- o Example: *right-click*

Activate an option by selecting a top-level menu item, followed by the option from a pull-down menu.

- o Format: Bold text for each item separate by ->
- o Example: **File->Save**

Identifying tab menu options from ribbon or other type of menu.

- o Format: Bold text (exactly as shown in user interface).
- o Example: **Developer** tab

Shortened term (abbreviation) used throughout document after definition presented in document (also added to glossary).

- o Format: Bold text followed by upper case abbreviation.
- o Example: **Visual Basic for Applications (VBA)**

A setting within the user interface (shown as a shortened form) either in the form of a checkbox or radio button (where only one can option can be selected).

- o Format: Text in quotes followed by ellipsis.
- o Example: "Trust access to the VBA project ..."

A keyboard key combination (keys held down together).

- o Format: Keys separated by the + sign.
- o Example: **CTRL+F8**

SECTIONS

TABLE OF FIGURES

1

INTRODUCTION

1 - INTRODUCTION

Aims

This guide is aimed at users who already have a grasp of the basics but want to enhance their workbooks by:

- o Improving performance.
- o Automating common tasks.
- o Simplifying and reducing clutter.
- o Extending functionality.
- o Maintaining robust and flexible workbook solutions.

Objectives

The key objectives are:

- o Methods for improving, simplifying and extending workbooks using best practices.
- o Coding techniques using the in-built Visual Basic for Applications (VBA) programming language for automating and improving performance.
- o Troubleshooting issues and providing a robust platform for future enhancements to workbook solutions.

Some methodologies are included as a foundation for introducing other alternative or preferred techniques as recommended by the author.

This guide covers only those features identified as being part of the aims and objectives as outlined above and is neither a general user's guide or programmer's guide but instead a document designed to help get the best out of the product.

Note: Some methods as described may be proven to perform better only in a certain set of circumstances i.e. very large workbooks.

The ribbon user interface

In recent versions, the menu user interface was changed with the introduction of the ribbon (Figure 1-1).

Each menu item on the ribbon is activated as a tab page showing options contained in logical groups.

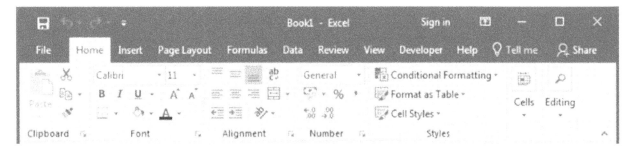

Figure 1-1. The ribbon user interface.

Excel options

On first use, various options may need to be set such as activating developer mode, so that macros can be recorded/edited and enabled to run.

To change the default options, use the **Excel Options** dialog (Figure 1-2).

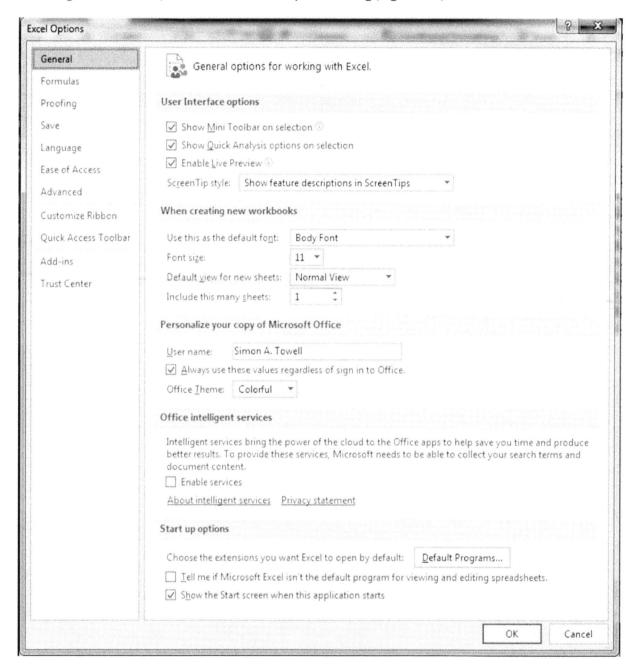

Figure 1-2: Excel Options dialog

To load the **Excel Options** dialog, *click* the **File** tab from the ribbon, then in the left bar *click* **Options**, the last option on the side bar (Figure 1-3).

Figure 1-3: File side bar menu

Note: In this guide selecting options such as **File**->**Options** infers the use of a *click* to choose each option in turn.

The **Excel Options** dialog displays the **General** options by default.

Developer mode

By default, the ribbon does not contain the Developer tab. To activate it, from the **Excel Options** dialog *click* the **Customize Ribbon** tab (Figure 1-4) and then *click* the **Developer** checkbox (it should have a tick alongside it).

Finally *click* the **OK** button to return back to the current worksheet. The **Developer** tab should now be available (Figure 1-5).

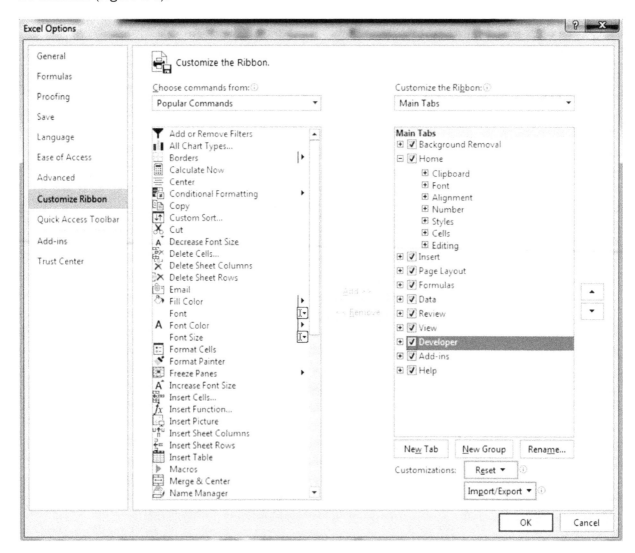

Figure 1-4: Customise ribbon (Developer option)

Figure 1-5: Developer tab

Management options

The **File** menu also displays the **Info** workbook management options (Figure 1-3).

The **Protect Workbook** option (Figure 1-6) can be used to restrict access and/or protect all or parts of the workbook.

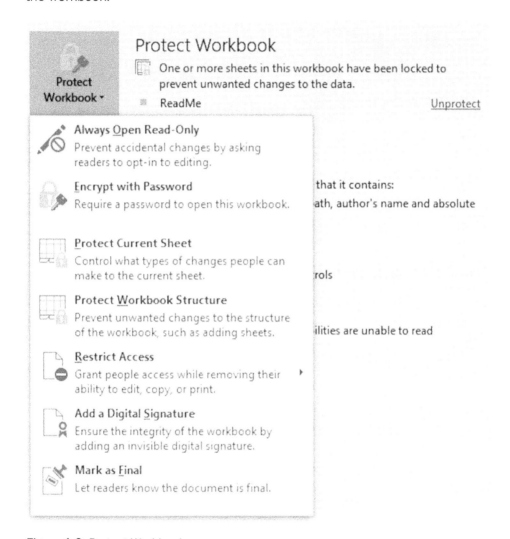

Figure 1-6: Protect Workbook

Below the **Protect Workbook** heading is the current status including details of protected sheets.

Other information relating to the currently open workbook is shown to the right-hand side of the pane including ownership, title, comments, size, dates of creation/modification and other pertinent details.

1 - INTRODUCTION

Click the **Check for Issues** button to highlight potential issues and then choose one of the possible options from the dropdown list (Figure 1-7).

Figure 1-7: Check for Issues

To the right-hand side of the **Check for Issues** button is the **Inspect Workbook** heading detailing the important features of the current workbook.

In Figure 1-8, the **Inspect Document** option checks selected content in the workbook. Select items to inspect and then *click* the **Inspect** button to start the inspection process. After completion of the inspection any items found to have issues are shown with further information, so that appropriate action can be taken if necessary.

Figure 1-8: Document Inspector

There are normally two types of action buttons available after a document inspection:

- o More Info – directs the user to web based information.
- o Remove All – removes the data referenced.

Figure 1-9 shows the **Check Compatibility** feature which can check for compatibility of the current workbook with previous versions, useful when migrating from one version to another or for backward compatibility testing. A dropdown list of versions to check against is available on the **Select versions to show** button. Other options include a checkbox to always **Check compatibility when saving this workbook** and a button which copies the report to an additional sheet named **Compatibility Report**. Links are available to jump to the issue; the **Find** link in the dialog or a **hyperlink** from an option on the **Compatibility Report** worksheet.

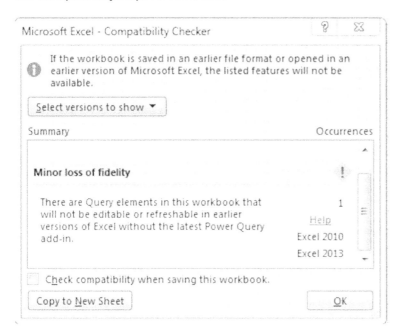

Figure 1-9: Compatibility checker

The **Manage Workbook** option (Figure 1-10) can be used to recover workbooks which may have become corrupted. *Clicking* on the **Recover Unsaved Workbooks** option displays the file dialog from where recoverable files can be opened.

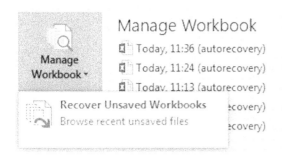

Figure 1-10: Manage Workbook

Macro settings

To use macros in newer versions, save the workbook as an **Excel Macro-Enabled Workbook** and make sure that macros are enabled when it is re-loaded, otherwise a warning message indicating that macros are disabled will be displayed.

To enable macros, *click* the **Developer** tab on the ribbon (once enabled), then *click* the **Macro Security** button in the **Code** group to view the **Macro Settings** options (Figure 1-11) in the **Trust Center** dialog.

An alternative, if the **Developer** tab is disabled is to *click* the **File** tab from the ribbon, then in the left bar *click* **Options** to load the **Excel Options** dialog.

Next *click* the **Trust Center** tab, followed by the **Trust Center Settings...** button and then in the **Trust Center** dialog *click* the **Macro Settings** tab (Figure 1-11).

Click the "Enable all macros ..." option and *tick* the "Trust access to the VBA project ..." box (if unticked) to allow macros will run without hindrance.

Finally *click* the **OK** button to return back to the current worksheet.

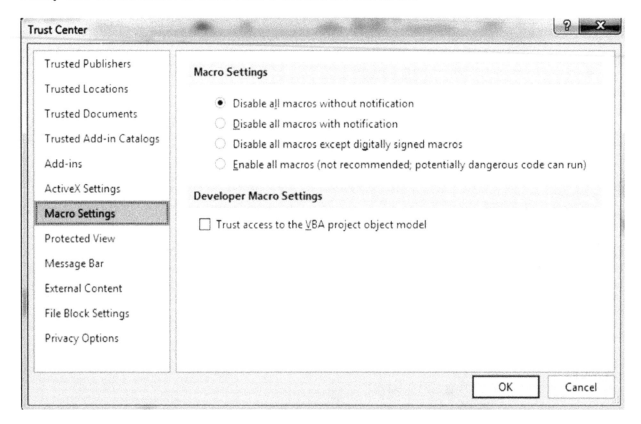

Figure 1-11: Macro Settings

Note: Macros are recorded as sub-routines (without parameters) within VBA code and run from the Macro dialog or via a defined shortcut key combination. User defined functions (which return a value) are added to the list of worksheet functions and available directly within formulas.

Recording a macro

Macros are recorded as a series of key strokes. To record a macro, *click* the **Developer** tab, then *click the* **Record Macro** button in the **Code** group (Figure 1-5), which will display the **Record Macro** dialog (Figure 1-12).

In the dialog, the macro default name can be changed, a shortcut key sequence can be assigned, a description identifying its purpose and a storage location from the following:

- o Personal Macro Workbook
- o New Workbook
- o This Workbook

By default, the macro is stored in the current workbook. The **Personal Macro Workbook** option enables macros to be available every time Excel is loaded (in a hidden workbook).

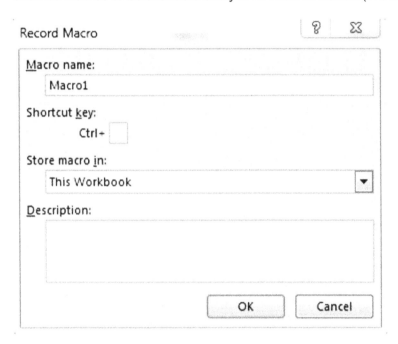

Figure 1-12: Record Macro dialog

Click the **OK** button to create the macro and then immediately start the process of recording keystrokes. Upon completion, *click* the **Stop Recording** button in the **Code** group from the **Developer** tab (Figure 1-5).

2

THE VISUAL BASIC EDITOR

2 - THE VISUAL BASIC EDITOR

The quickest way to view code created by the **Macro Recorder** is to use the **ALT+F11** key combination which loads the **Visual Basic Editor (VBE)** (Figure 2-1) a powerful design, editing and debugging tool also known as an Integrated Development Environment (IDE).

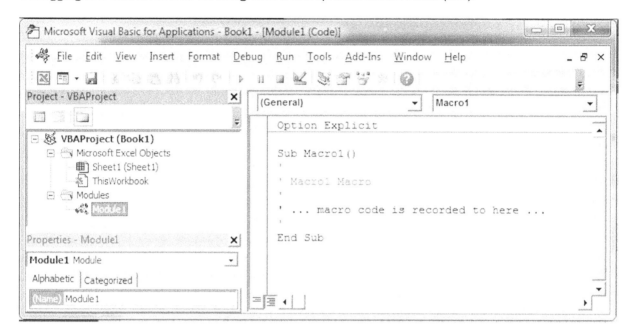

Figure 2-1: Visual Basic Editor

Note: To view the code (for the first time), it may be necessary to expand the **Modules** folder and then *double-click* on **Module1**.

Another way to activate the VBE is to *click* the **Visual Basic** button in the **Code** group from the **Developer** tab (if enabled) on the ribbon.

When a macro is recorded it creates a sub-routine with the code for the named macro contained between **Sub** and **End Sub** statements.

A macro is deemed public by default i.e. available from any module in the project. By prefixing with the word **Private** a sub-routine (or function) is available only in the module in which it was declared and is not listed in the run **Macro** dialog.

An alternative at the global module level is to add the statement **Option Private Module** to prevent a module's contents from being referenced outside its project. An individual macro hidden in this way can still be run from the Macro dialog, by typing the name (if known) and then *click* the **Run** button.

The code created by the macro recorder can be rather verbose. In many cases code can be written directly within the VBE both to do the same task more efficiently and in fewer lines.

To activate a context sensitive pop-up menu either *click* on an option in the main menu at the top of the VBE dialog or *right-click* on an object or code element. Some menu options also have keyboard shortcuts.

Main toolbar

The **Main toolbar** (Figure 2-2) located below the main menu duplicates the most common options found in the various menus.

Figure 2-2: Main toolbar

File menu

The **File** menu (Figure 2-3) is rarely used except for the print option as all the other options are available more conveniently elsewhere within the VBE.

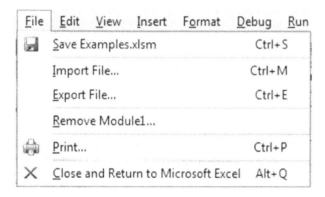

Figure 2-3: File Menu

To **Save** work from within the VBE either *click* the **Save** button in the main toolbar (Figure 2-2) or choose the **File->Save (CTRL+S)** option.

To return to the worksheet *click* the **Excel** button in the main toolbar or choose the **File->Close and Return to Microsoft Excel (ALT+Q)** option.

The **File** menu dropdown has options to **Import File... (CTRL+M)** or **Export File... (CTRL+E)** code objects, which are also available directly via the *right-click* context sensitive menu when an object is selected.

File types which are supported (a text (.txt) file can also be inserted) are as follows:
  o Basic Files (Modules) (.bas)
  o Class Modules (.cls)
  o Forms (.frm)

The **Import** and **Export** options both use the standard file dialog for opening and saving files. The export option defaults to the correct file extension for the file type. When importing files, a filter can be set for a specific file type.

To remove a code object, select the object then either *right-click* to activate the pop-up menu and *click* the option to **Remove** or choose the **File->Remove** option (for the currently selected module or form). A code object being removed can be exported to a file before it is permanently removed, or the option to remove can be cancelled.

VBA Code and/or a **Form Image** can be printed by choosing **File->Print** (**CTRL+P**) which activates the Print dialog (Figure 2-4).

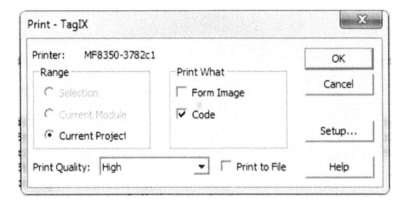

Figure 2-4: Print dialog

A selected block of code can be printed by choosing the **Selection** option (it is unavailable if no code is selected).

Likewise, the currently selected Module can be printed if selected by choosing the **Current Module** option.

The entire project can be printed by choosing the **Current Project** option.

When a form is selected both **form image** and the attached **code** can be printed from the **Print What** section of the **Print** dialog, by ticking the relevant checkbox.

Click the **Setup...** button to activate the **Windows Print Setup** dialog where the printer destination, paper size, paper source and orientation can be changed.

Click the **OK** button to proceed with printing or *click* the **Cancel** button to cancel the operation and close the **Print** dialog.

Edit menu

The **Edit** menu has many standard options such as **Cut** (**CTRL+X**), **Copy** (**CTRL+C**), **Paste** (**CTRL+V**), **Undo** (**CTRL+Z**), **Redo, Clear** (**Del**) and **Select All** (**CTRL+A**), some of which are also available directly from the main toolbar (Figure 2.2).

The Edit menu also has other useful features in the VBE context.

Note: Some toolbars have additional options not shown on the menus. For example, the **Edit** toolbar has the **Comment Block** and **Uncomment Block** options. When coding, these two options are quite useful for commenting or uncommenting large blocks of code.

Figure 2-5: Edit Menu

The **Edit->Find** (**CTRL**+F) dialog (Figure 2-6) provides options to search for a phrase within the **Current Procedure**, **Current Module** and **Current Project**. **Edit->Find Next** (**F3**) continues the search.

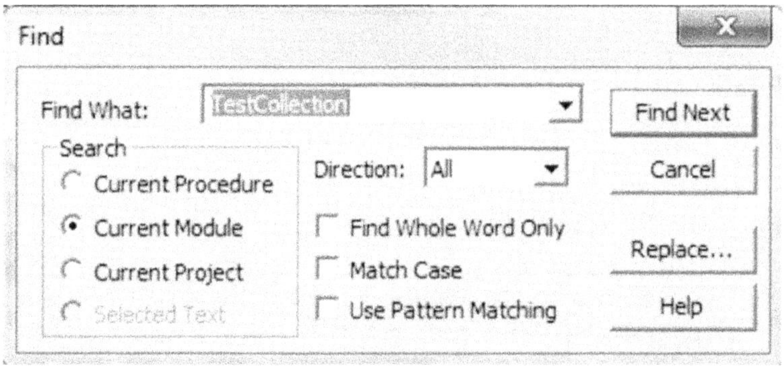

Figure 2-6: Find dialog

The **Edit->Replace** (**CTRL+H**) dialog (Figure 2-7) has the same functionality as the **Edit->Find** option but with the ability to replace the found phrase with a different one for one or more occurrences.

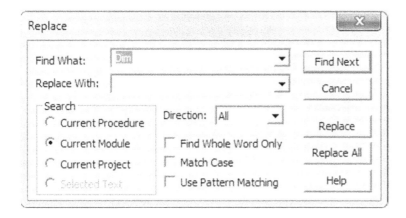

Figure 2-7: Replace dialog

Code layout can be organised using the **Edit->Indent** (**TAB**) and **Edit->Outdent** (**SHIFT+TAB**) options, alternatively using the **TAB** (→|) and **BACKTAB** (|←) keys on the keyboard.

The **Tab Width** used by the tabbing options and the **Auto Indent** setting are configured from the **Tools->Options** dialog.

Other **Edit** options available during coding include:
- o List Properties/Methods
- o List Constants
- o Quick Info
- o Parameter Info
- o Complete Word

To aid in selecting **Properties** or **Methods** for code input the **Edit->List Properties/Methods** (**CTRL+J**) (Figure 2-8) option may prove useful.

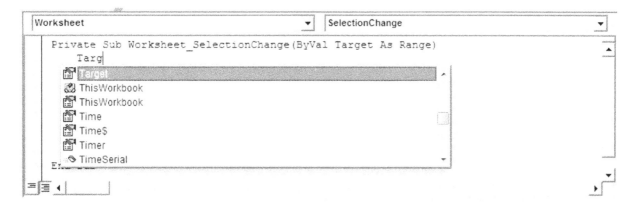

Figure 2-8: List Properties/Methods

Properties and **Methods** matching the characters typed are shown in the popup list, to aid in inputting the correct syntax.

When entering application **Constants,** the **Edit->List Constants** (**CTRL+SHIFT+J**) option (Figure 2-9) may be useful. The list of **Constants** displayed in the popup list are those in-built values available for the current object property.

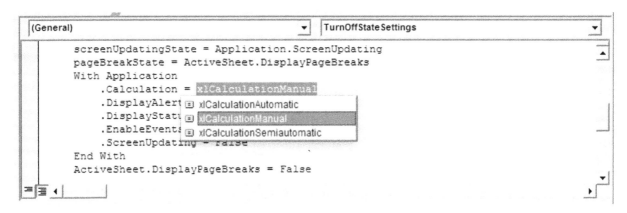

Figure 2-9: List Constants

To assist in coding the **Edit->Quick Info** (**CTRL+ I**) option (Figure 2-10) shows useful information at the current cursor location such as the value if it is a constant, data type if an argument and so on. When the cursor is located over a sub-routine or function name the information contains all of the parameters which are required, to help complete the argument input.

```
(General)                                    ufDAILYRATE

Option Explicit
Private Const itDaysInYear As Integer = 365
Private Const itDaysInLeapYear As Integer = 366

' return daily rate when passed an annual rate and year
Public Function ufDAILYRATE(dbAnnualRate As Double, lnTheYear As Long)
    If (lnTheYear Mod 400) = 0 _
        Or ((lnTheYear Mod 100) <> 0 And (lnTheYear Mod 4) = 0) Then
        ufDAILYRATE = dbAnnualRate / itDaysInLeapYear
    Else
        ufDAILYRATE = dbAnnualRate / itDaysInYear
    End If                           itDaysInYear = 365
End Function
```

Figure 2-10: Quick Info

The **Edit->Parameter Info** (**CTRL+SHIFT+I**) (Figure 2-11) will display the parameters required during input of arguments for a function or sub-routine. The current parameter required is highlighted within the list of parameters. The equivalent information if available when the Quick Info option is used and the cursor is located over the named function or sub-routine.

```
(General)                                    smartRecalc

Public Sub smartRecalc()
    getRecalcTime "SmartRecalc"
End   getRecalcTime(stCalcOption As String)
```

Figure 2-11: Parameter Info

The **Edit->Complete Word** (**CTRL+SPACE**) (Figure 2-12) will help complete the input of statement syntax when only partly known, showing possible matches to the typed code.

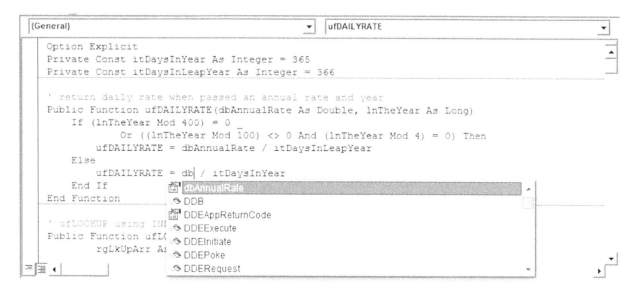

Figure 2-12: Complete Word

Note: When the **Edit->Complete Word** option is selected on a partially input word and there is only one possible word which matches, the word is automatically completed for you.

Bookmarks can be set then used using the **Edit->Bookmarks** options as follows:
  o Toggle Bookmark
  o Next Bookmark
  o Previous Bookmark
  o Clear All Bookmarks

A **bookmark** is displayed in the side margin to the left of the line (Figure 2-13).

Alternatively, display the context sensitive pop-up menu using the *right-click* option and then choose **Toggle->Bookmark**.

Figure 2-13: Bookmark

Note: The side margin is also where a breakpoint can be set when debugging, so it is possible to have both markers present at the same time.

View menu

The **View** menu dropdown contains options to open the various Windows used in the VBE.

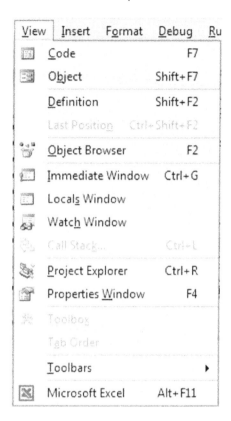

Figure 2-14: View Menu

View->Code (**F7**) displays code for the currently selected object and multiple code windows can be open at the same time (Figure 2-15). Alternatively, use the *right-click* option to display the context sensitive pop-up menu and choose the **Code** option to show an object's code window.

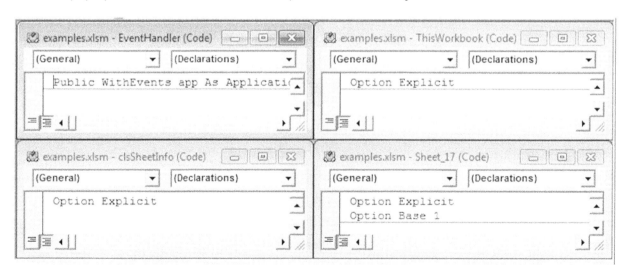

Figure 2-15: Multiple open code windows

The state of the **Code Window** (Figure 2-15) is saved between sessions but individual layout for code windows can be changed manually, or automatically from the **Window** menu.

Windows within the VBE (as with most IDE's) can be configured according to the user's requirements.

When individual code modules are opened they create their own **Code Window** and are sized according to either the restore state or as the only displayed window, if the current window setting is maximized.

Code windows can be arranged in different ways in relation to each other. In Figure 2-15 the code windows are Tiled Horizontally.

A code window can be maximised to fill the entire code window area, displayed as a series of windows using one of the Window menu options or manually managed. When maximised to fill the entire code window area, a *double-click* or *right-click* and then a *click* of the **View Code** option from the context sensitive pop-up menu will replace the current code window with the selected module's code window.

Note: The **Window** menu displays a list of all open code windows (each being an entire module) from which one can be selected. However, it is generally quicker to select the module (*double-click*) from the **Project Explorer**, especially when it is not known if it is already open or not.

Text can be copied between two code windows and to the **Immediate** and **Watch** windows.

Any window can be closed using the **Close** button and the VBE window can be also be closed by the **File**->**Close** (**ALT+Q**) option.

At the top of each code window (Figure 2-16) are two context sensitive dropdown menus.

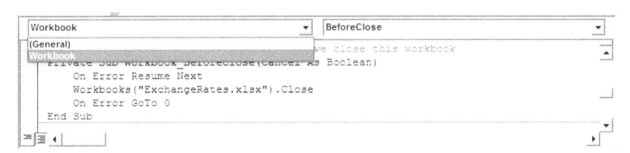

Figure 2-16: Code Window dropdown options

The **left-hand** dropdown will show object specific options. For example, the **ThisWorkbook** object will show **(General)** for generic procedures created in the code window or **Workbook** for available event methods which are then shown in the right-hand dropdown and highlighted in **bold** where used.

Selecting a method in the **right-hand** dropdown will position the cursor to the existing routine with that name or automatically create a sub-routine with that name. For example, selecting **Open** for the first time will create the **Workbook_Open** event method and once created subsequent selections will position the cursor within the named routine.

The **View->Object** (**SHIFT+F7**) option, when available will **activate** the selected object including returning to the selected or current worksheet which is the same as using the **View->Microsoft Excel** (**ALT+F11**) option.

Whilst coding **View->Definition** (**SHIFT+F2**) will re-position the cursor to the definition of a selected item, and the **View->Last Position** (**CTRL+SHIFT+F2**) option will move the cursor to its previous location.

The **View->Object Browser** (**F2**) lists all objects (Figure 2-17) and can be filtered to just the current project; useful in pinpointing the location of an object and its dependencies.

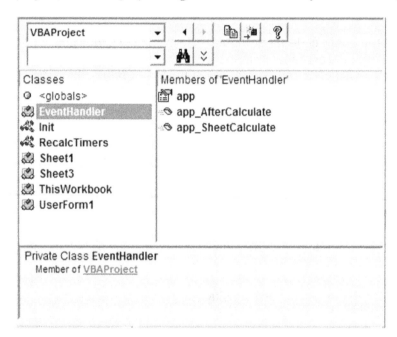

Figure 2-17: Object Browser Window

Once an object has been selected a view of the dependencies is displayed in the preview pane and a description in the bottom pane. *Double-click* on the item selected to open any associated code window and position the cursor to the definition.

View->Immediate (**CTRL+G**) when visible (Figure 2-18) can be used for typing single line VBA statements which are immediately executed. Preceding a statement with the "**?**" symbol prints the result.

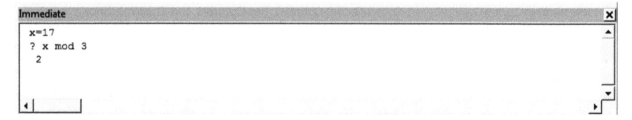

Figure 2-18: Immediate Window

Note: Hovering over a variable when suspending a routine shows its value (Figure 2-19)

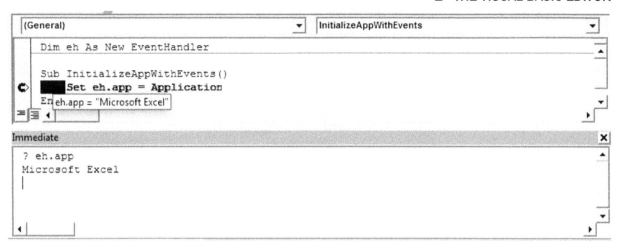

Figure 2-19: Immediate Window Example

View->**Locals Window** when visible (Figure 2-20) shows all the property values of objects and declared variables at runtime when in break mode or navigating the call stack.

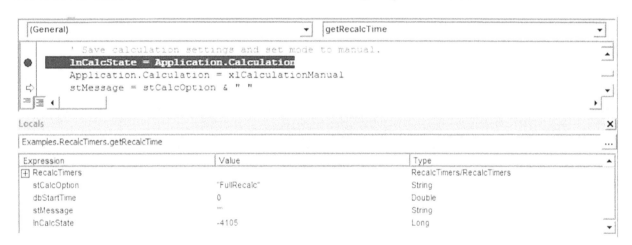

Figure 2-20: Locals Window

In Figure 2-20, breakpoints have been set, so at runtime when the second breakpoint is reached the **Locals Window** shows that **stCalcOption** has a **string** value of **"FullCalc"**. At this point **lnCalcState** which has been declared as type **long** has a value of **-4105** (**Application.Calculation** now has a setting of **xlCalculationManual** which is a value of **-4135**).

The **Locals Window** also shows a header (Figure 2-21) with the current routine name and **...** button which when *clicked* displays the call stack.

Figure 2-21: Locals Window Header

Changing the routine to view in the call stack will change the Locals Window accordingly.

View->**Watch Window** when visible (Figure 2-22) displays any values of declared variables or expressions.

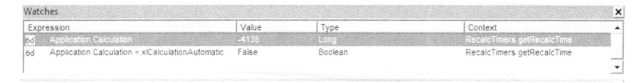

Figure 2-22: Watch Window

One method of adding a **Watch** expression is with the **Debug**->**Add Watch** option. In Figure 2-22 the **Application.Calculation** expression has been added, which shows it is set to manual (value -4135).

In Figure 2-23, the **Immediate Window** is used to verify that **Application.Calculation** is set to **xlCalculationManual** and **InCalcState** was set to **xlCalculationAutomatic** both returning the result **True**.

```
? application.Calculation = xlCalculationManual
True
? lnCalcState = xlCalculationAutomatic
True
```

Figure 2-23: Using the Immediate Window to verify settings

To select a **Watch** expression, click on the **Spectacles** icon. Selecting and then *right-clicking* a **Watch** expression displays the context sensitive pop-up menu (Figure 2-24).

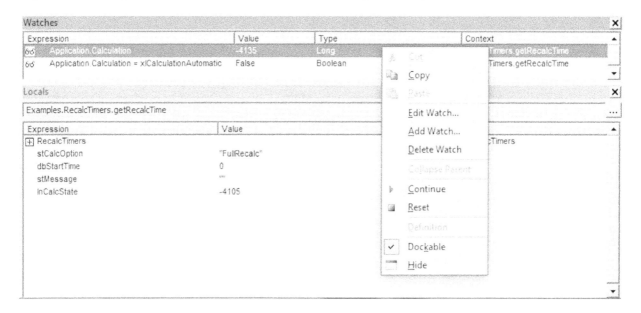

Figure 2-24: Watches context sensitive popup menu

The popup menu has the **Edit Watch**, **Add Watch** and **Delete Watch** options.

Also, options to **Continue** (continuing running the code) and **Reset** (break the code) are available. The **Local** and **Watch Windows** can be changed as follows:

- o Dragged and positioned anywhere on the screen.
- o Columns resized by dragging the column separator (resizing cursor) left or right.
- o Resized.
- o Docked.
- o Closed (Hide).

Unlike properties in the **Locals Window**, **Watches** are retained until they are deleted.

Note: Whilst the **Local Window** variables change according to breakpoint location, the **Watches Window** variables remain static, either displaying a **Value** or the **<Out of context>** message.

The **View->Call Stack** (**CTRL+L**) option (Figure 2-25) is used to view the program call stack when runtime VBA code is paused such as at a breakpoint and when it stops due to an error.

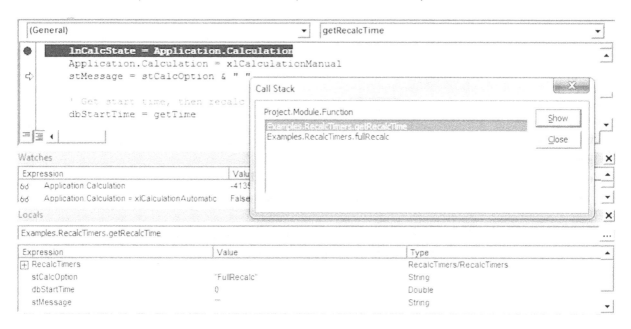

Figure 2-25: Call Stack dialog

In the **Call Stack** dialog *clicking* on an item in the list and then the **Show** button or alternatively *double-clicking* on the item will display the code for that item.

The **View**->**Project Explore**r (**CTRL+R**) window (Figure 2-26) is normally visible by default but can be closed. It shows the Project objects, including sheets, this workbook, modules, class modules and forms. *Double-clicking* an object activates the appropriate window for editing.

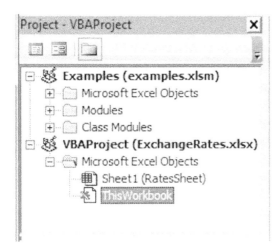

Figure 2-26: Project Explorer Window

The **View**->**Properties** (**F4**) Window (Figure 2-27) is normally visible by default but can be closed. It displays the object properties selected in the **Project Explorer** window which can be changed at design time, although if allowed they may also be changed at runtime.

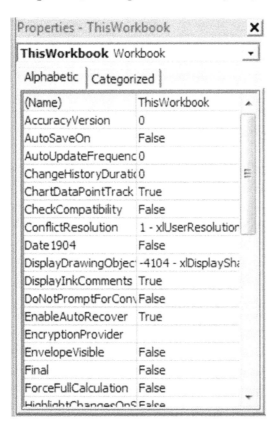

Figure 2-27: Properties Window (for ThisWorkbook selected in Project Explorer)

There are two View menu options specific to form design. The **View**->**Toolbox** option (Figure 2-28) activates the **Toolbox** dialog, from where the **ActiveX** controls can be selected and placed on the form.

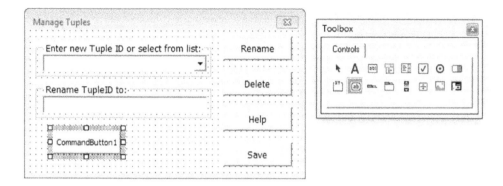

Figure 2-28: Toolbox controls

The **View**->**Tab Order** option (Figure 2-29) manages the sequence the tab key traverses' controls on a form during runtime.

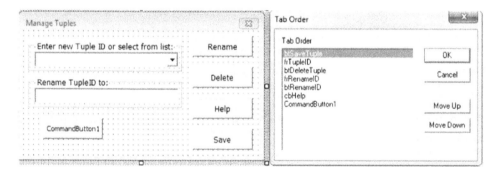

Figure 2-29: Tab Order dialog

Toolbars may open automatically but are also available from either the menu system, the context sensitive pop-up menu (accessed by using *right-click* on a selected item), the customizable toolbar (immediately below the menu bar) or by toggling (*click* in the Code Window left side bar).

Toolbars can be managed from the **View**->**Toolbars** option and can be permanently docked on the main toolbar or kept as a separate window.

The **View**->**Toolbars**->**Customize** dialog also has features to change the "look and feel" of the **Toolbars** and **Commands** within the VBE.

The **View**->**Toolbars** option (Figure 2-30) displays a separate sub-menu of toolbars, those already activated indicated by a tick.

Selecting an already activated toolbar will deactivate it. A newly activated toolbar can be moved to a new position by dragging it and/or docking it on the main menu.

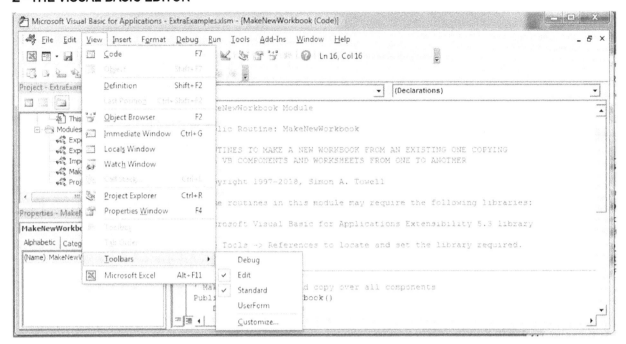

Figure 2-30: Toolbars menu options

Insert menu

The **Insert** menu (Figure 2-31) can also be used to add a new form or module. A new folder is created if this is the first object of its type to be inserted.

Most options on the **Insert** menu are available from the *right-click* context sensitive pop-up menu for the object or currently open code window.

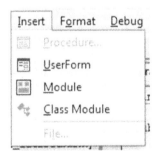

Figure 2-31: Insert Menu

When inside a VBA code window, the **Insert->Procedure** option (Figure 2-32) will activate the **Add Procedure** dialog which assists in the creation of a routine construct.

Within the Add Procedure dialog enter the **Name** of the routine, the **Type**, **Scope** and tick the checkbox if **All Local variables** are declared **as Statics**, then *click* the **OK** button to create or **Cancel** to close.

Figure 2-32: Add Procedure dialog

The **Insert**->**File** option is also available when inside the code window, allowing new code to be added to the current window from an external file.

Format menu

The **Format** menu options (Figure 2-33) are primarily used during **Form** design, with most options also being available from the *right-click* context sensitive pop-up menu. Options on the **Format** menu are made available when a **Form** is visible in the main window.

To select multiple controls to format, keep the **CTRL** key depressed and then *right-click* on each control. Alternatively, controls can be selected by rubber banding i.e. *click* and *drag* a corner of an area and then select to an opposite corner and *release*.

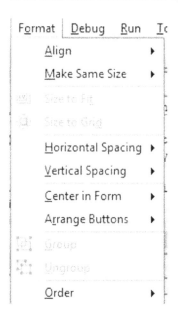

Figure 2-33: Format Menu

Spacing of controls using the various menu options uses the current setting for the form grid as set in the **Options** dialog **General** tab from the **Tools->Options** menu option (Figure 2-34).

Grid Units are set in **Points** and are shown on the form providing the **Show Grid** option is *ticked*. Controls are aligned automatically providing the **Align Controls to Grid** option is also *ticked*.

If controls are grouped, some of the formatting options will not be available.

Note: Controls are grouped by using the **Format->Group** option.

Selecting a group of controls for formatting purposes is a temporary operation, unlike setting them as a group which then always act as a single unit until being ungrouped.

Cut, **Copy**, **Paste** and **Delete** provide the normal operations associated with these options including cloning a control (via Copy & Paste).

Double-clicking a control, loads code associated with the control into the main (code) window.

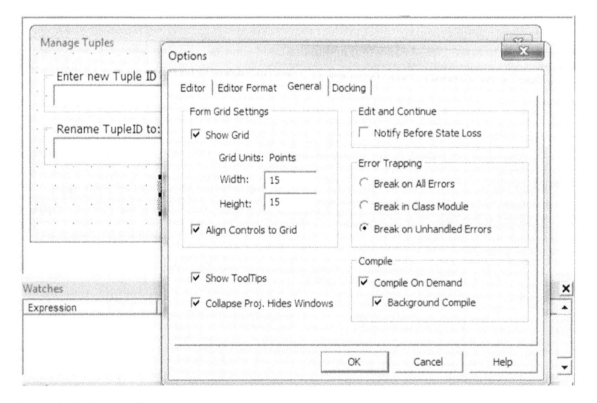

Figure 2-34: Options dialog

Selected controls can be aligned using the **Format**->**Align** options (Figure 2-35).

Both Horizontal (Lefts, Centers, Rights) and Vertical alignment (Tops, Middles, Bottoms) options are available including aligning to the Grid.

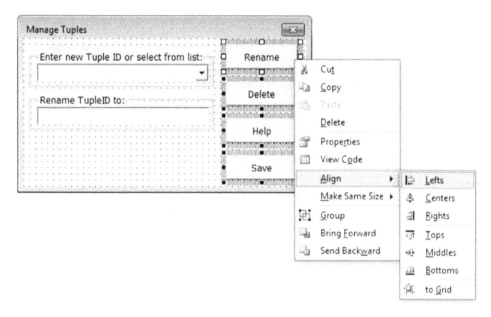

Figure 2-35: Format Align options menu

The **Format**->**Make Same Size** option (Figure 2-36) can be used to resize a selected group of controls, especially useful with Command (button) controls.

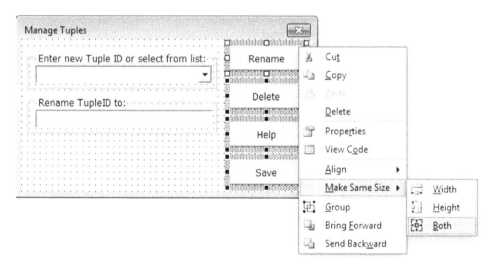

Figure 2-36: Format Make Same Size menu options

The **Format**->**Size to Fit** option resizes a selected control to fit the size of the caption contained within it.

The **Format**->**Size to Grid** option resizes a selected control according to the current grid sizing.

A selected control can be resized by dragging its sizing handles.

The **Format->Horizontal Spacing** menu option (Figure 2-37) manages the spacing between **selected** form controls.

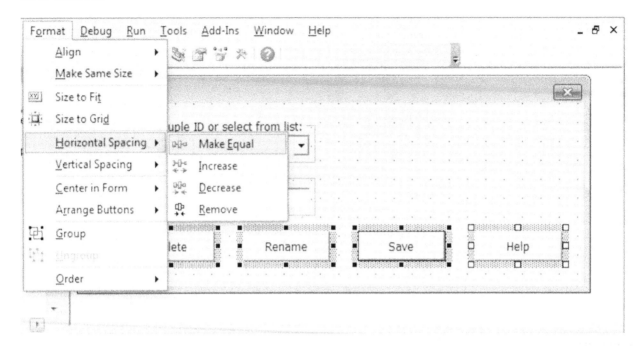

Figure 2-37: Horizontal Spacing options

The **Make Equal** option can be used, to create equal spacing and then adjusted using the **Increase** and **Decrease** options or completely spacing completely removed with the **Remove** option.

The **Format->Vertical Spacing** menu option works in the same fashion as the **Horizontal Spacing** option except for selected vertically spaced controls instead.

Selected controls can be formatted in the centre of the form either **Horizontally** or **Vertically** from the **Format->Center in Form** menu option.

The **Format->Arrange Buttons** menu option can be used to format selected controls either at the **Bottom** or to the **Right** part of the form.

Controls can be selected and then set as a **group**, so they can be managed as a permanent single unit.

To create a group, keep the **CTRL** key depressed and then *right-click* on each control required in the group.

To complete the grouping of controls, *right-click* to activate the pop-up menu, next *click* the **Group** option or use the **Format->Group** option.

To ungroup use the **Format->Ungroup** option or right-click and click the **Ungroup** option from the context sensitive pop-up menu.

The **Format**->**Order** feature (Figure 2-38) is used with controls to re-order them for viewing, such as changing precedence where they overlap.

Bring to Front promotes the selected control to be the first in the order of either all controls or if a sub-element within a group the first in the group.

Send to Back demotes the selected control to be the last in the order of either all controls or if a sub-element within a group the first in the group.

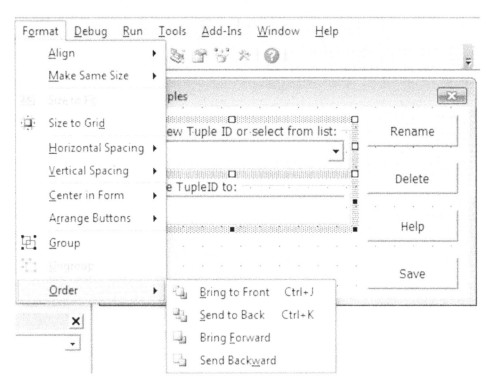

Figure 2-38: Format Order menu options

Bring Forward promotes the control one place up in the order and **Send Backward** demotes the control one place down in the order.

Right-clicking on a selected group of controls enables the **Bring Forward** and **Send Backward** options on the context sensitive pop-up menu.

Note: Formatting options specific to the type of control are only available from the **Properties** window.

Debug menu

The Debug menu (Figure 2-39) has features for compiling and debugging VBA code.

Although VBA does not produce "true" compiled code the VBE does have the **Debug**->**Compile VBAProject** option.

To check whether code has been compiled (or will compile subject to not having syntax errors) *click* **Debug** from the VBE menu and then *click* the **Compile VBAProject** option (if selectable) from the pull-down menu.

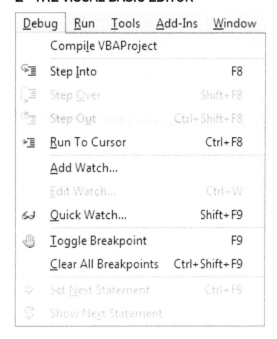

Figure 2-39: Debug Menu

A dimmed (non-selectable) **Compile VBAProject** option indicates that the code has been compiled successfully (so does not need to be executed again in the current environment).

After typing a line of code in VBA and submitting it (by pressing the ENTER key) it is checked for errors and then compiled and stored in an intermediate code format, called Op-code both in the file and in memory. It is the Op-code that is compiled into executable code either at runtime or via the **Compile VBAProject** option and stored as well. Executable code is then further compiled into native code at runtime but this is not stored.

There is potential for code corruption to occur between different states both in the file and in memory.

Note: When the VBA code appears corrupted, try removing the latest line of code, inserting or removing blank lines and re-entering the offending line. Also, re-compile to see if this cures the problem.

It is possible for code to work in one environment but fail in another which may require re-compilation and/or cleaning up of the code.

Note: When opening a workbook containing macros in a newer version of Excel or running on a different operating system, it is advisable to re-compile first to check for any errors and create a clean compilation.

The **Debug->Step Into** (**F8**) option can be used to step into the code at the selected cursor.

Code can be stepped over using the **Debug->Step Over** (**SHIFT+F8**) option and stepped out using the **Debug->Step Out** (**CTRL+SHIFT+F8**) option.

Code can be run up to the current cursor position using the **Debug->Run to Cursor** (**CTRL+F8**) option.

Watch expressions can be added with the **Debug**->**Add Watch** option (Figure 2-40).

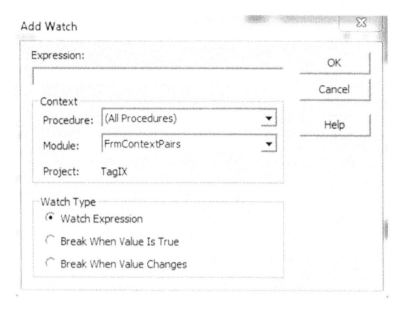

Figure 2-40: Add Watch dialog

Once created the **Debug**->**Edit Watch** (**CTRL+W**) option (Figure 2-41) is available to edit the watch.

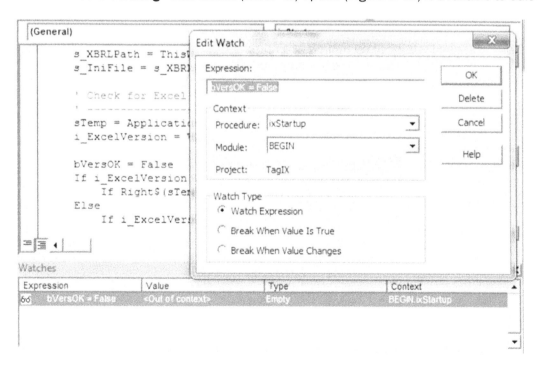

Figure 2-41: Edit Watch dialog

Managing a **Watch Expression** is via the **Watch** dialog. Any valid expression can be added and the result viewed in the **Watch Window**. The **Watch Type** can be set to determine what happens with the expression as follows:

- o Watch Expression – display only
- o Break When Value is True
- o Break When Value Changes

The **Debug->Quick Watch** (**SHIFT+F9**) option (Figure 2-42) can be used to quickly set up a watch based on a valid selected expression which then shows the value in the **Watch Window**.

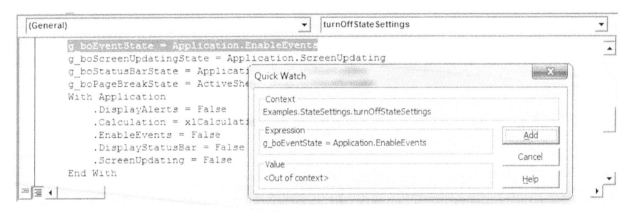

Figure 2-42: Quick Watch dialog

Breakpoints (Figure 2-43) can be toggled on and off in a number of ways, directly with a *click* within the left-hand margin of the **Code Window** on the line required, **Debug->Toggle Breakpoint** (**F9**) or right-click to show the context sensitive pop-up menu, then the **Toggle->Breakpoint** option.

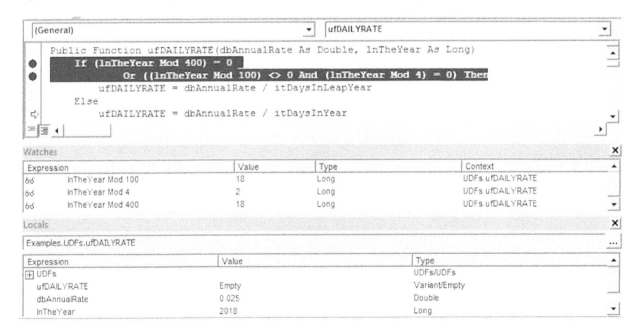

Figure 2-43: Breakpoint example

Once a breakpoint is set it shows as a highlighted line. When at runtime the breakpoint is reached it stops the running code and shows with an arrow and a different colour highlight. When code is suspended both the **Locals** and **Watches Windows** show the various object properties and variable values declared within the VBA code (Figure 2-43).

The **Run** (**F5**) option continues execution, although the other options to control code execution flow can be used for debugging purposes.

All breakpoints can be removed using the **Debug->Clear All Breakpoints** (**CTRL+SHIFT+F9**) option.

Code flow can be changed using the **Debug->Set Next Statement** (**CTRL+F9**).

During code debugging the **Debug->Show Next Statement** returns the cursor to the next statement where the code has been suspended.

Run menu

The **Run** menu (Figure 2-44) has the same options as those on the main toolbar, so either can be used.

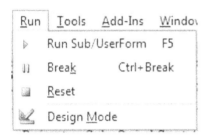

Figure 2-44: Run Menu

A selected user form or sub-routine can be executed using the **Run** (**F5**) button from the **main toolbar** (Figure 2-45). If the cursor is placed anywhere within a sub-routine its code will be executed when the **Run** option is selected.

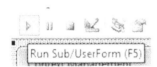

Figure 2-45: Run button

To stop the code for debugging purposes use the **Break** (**CTRL+BREAK**) button (Figure 2-46).

Normally breakpoints would be set for this purpose.

Figure 2-46: Break button

Code can be stopped permanently using the **Reset** button (Figure 2-47).

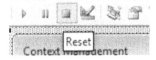

Figure 2-47: Reset button

The **Run**->**Design Mode** option (Figure 2-48) enters design mode which automatically stops all code execution and events are disabled. The associate **Run** menu option changes to **Exit Design Mode** which can then be used to exit design mode, alternatively *click* the main toolbar **Design Mode** button.

Figure 2-48: Design Mode button

For some operations **Design Mode** may not be required, although can be used to stop untoward events occurring whilst editing controls.

Tools menu

The **Tools** menu (Figure 2-49) is used to set default options and properties for the project.

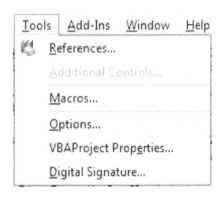

Figure 2-49: Tools Menu

Every project comprises a number of libraries which may add additional features. These can be viewed via the **Tools**->**References** option.

Note: When opening a workbook, the error message **"Cannot find Project or Library"** might occur. This may indicate an incompatible or missing library reference i.e. one used in an earlier version which is no longer available, not required or requires updating.

Another possibility is that the library reference has not yet been added to the current installation, such as the use of a third-party add-on.

Figure 2-50 displays the libraries currently in use for a project known as TagIX. The **Microsoft Windows Common Controls 6.0 (SP6)** is missing. The file and path are shown at the bottom of the References dialog.

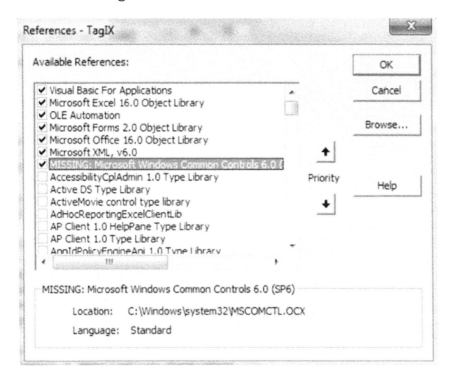

Figure 2-50: References dialog

In the **References** dialog missing references will be shown preceded by the phrase **"MISSING:"**, so can be easily identified and either removed or added, depending on their purpose. Some may have been added in the past and not used or have been superseded by a more up to date version.

To remove the missing reference, *un-tick* the reference and then *click* the **OK** button. Alternatively, locate the missing file and place it in the relevant location (it may require registering with the operating system).

The library references normally included are:
   o Visual Basic for Applications
   o Microsoft Excel 16.0 Object Library
   o OLE Automation
   o Microsoft Office 16.0 Object Library

Note: A common reference which might be listed as being in use is the Microsoft Forms 2.0 Object Library, which is automatically added when inserting a user form within the VBE. This library uses the FM20.DLL file which is located in the \Windows\SysWOW64 folder.

Many object libraries are available and can be added to a project, simply by ticking the reference to it in the References dialog.

Tools->Additional Controls (Figure 2-51) is only available when the **Controls Toolbox** is visible and shows the additional controls which can be added to the toolbox and used on forms.

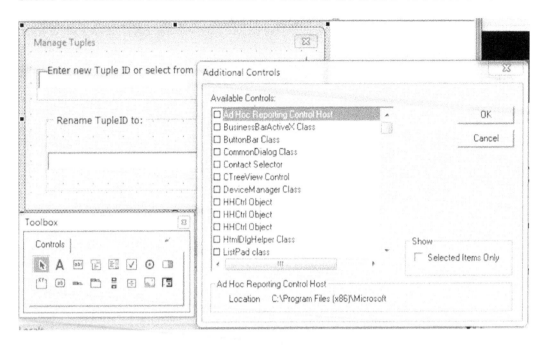

Figure 2-51: Additional Controls dialog

The **Tools->Macros** option shows all macros not defined as private in the **Macros** dialog (Figure 2-52).

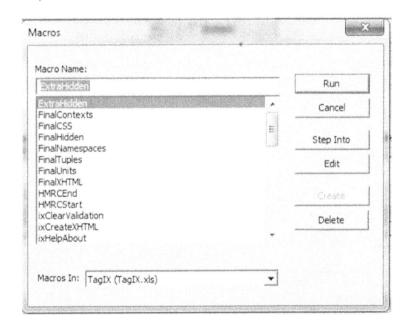

Figure 2-52: Macros dialog

The **Macros** dialog provides an alternative method to run, debug, edit and delete macros.

The **Tools**->**Options** option (Figure 2-53) activates the Options dialog where project settings can be managed.

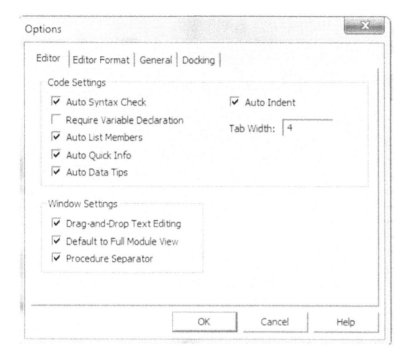

Figure 2-53: Options dialog

Project options are categorised and managed via the tabbed pages as follows:

- o Editor
- o Editor Format
- o General
- o Docking

When the **Require Variable Declaration** is set on the **Editor** tabbed page the **Option Explicit** statement is added as the first line of a newly created module.

Code formatting is controlled by the **Auto Indent** and **Tab Width** features which are set on the **Editor** tabbed page.   The **Tab** key is used to indent code according to the width set on the **Tab Width** option. When pressing the **Enter** key at the end of line the next new line will respect the current indentation setting if the **Auto Indent** feature is set.

Note: If the **Default to Full Module View** option is not set on the **Editor** tabbed page, individual routines can only be viewed by selecting them from the dropdown lists at the top of the code window.

The **Editor Format** tabbed page controls how different types of text used for highlighting within the code window are displayed including font, font size, foreground and background colours. There is also an option to toggle the indicator margin which is normally on by default.

The **General** tabbed page has options useful in form design such as grid spacing, align controls to the grid and whether to show the grid. Other useful settings include compiling on demand and in the background as well as when to break on errors.

2 - THE VISUAL BASIC EDITOR

The **Tools->VBAProject Properties** option (Figure 2-54) activates the **Project Properties** dialog. The name of the project defaults to **VBAProject** but can be renamed, which changes the caption shown as the menu option and there are other options to add a description, attach a help file and set conditional compilation arguments which can be used for debugging using assertions.

The **Protection** tab can be used to protect the project from viewing by assigning a password to it.

Figure 2-54: Project Properties dialog

The **Tools->Digital Signature** option (Figure 2-55) can be used to digitally sign a macro project using a certificate, either from a commercial certificate authority (CA) or by self-signing certification using the Selfcert.exe tool.

Figure 2-55: Digital Signature dialog

Normally a project is only digitally signed once it is complete and ready for distribution, which proves to users that it has not been tampered with since being signed. It is important to obtain a time stamp so that other users can verify the authenticity of the signature if for example it has expired or has been revoked after signing.

Self-signed projects are only trusted by a computer that has the self-signing certificate added to the **Trusted Root Certification** folder in the **Certificates – Current User** store.

The https://msdn.microsoft.com/en-us/library/bb669658.aspx page details the adding of certificates to the **Certificates Store** on the **Client**.

Add-Ins menu

The **Add-Ins** menu (Figure 2-56) in the VBE has one option (Figure 2-57), the **Add-In Manager** which activates a dialog for managing Add-Ins specific to the editor and registered with the operating system.

Figure 2-56: Add-Ins Menu

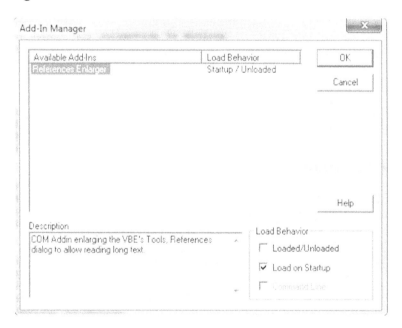

Figure 2-57: Add-In Manager dialog

COM Add-ins such as that shown in Figure 2-57 have to be registered with the host operating system and are supplied as dll files. To **register** a dll a **Command Prompt** is loaded and "**Run As Administrator**" (with administrator privileges) for example:

regsvr32 filename.dll

To **unregister** the dll the **/u** option is supplied after the regsvr32 command.

In the **Tools->References** dialog some library references have the full path truncated. There are third-party VBE add-ins which attempt to correct this problem such as that shown in Figure 2-57, showing the path over two lines or increasing the width of the dialog.

A VBA sub-routine could be coded to list the library references currently in use for the current project.

In Figure 2-58 a routine has been coded to print out a list of library references for all open projects (available in the **ProjectExamples.xlsm** workbook).

The **Microsoft Visual Basic for Applications Extensibility 5.3** library reference is required for the example in Figure 2-58 which can be added via **Tools->References**.

The **Immediate Window** needs to be open to view the output from the **Debug.Print** statements.

```
(General)                                                    listLibraryReferences

' Prints active library information from Tools->References dialog to Immediate Window.
' Note: The standard dialog window may not be wide enough to display full path.

Public Sub listLibraryReferences()
    Dim vbp As VBProject
    Dim rf As Reference
    ' Traverse all open projects and for print each reference in references collection.
    For Each vbp In Application.VBE.VBProjects
        Debug.Print "Project Name: " & vbp.Name
        For Each rf In vbp.References
            Debug.Print "Library Reference: " & rf.Name
            Debug.Print "Path: " & rf.FullPath
        Next rf
        Debug.Print "----------------------------------"
    Next vbp

End Sub
```

Figure 2-58: The listLibraryReferences sub-routine (ProjectInformation module)

The type of output from the sub-routine in Figure 2-58 is shown in Figure 2-59 which prints the Project Name, the Library Reference followed by the Path of that reference.

```
Immediate                                                                    ×
Project Name: Examples
Library Reference: VBA
Path: C:\Program Files (x86)\Common Files\Microsoft Shared\VBA\VBA7.1\VBE7.DLL
Library Reference: Excel
Path: C:\Program Files (x86)\Microsoft Office\Root\Office16\EXCEL.EXE
Library Reference: stdole
Path: C:\Windows\SysWOW64\stdole2.tlb
Library Reference: Office
Path: C:\Program Files (x86)\Common Files\Microsoft Shared\OFFICE16\MSO.DLL
Library Reference: MSForms
Path: C:\Windows\SysWOW64\FM20.DLL
----------------------------------
Project Name: VBAProject
```

Figure 2-59: Library references example output

Window menu

The **Window** menu option (Figure 2-60) has options to rearrange or select the **Code Window** for currently open code modules.

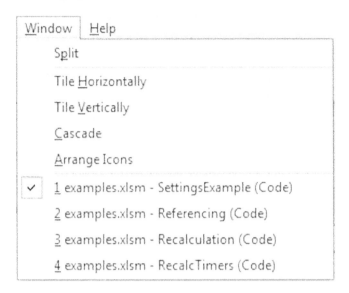

Figure 2-60: Window Menu

The **Window->Split** option only works on the active code window.

Figure 2-61, shows the arrangement of windows from using the **Cascade** option.

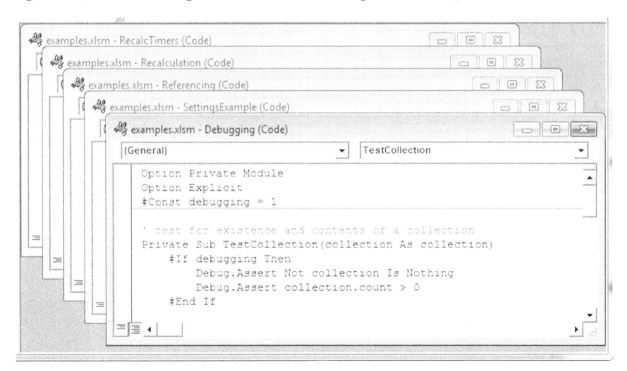

Figure 2-61: Cascaded Windows

Note: Choosing a different **Window** menu option will re-arrange all **Code** windows.

Help menu

The Help Menu options (Figure 2-62) activate VBA help, MSDN on the Web and display details of the current version of VBA.

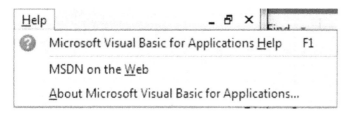

Figure 2-62: Help Menu

3

MACROS AND VBA

3 - MACROS AND VBA

Whilst Macros can be created from recording keystrokes, it is generally better to either edit this code or write code from scratch to make sure the task is executed as efficiently and as reliably as possible.

There are ways to check that the code is working correctly by the use of assertions and conditional compilation features in VBA.

Avoiding use of features that can cause issues

There are many features which should be avoided as they:
- Slow down running of code.
- Can cause runtime errors.

Where possible avoid using the following statements (or any that activate or select the object):
- Select.
- Activate.
- Selection.
- ActiveCell.
- ActiveSheet.
- ActiveWorkbook.

Instead where possible create a reference to objects and then use this reference rather than selecting or activating them.

In many cases, there is no need to select or activate objects before working with them. Objects and ranges can be declared using the **Dim...As** style construct. The **Set** command can then be used to reference the object (such as a workbook, worksheet or range).

Where worksheet values are used repeatedly, it may be better to save them to variables (such as to an array or a collection) manipulate them in memory via the code and then update the worksheet later (if necessary).

In Figure 3-1, **ThisWorkbook** could be referenced and then used throughout VBA code and can be passed as an argument to other sub-routines or functions. In the example a variable named **wb** is used to hold a reference to a **Workbook** object and then a reference is set to **ThisWorkbook**, the workbook which holds the code currently being executed.

Figure 3-1: Creating a reference to ThisWorkbook

Note: The **ActiveWorkbook** (the workbook currently active) may not necessarily be the same as **ThisWorkbook** when more than one workbook is open.

In Figure 3-2, the application, workbooks and worksheets are referenced and used without selecting or activating them as follows:

- o The **app** variable is declared and set to the **Application** object
- o The **wb** variable is declared and then used as a reference in the **For…Each** statement for each **Workbook** in the **app** (Application) **Workbooks** collection. A message box is used to display each workbook name.
- o The **ws** variable is declared for use as a reference in the **For…Each** statement for each **Worksheet** in the **Worksheets** collection in the currently referenced **Workbook** (**wb**).
- o For each worksheet a message box is used to display the worksheet name and its code name.

A **Debug.Print** statement could have been used to direct output to the **Immediate Window**.

```
(General)                                              referencingExample1

Public Sub referencingExample1()
    ' Set up application object.
    Dim app As Application
    Set app = Application

    ' Process each workbook within the collection of workbooks in this application.
    Dim wb As Workbook, ws As Worksheet
    For Each wb In app.Workbooks
        MsgBox "Workbook: " & wb.Name

        ' Process each worksheet within the collection of worksheets in our workbook.
        For Each ws In wb.Worksheets
            MsgBox "Worksheet name: " & ws.Name _
                & "  Code name: " & ws.CodeName
        Next ws
    Next wb
End Sub
```

Figure 3-2: Referencing example 1 (Referencing module)

Note: Setting a reference to the **Application** is not always necessary. The **Workbooks** collection can be referred to directly so the **app.Workbooks** statement is not actually required, instead just **Workbooks** would suffice.

Declarations can be placed anywhere before they are referenced. Some developers recommend they are placed together at the beginning of the routine and in some languages, this is actually a requirement.

Some of the examples are arranged in blocks for readability purposes. Declarations should be placed before they are used in a particular block of code avoiding being placed inside loops. In Figure 3-2, the **Worksheet** declaration is not used until the inner loop but is declared next to the **Workbook** declaration outside and before the nested loops are executed. Notice it has been placed on the same line separated by a comma (**,**) which is allowed but remember to declare it in full i.e. with the "As" part of the statement.

Variable naming should be consistent such as indicating the data or object type and some meaningful name for the task being executed. For example, a filename variable might be **stFileName** where the prefix "**st**" indicates a String and "**FileName**" indicates it is a filename (see the Appendices for more information).

Figure 3-3 shows a method of how to "copy and paste" between worksheets without selecting or activating the workbook, worksheets, cells or using the copy and paste options.

```
(General)                                          ▼   referencingExample2                                 ▼

Public Sub referencingExample2()
    ' Reference the newly added workbook.
    Dim wb As Workbook
    Set wb = Workbooks.Add

    ' Add another worksheet if less than 2.
    If wb.Worksheets.count < 2 Then
        wb.Worksheets.Add After:=Sheets(Sheets.count)
    End If

    ' Reference the two new worksheets.
    Dim ws1 As Worksheet
    Dim ws2 As Worksheet
    Set ws1 = wb.Worksheets(1)
    Set ws2 = wb.Worksheets(2)

    ' Create some example data in worksheet 2.
    ws2.Cells(1, 1) = "Example"

    ' Copy from worksheet 2 to worksheet 1 and add "2".
    ws1.Cells(1, 1).Value2 = ws2.Cells(1, 1).Value2 & "2"

    ' Remove the example workbook
    ' wb.Close savechanges:=False
End Sub
```

Figure 3-3: Referencing example 2 (Referencing module)

In Figure 3-3 a reference is set to a newly added workbook and then an additional worksheet is added to this new workbook, if there are less than two sheets i.e. it has only one sheet.

Next, references are declared and set to the two worksheets, namely the variables **ws1** and **ws2**.

The text "Example" is then added to the second of the two worksheets at row 1, column 1.

Finally, the string value "2" is added to the row1, column 1 value and this is copied to the first worksheet at row 1, column 1.

At no time are any of the referenced objects selected or activated.

Note: The **Value2** property is used to store the information. **Value2** only contains the actual data without any formatting, so aids performance when used to copy to and from cells.

Once a reference is set to a workbook, the reference can be used throughout. In Figure 3-3 the workbook could be closed using the **wb.Close** statement (although it is commented out so that the user can satisfy themselves that this method of referencing does actually work).

A more complicated referencing example is shown in Figure 3-4 where for each open workbook the workbook name is printed to the **Immediate Window** and then for each individual worksheet in the worksheets collection the worksheet name and used range information is printed to the **Immediate Window**.

```
(General)                                              referencingExample3

    Public Sub referencingExample3()

        ' Set up our application.
        Dim app As Application
        Set app = Application

        ' Declare references for a workbook and worksheet.
        Dim wb As Workbook
        Dim ws As Worksheet
        ' Process each workbook within the collection of workbooks.
        For Each wb In app.Workbooks
            Debug.Print "Workbook: " & wb.Name

            ' Process each worksheet in the worksheet collection.
            For Each ws In wb.Worksheets
                Debug.Print "Worksheet name: " & ws.Name _
                    & "  Code name: " & ws.CodeName

                ' Print the used range on the worksheet.
                Debug.Print "Range extends to row: " & _
                    CStr(ws.Cells.Find("*", SearchOrder:=xlByRows, _
                    searchdirection:=xlPrevious).row) _
                    & " to column: " & _
                    CStr(ws.Cells.Find("*", SearchOrder:=xlByColumns, _
                    searchdirection:=xlPrevious).Column)
            Next ws
        Next wb
    End Sub
```

Figure 3-4: Referencing example 3 (Referencing module)

Note: In Figure 3-4, the declaration for workbook and worksheet are handled outside of the two loops on separate lines.

Assertions and conditional compilation

When developing in VBA the interpreter checks each line as it is written and warns of errors when the return key is pressed.

The compiler checks code when the **Debug->Compile VBAProject** option is used and will detect other types of errors, not directly related to any one individual line, for example an **If** statement without a corresponding **End If** statement.

Some errors may only occur at runtime, so error checking should be included to catch and deal with them as they occur. During testing it may be difficult to spot some errors, so methods need to be employed to more easily detect them.

Assertions are one way of debugging internal errors at runtime when testing code and not intended for the user and as such should be not required as part of the runtime code. However, they may be useful for future maintenance and testing, so need to be retained within the code.

To include the actual assertion, the **Debug.Assert** function can be used followed by a **condition** that requires testing. The **#If...Then...#Else...#End If** directive then informs the compiler that this code is not required at runtime.

To facilitate ignoring of code **Conditional Compilation Argument** can be set to use in the directive which is added either from the **Tools**->**VBAProject Properties** dialog (Figure 3-5) or as a **#Const** conditional compiler constant within the VBA code.

In Figure 3-5, **c_debugging = 1** has been set. Any name can be used and the value is set to **0** to **turn off** assertions, any other value such as **1** indicating that assertions are switched **on**.

Figure 3-5: Project Properties dialog

In Figure 3-6, the **testCollection** procedure tests if the collection (**cnExample**) exists and then if it has any items. It will stop execution at any assertion which is **false**. The alternative method to setting **c_debugging = 1** with the **#Const** directive in code is shown in Figure 3-6.

The **createCollection1** sub-routine (Figure 3-6) will stop on the first test as the collection has not yet been set to a new collection, it has only been declared so does not yet exist.

The **createCollection2** sub-routine (Figure 3-6) will stop at the second test as it does exist but does not contain any items.

The **createCollection3** sub-routine (Figure 3-6) passes both tests as one item has been added.

Note: For the declaration of a **collection** the **cn** prefix has been used, thus **cnExample** is defined as a collection. Other prefixes used throughout this document are shown in the **Appendices**.

```
(General)                                    ▼   testCollection                              ▼

    Option Private Module
    Option Explicit
    #Const c_debugging = 1

    ' test for existence and contents of a collection
    Private Sub testCollection(cnExample As collection)
        #If c_debugging Then
            Debug.Assert Not cnExample Is Nothing
            Debug.Assert cnExample.count > 0
        #End If
    End Sub

    ' declare a collection (without declaring as new)
    Sub createCollection1()
        Dim cnExample As collection
        Set cnExample = New collection
        testCollection cnExample
    End Sub

    ' declare and set as a new collection
    Sub createCollection2()
        Dim cnExample As New collection
        testCollection cnExample
    End Sub

    ' declare and set as a new collection with an item
    Sub createCollection3()
        Dim cnExample As New collection
        cnExample.Add "first item"
        testCollection cnExample
    End Sub
```

Figure 3-6: Debugging examples (Debugging module)

Changing the debugging value to 0 ensures the code is ignored in the final version of the project.

The conditional compilation option could be used for other purposes, such as ignoring code only required in specific versions of VBA or the application.

Speeding up object referencing
Code will run faster by optimizing the way VBA resolves object references.

This can be affected by:

o How an ActiveX component has been implemented i.e. in-process or out-of-process server.
o Whether an object reference is early or late bound.

In general, if an ActiveX component has been implemented as a dynamic-link library, it is an in-process server, whereas when part of an executable file it is an out-of-process server.

In-process servers normally run faster since the application does not have to cross process boundaries to use an object's properties, methods and events.

When an object reference has been declared with a specific class it is early-bound and generally will run faster since its attributes are known at compile time.

Late-bound objects use the generic Object class, so cannot determine until run time reference type and other attributes, so may show up errors not known at compile time. However, they have an advantage of negating the need to set a reference to non-default objects in the object library, which makes them more portable.

In figure 3-7, **app1** is early bound, whilst **obApp2** is late bound.

```
(General)                                          ▼   referencingExample3                ▼

    ' Object referencing examples.
  Sub objectReferencing()

      Dim app1 As Excel.Application
      Set app1 = New Excel.Application

      Dim obApp2 As Object
      Set obApp2 = CreateObject("Excel.Application")
```

Figure 3-7: Types of referencing (Referencing module)

Note: The **app** prefix has been used to define a known object type, the **Application** object type. However, **App2** is declared as an ordinary object, hence the use of the **ob** prefix (see Appendices).

A new object can be directly declared as part of the **Dim** statement as in Figure 3-8. Again, **app3** is a known object type where **app** is the prefix.

```
(General)                                          ▼   referencingExample3                ▼

      Dim app3 As New Excel.Application
```

Figure 3-8: Declaration of a new object (Referencing module)

Other techniques to speed up processing

There are various techniques one can use to help speed up processing within VBA code including:

- o   Pass arguments by reference rather than by value.
- o   Declare data types and use those which require less memory such as avoiding variants.
- o   Reduce the frequency of interactions between workbook and VBA code.
- o   For frequently used functions within code avoid using the WorksheetFunction object but instead implement them directly.
- o   Use the **Value2** property of a range to retrieve data from a cell as it is faster than **Value** or **Text**.
- o   Process a range as a single item rather than the individual cells it contains where feasible e.g. assign an array to a range or join ranges into one unit using the **Union** statement.

Controls

Although controls can be added via adding the appropriate library references in the **References** dialog some **Windows Form** controls and **Active-X** controls are automatically made available for use on worksheets.

Additional and custom worksheet ActiveX controls can be added to those already available.

Some controls such as the **Form** are added directly within the VBE and some are only available once added by directly coding them in VBA.

In Figure 3-9, a **TreeView** control has been used on a form with each node having an associated image stored as an item in an image list collection. A variable is declared as type **ListImage** within VBA code, so that the image list collection can be created from a series of images.

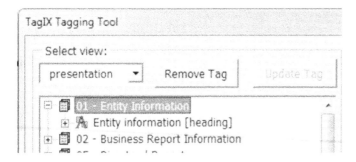

Figure 3-9: TreeView control

Note: The **TreeView** control is available from the **Microsoft Windows Common Controls 6.0 (SP6)** contained in the **MSCOMCTL.OCX** library and stored in **\Windows\SysWOW64** when added.

The **TreeView** control is added via the **Tools->Additional Controls** option (Figure 3-10) and is listed as **Microsoft TreeView Control, version 6.0**.

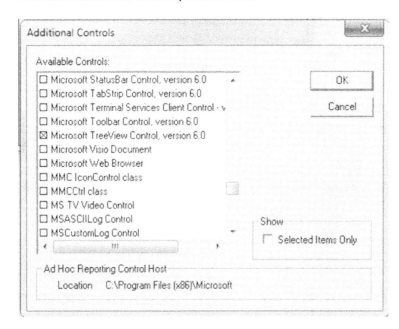

Figure 3-10: Additional Controls dialog

Once added, the **TreeView** control becomes available on the **Toolbox** (Figure 3-11) and can be added to a form.

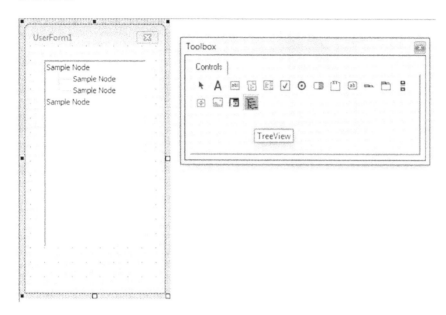

Figure 3-11: Toolbox and TreeView control placed on form

Section 18 of this document shows an example application which uses a **Form** with various controls added within the VBE. The VBA code is attached to the **Form** object and accessible from the Project Explorer.

Worksheet Controls are shown in more detail in **Section 5**. When a control is placed on a worksheet its VBA code is attached to the **Worksheet** object accessible from the Project Explorer.

4

ADD-INS

4 - ADD-INS

Add-ins extend the functionality of the application and can be developed directly by the user or supplied by third parties.

Types of add-in

There are various types of add-ins available. There is an **Add-ins** group from the **Developer** tab (Figure 4-1) on the ribbon with options for:

- o Add-ins (newer style Office Add-ins for Excel)
- o Excel Add-ins including Automation Add-ins
- o COM Add-ins

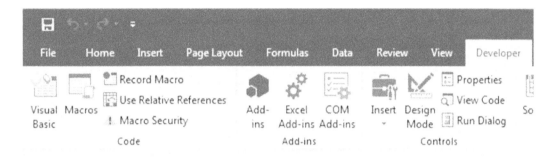

Figure 4-1: Add-ins group on Developer tab

Automation add-ins are available from the **Excel Add-ins** option.

Alternatively, the **Excel Options** dialog has an **Add-ins** page with a **Manage** dropdown (Figure 4-2) which shows the following options:

- o Excel Add-ins
- o COM Add-ins
- o Actions
- o XML Expansion Packs
- o Disabled Items

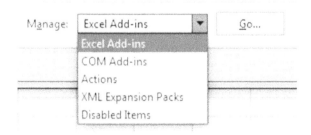

Figure 4-2: Manage dropdown

Choose **File->Options** then *click the* **Add-ins** tab from the **Excel Options** dialog.

Next, on the **Manage** drop-down menu *click* the type of **Add-ins** required and then *click* the **Go...** button.

4 - ADD-INS

The **Add-ins** page (Figure 4-3) displays both the **Active** and **Inactive** Application Add-ins. Selecting an item in the list details relevant information pertaining to that Add-in. Add-ins can be enabled or disabled, added via the **Browse** dialog or via the **Automation Servers** dialog.

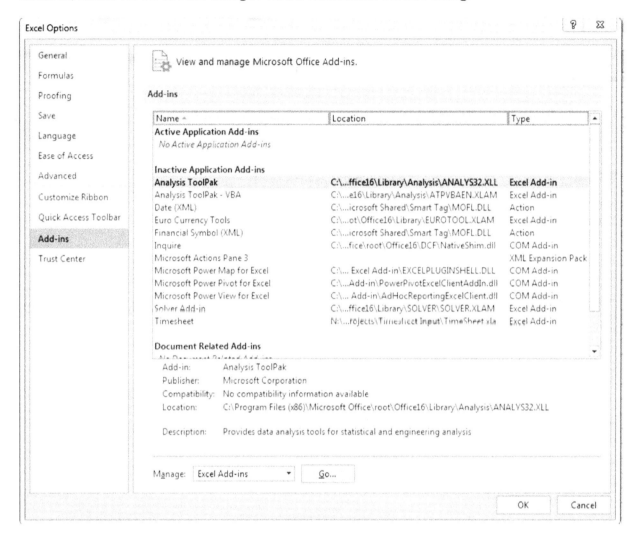

Figure 4-3: Add-ins page

The newer **Office Add-in** category does not involve code hosted on the user's device, instead using Javascript and HTML via the web and totally independent from the application, as well as being cross platform.

The older style **Excel Add-in** option may list add-ins in the dialog created from different sources such as:

  o Directly within VBA.
  o Visual Studio Tools for Office (VSTO).
  o Automation Servers.

An add-in created directly using VBA code is hosted within a workbook which is subsequently saved as an add-in file. When loaded as an add-in the workbook it is hidden from the user. Unless protected, the add-in project and all of its objects are still present and available to the user.

Changing the add-ins **ThisWorkbook** object **IsAddin** property (Figure 4-4) from **True** to **False** will make the workbook visible again and treat it as an ordinary workbook.

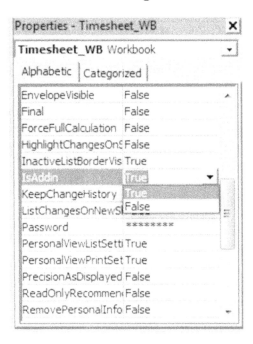

Figure 4-4: IsAddin property

Some of those listed in the **Add-ins** dialog (Figure 4-5) may be built into the application when it was first installed.

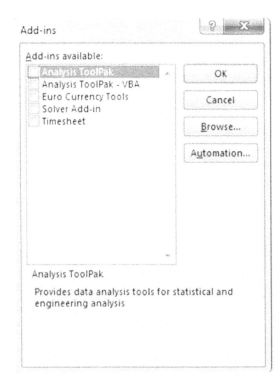

Figure 4-5: Add-ins dialog

Note: When an add-in not listed is added for the first time, a prompt requests confirmation to save it in the default add-ins folder for the user. For add-ins hosted on a network server, it is normal to ignore this request, to ensure that the correct version of the add-in is always loaded.

COM Add-ins

The COM style add-in is used to extend the functionality of the application by automation through objects, events and controls but not directly from cell formulas in worksheets.

A COM Add-in is an in-process COM server (an ActiveX DLL) and must implement the methods of the IDTExtensibility2 interface. A registry entry is created under the following key:

HKEY_CURRENT_USER\Software\Microsoft\Office\Excel\Addins

The COM Add-ins dialog (Figure 4-6) can be used to enable or disable, add or remove add-ins.

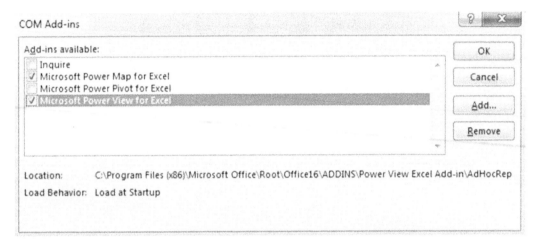

Figure 4-6: COM Add-ins dialog

Note: COM Add-ins loaded as part of the VBE are handled directly by the **Add-Ins Manager** within the VBE.

Automation Add-ins

Automation Add-ins build on COM Add-ins by supporting calling from formulas on worksheets and can be in-process and out-of-process COM servers and implementation of IDTExtensibility2 is optional.

The **Automation Servers** dialog (Figure 4-7) is accessed from the **Excel Add-ins** dialog as a separate **Automation** button.

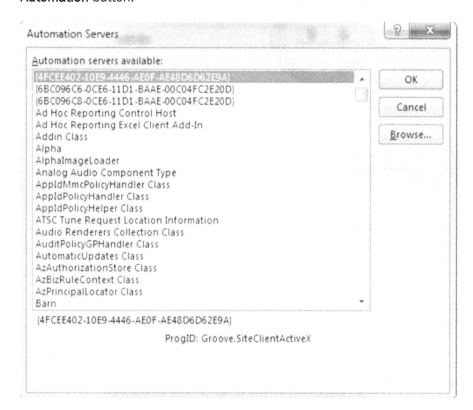

Figure 4-7: Automation Servers dialog

To add an item, select it from the list and *click* the **OK** button. It will then appear within the **Add-Ins** dialog (Figure 4-5) as an available and installed item.

To add externally available **Automation Servers,** click the **Browse...** button and select the new server in the file dialog.

5

WORKSHEET CONTROLS

5 - WORKSHEET CONTROLS

Worksheets can be enhanced by the use of **Controls** such as a button to run a macro, a checkbox to enhance formatting and so on.

To add an existing control to the worksheet, *click* the **Developer** tab, then from the **Controls** group, *click* the **Insert** button.

Next, *click* the control required from the list of available controls (Figure 5-1) and apply to the worksheet at the desired location.

Figure 5-1: Controls list

A control can be resized by dragging its sizing handles (Figure 5-2), moved and associated text edited whilst it is initially activated.

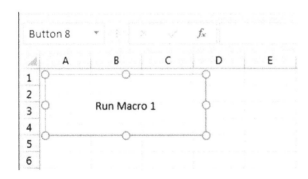

Figure 5-2: Control sizing handles

There are two types of control available, **Form** controls, which are built in and **ActiveX** controls which provide more flexibility but are loaded separately.

5 - WORKSHEET CONTROLS

Additional **ActiveX** controls are available via the **More Controls** option (Figure 5-3).

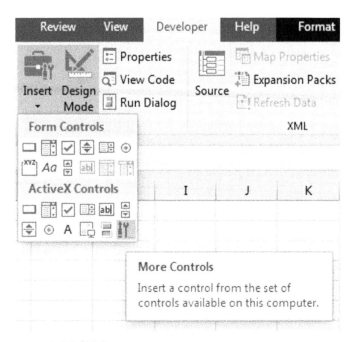

Figure 5-3: More Controls option

To add a control which is not built in select it from the list of controls in the **More Controls** dialog (Figure 5-4) and then *click* the **OK** button.

As with built in controls, the cursor will change (auto fill style), so that the new control can be placed at the desired location on the worksheet.

If the required control is not listed but is available within the operating system the **Register Custom** button is used to locate and add it.

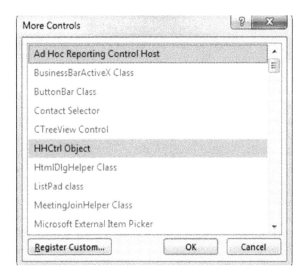

Figure 5-4: More Controls dialog

To edit an **ActiveX** control, *click* the **Developer** tab, then *click* the **Design Mode** button (Figure 5-5) in the **Controls** group.

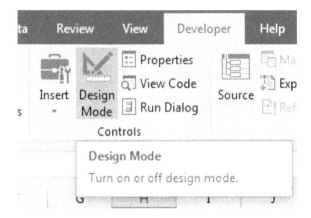

Figure 5-5: Design Mode option

Right-click the control to either resize it or reveal the associated pop-up menu options depending on type, which include:

- o Cut, Copy & Paste (all).
- o Edit Text (Form).
- o Properties (ActiveX).
- o View Code (ActiveX).
- o ActiveX Object - Edit (those with captions).
- o Grouping (all).
- o Order or Bring to Front and Send to Back for a group.
- o Link (Group).
- o Assign Macro... (all).
- o Edit Alt Text... (Group).
- o Set as Default (Group/Shape)
- o Size and Properties... (Group/Shape).
- o Format Shape (Shape).
- o Format Control... (all).

Note: When a control is selected a **Format** tab on the ribbon is made available which provides various **Drawing Tools** some of which are the same as or similar to those provides via the **Format Control** dialog.

Cut, **Copy** and **Paste** provide the normal operations associated with these options including cloning a control (via Copy & Paste).

Edit Text is used to change the caption associated with the control.

Properties activates the ActiveX **Properties** dialog where most of the control's properties can be changed.

View Code opens the VBE so that code can be added for the ActiveX control.

5 - WORKSHEET CONTROLS

The **Object->Edit** option is used to change the text shown as the **caption** on the control. The actual menu option prompt is the name of the ActiveX control e.g. **CommandButton**.

Grouping will activate a sub-menu with options to **Group**, **Regroup** and **Ungroup** controls. Grouping controls enables formatting as if a single unit.

To create a group, keep the **CTRL** key depressed and then *right-click* on each control required in the group. To complete the grouping of controls, *right-click* to activate the pop-up menu, next *click* the **Group** option (Figure 5-6) to display the sub-menu, then *click* the **Group** option.

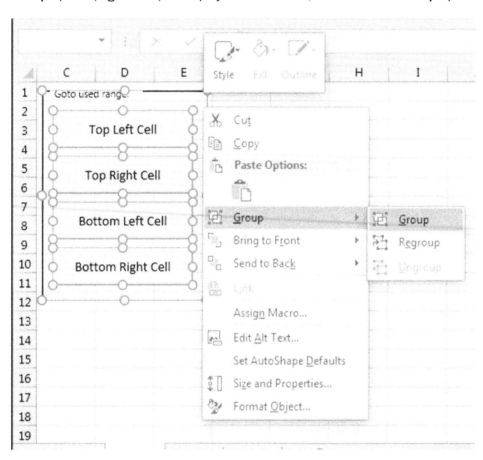

Figure 5-6: Group menu options

Once a group has been created, the context sensitive pop-up menu will update to show the extra group options.

A group of controls can be moved by a *click* and *drag* action when the cursor changes to a "click and drag" type as it is moved over the group of controls providing none of the controls are already selected.

Note: If a **Group Box** type control has been added with other controls contained within it *clicking* the group will select the **Group Box** first. *Right-clicking* on another control thereafter will then select that control for formatting. If a macro has been assigned to a control it will execute if the control is selected with a *click* instead of a *right-click*.

The **Link** option (Figure 5-7) for a group is used to set a **hyperlink** which can load a file or web page, go to a place in the workbook, create a new document or send to an email address.

Once a hyperlink has been attached to a group the pop-up menu is updated with additional options:
- o Edit Link.
- o Open Link.
- o Remove Link.

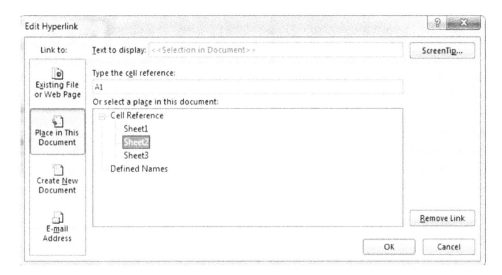

Figure 5-7: Edit Hyperlink dialog

To activate a **hyperlink** which is attached to a group, move the cursor over the group and *click* when it changes to the hand icon.

By adding a **Group Box** (Form Control) it is possible to create framed controls. To select a **Group Box,** move the cursor over its edge and *right-click* when it changes (click and drag cursor).

The **Ungroup** option will remove the grouping, whereas **Regroup** will regroup previously grouped controls.

The **Order** feature is used with controls to re-order them for viewing, such as changing precedence where they overlap and has the following sub-menu options:
- o Bring to Front.
- o Send to Back.
- o Bring Forward.
- o Send Backward.

Bring to Front promotes the selected control to be the first in the order of either all controls or if a sub-element within a group the first in the group.

Send to Back demotes the selected control to be the last in the order of either all controls or if a sub-element within a group the first in the group.

Bring Forward promotes the control one place up in the order and **Send Backward** demotes the control one place down in the order.

5 - WORKSHEET CONTROLS

To assign a macro to a control, *right-click* on the control to reveal the pop-up menu and then click the **Assign Macro** option to activate the **Assign Macro** dialog (Figure 5-8). In the dialog *click* on the macro name to assign and then *click* the **OK** button to complete the process.

An attempt to add a **Button** (Form control) or **Command** (ActiveX control) before any macros have been created causes the **Assign Macro** dialog to be activated but with the **New** button (to create a new macro directly within the VBE by writing VBA code) and the **Record** button (for recording the new macro).

If the **Record** button is *clicked*, the **Record Macro** dialog is activated. *Clicking* the **OK** button, adds the control but no further action is taken.

Figure 5-8: Assign Macro dialog

Note: Sometimes a macro assigned to a Button (Form control) may not work in a workbook from a previous version of Excel. Changing the assignment to the Command (ActiveX control) may resolve the issue.

When adding a new macro for an **Active-X** control such as a **CommandButton** the code is attached to the **Worksheet** object instead of a new standalone module. In Figure 5-9 a Private sub-routine is automatically created for the **CommandButton1 Click** method.

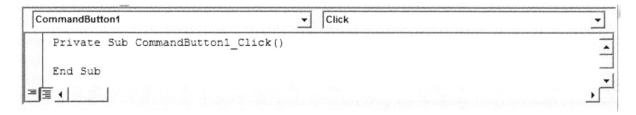

Figure 5-9: New macro assigned to Active-X control

The **Format Control** option activates the **Format Control** dialog (Figure 5-10) which comprises a varying number of tabbed pages, depending on the type of control being formatted.

Figure 5-10: Format Control dialog

The **Format** tab (**Drawing Tools** version - Figure 5-11) is also available when formatting a worksheet control and has the following groups:

- o Insert Shapes.
- o Shape Styles.
- o WordArt Styles.
- o Arrange.
- o Size.

Figure 5-11: Format tab

Some of the options in the **Format** tab groups, may be similar or the same as those available from the *right-click* **Worksheet Control** pop-up menu.

Shapes and the **Text Box** from the **Insert Shapes** group can be combined with other **Drawing Tools** and **Worksheet Controls** to enhance the look of the objects being used.

5 - WORKSHEET CONTROLS

More granular control of the objects is available via the **Selection Pane** option (Figure 5-12) in the **Arrange** group from the **Format** tab on the ribbon.

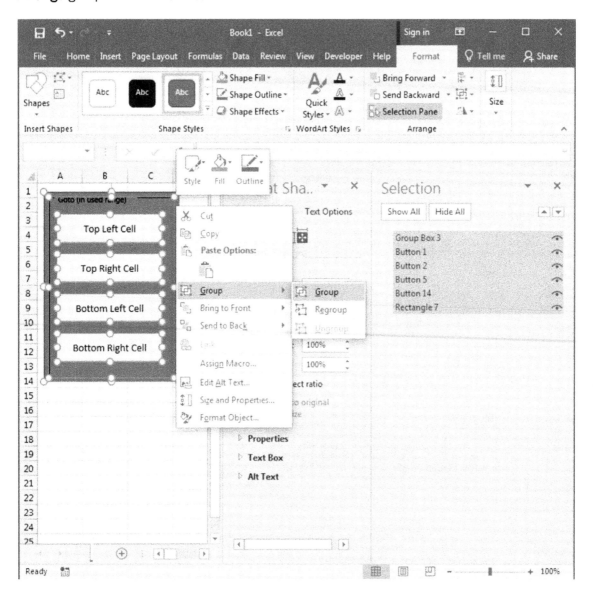

Figure 5-12: Selection pane

The **Format Shape** pane also has more options specific to the properties of the shape.

The example above, combines a **Shape** (Rectangle), **Group Box** (Form Control) and four **Buttons** (Form Controls) as a group.

Note: A Command Button (ActiveX control) has more flexibility than a Button (Form control) including the ability to disable it based on a set of criteria.

6

CONTROLLING CALCULATION MODES

6 - CONTROLLING CALCULATION MODES

Calculation performance can be improved by good design and understanding how the calculation engine works.

Smart recalculation technology ensures that only factors which necessitate a re-evaluation are included in the calculation process. The calculation engine dynamically determines the calculation sequence by creating and then continually revising the calculation chain, so as to optimize future calculations.

Some actions can also trigger a recalculation, so there may be occasions when manual control of this process may be desirable.

Calculation options

Various settings can be changed in the **Calculations options** group from the **Formulas** tab in the **Excel Options** dialog (Figure 6-1).

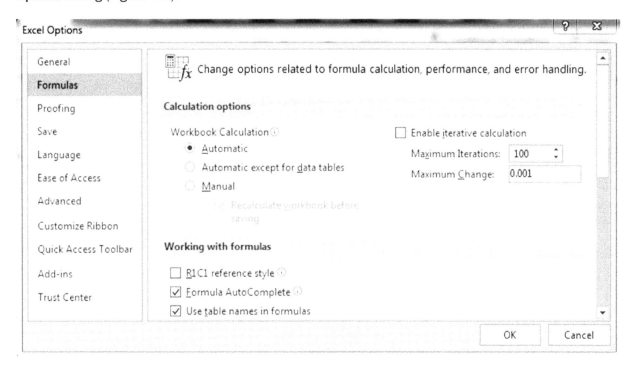

Figure 6-1: Excel Options - Formulas

To activate the **Excel Options** dialog from the ribbon, *click* **File**, then *click* **Options** from the left bar. Most of these options are also available directly from the ribbon from the **Formulas** tab.

More advanced features are available from the **Advanced** tab in the **Excel Options** dialog in the **Formulas** group.

Generally, the default settings are recommended but in special circumstances such as with very large workbooks, other settings may be preferred e.g. turning off automatic recalculation.

Calculation options on the ribbon

Many users default to the automatic calculation method relying on the smart calculation features which have been improving both with newer versions and advances in technology.

The options available directly from the ribbon via the **Formulas** tab are:

- o Automatic (in VBA - **xlCalculationAutomatic** mode).
- o Automatic except for data tables (in VBA - **xlCalculationSemiAutomatic** mode).
- o Manual (in VBA - **xlCalculationManual** mode).

There are also options to recalculate the entire workbook, **Calculate Now** or just the current active sheet, **Calculate Sheet**.

Manual recalculation options

Some users may not be aware of the various shortcut key combinations available to trigger the different methods of recalculation. In manual recalculation mode pressing the **F9** key triggers a **smart recalculation** which only evaluates the following:

- o Changes which require or are flagged as requiring recalculation.
- o Dependencies which require recalculation.
- o Volatile functions and visible conditional formats.

To force a recalculation of all formulas requires the **CTRL+ALT+F9** key combination. To force a full-rebuild which includes all formulas and dependencies use the **SHIFT+CTRL+ALT+F9** key combination. If multiple sheets are selected these can also be recalculated by use of the **SHIFT+F9** key combination.

Volatility and its effect on recalculations

Volatile functions and actions can slow down recalculation, so minimizing volatility to improve the overall user experience is to be encouraged.

Methods which can be employed include:

- o Turning off automatic recalculation during any major changes.
- o Minimizing the use of volatile functions in formulas.
- o Using VBA code to control the recalculation process such as during data entry.

Control the recalculation process via coding

In **VBA**, code can be used to control the recalculation process (Figure 6-2). Selecting **xlCalculationManual** sets the calculation mode to manual.

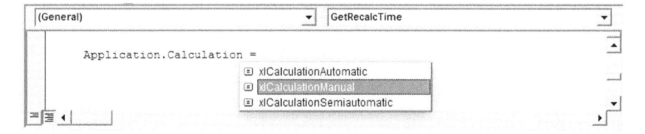

Figure 6-2: Calculation options

It may be necessary to force a recalculation before a workbook is saved (Figure 6-3).

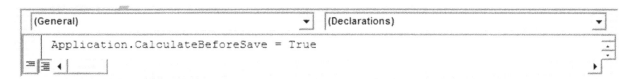

Figure 6-3: Calculate before saving

Interrupting a recalculation using the **CalculationInterruptKey** property may be necessary when the elapsed recalculation time is excessive. This feature can be coded using one of the **XlCalculationInterruptKey** constants (Figure 6-4).

The first two constants will interrupt a calculation whilst **xlNoKey** will disable the feature.

Figure 6-4: Calculation interrupt key

Various VBA methods, properties and events can be used to control the recalculation process including:
- o **AfterCalculate** application event occurs at application level after all calculation activities have completed, including the updating of the calculation state.
- o **Application.CalculateFull** method forces a full recalculation in all open workbooks.
- o **Application.CalculateFullRebuild** method forces a full recalculation including rebuilding dependencies.
- o **Calculate** method will recalculate all open workbooks, a specific worksheet in a workbook or a specified range of cells on a worksheet.
- o **Calculate** event occurs after the worksheet has been recalculated.
- o **CalculateRowMajorOrder** method calculates the range in left to right and top to bottom order but ignoring dependencies.
- o **CalculationState** property returns the calculation state as one of the following **XlCalculationState** constants:
- o **xlCalculating** indicates that calculations are in progress.
- o **xlDone** indicates calculations are complete.
- o **xlPending** indicates that recalculation has been triggered but not yet performed.
- o **CalculationVersion** property can be used to determine if a recalculation is required.
- o **ForceFullCalculation** property returns or sets the specified workbook to forced calculation mode.
- o **SheetCalculate** application event occurs after any worksheet is recalculated or after any changed data is plotted on a chart.

Using calculation application events

The **AfterCalculate** and **SheetCalculate** application events require the creation of an event handler for the **Application** object as follows:

- o Creation of a **class module** with a declaration of an Application object variable.
- o Inclusion within the new class module of specific event handling procedures.
- o Initializing the declared object from the module from where it will be used.

To add a class module (or standard module) *click* the option from the **Insert** drop-down menu (image on the left) or *right-click* any of the current project objects to reveal a pop-up menu (Figure 6-5).

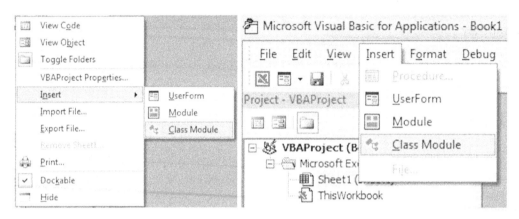

Figure 6-5: Inserting a class module

The **class module** in Figure 6-6 creates an object for handling the events. This is one of the differences between a class module and a standard module. The use of the **WithEvents** keyword with the **app As Application** statement automatically adds event handler methods for the **app** reference.

Figure 6-6: The clsEventHandler class module

A module name can be changed via the **(Name)** property in the **Properties** dialog.

To enable the event handlers within the class module, connect to the declared object (**app** in the example) with the **Application** object from a standard module as per Figure 6-7.

```
(General)                                    (Declarations)

    Public eh As New clsEventHandler

    ' Initialize the With Events event handler.

    Public Sub initializeAppWithEvents()
        Set eh.app = Application
    End Sub
```

Figure 6-7: Event handler coding (EventHandling module)

Once the **initializeAppWithEvents** sub-routine is executed events are trapped when they occur. For example, the routine can be executed from the **Workbook_Open** event as per Figure 6-8 to enable the event handlers coded within the **clsEventHandler** class module.

```
Workbook                                     Open

    Private Sub Workbook_Open()

        ' Initialize the with events event handler.
        initializeAppWithEvents

```

Figure 6-8: The initializeAppWithEvents example (ThisWorkbook object code)

Note: Figure 6-6 shows only two of the many **application events** which can be handled by the coding of an event handler. Other events related to the **Workbook**, **Sheet**, **PivotTable** and **Window** can be handled once the "with events" routine has been configured. There are also the two methods; **initialized** and **terminated** for the class module itself. Other specific methods and properties can be added to a class module for even greater flexibility and power.

Note: Application events occur after workbook events, which in turn occur after worksheet events. Thus, a workbook open event can be handled twice, when the workbook is opened and then again at application level when configured. It is important to remember that some events are only handled at application level.

Finding and minimizing calculation obstructions

VBA code can be used to find instances where calculation obstructions might be occurring, by timing different aspects of the recalculation process. For example, an extremely complex formula might be handled more easily with VBA code, removing the necessity to calculate the values in the worksheet.

A well-designed **user defined function** (UDF) may run much quicker than an equivalent method using worksheet functions in formulas.

Comparisons can be performed of both before and after any changes made to improve the speed of recalculation by employing macros for smart, full, full rebuild, range, range in row major order and worksheet timing.

6 - CONTROLLING CALCULATION MODES

In Figure 6-9 the **getTime** function returns an accurate time, for use when calculating elapsed time (in seconds including decimal fractions) which can then be used in combination with the **elapsedTime** function (Figure 6-10).

To retrieve an accurate time, calls are made to two system functions made available to interrogate the system hardware. The system functions are declared according to their specification, such as the required type and number of parameters. Some functions such as the **getVersion** function require no parameters.

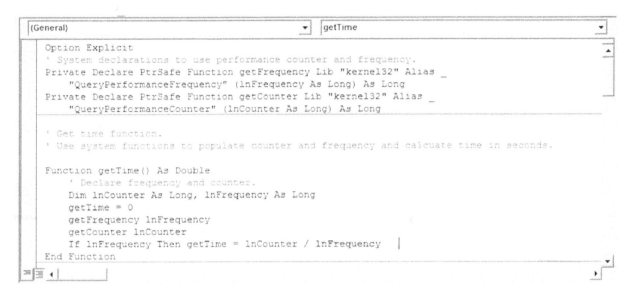

```
(General)                                      getTime

Option Explicit
' System declarations to use performance counter and frequency.
Private Declare PtrSafe Function getFrequency Lib "kernel32" Alias _
    "QueryPerformanceFrequency" (lnFrequency As Long) As Long
Private Declare PtrSafe Function getCounter Lib "kernel32" Alias _
    "QueryPerformanceCounter" (lnCounter As Long) As Long

' Get time function.
' Use system functions to populate counter and frequency and calcuate time in seconds.

Function getTime() As Double
    ' Declare frequency and counter.
    Dim lnCounter As Long, lnFrequency As Long
    getTime = 0
    getFrequency lnFrequency
    getCounter lnCounter
    If lnFrequency Then getTime = lnCounter / lnFrequency
End Function
```

Figure 6-9: The getTime function and required system declarations (RecalcTimers module)

Note: The **QueryPerformanceFrequency** system function retrieves the frequency of the performance-counter, in counts per second which is fixed at system boot and is consistent for all processors. If supported by the hardware it is a high-resolution performance counter. The **QueryPerformanceCounter** system function retrieves the current performance-counter value, in counts and can be used in conjunction with the frequency to get a time in seconds which is highly accurate.

In Figure 6-10 an argument for the start time is passed and then used with another call to the **getTime** function. The difference between the two times is calculated to give the elapsed time in seconds to five decimal places.

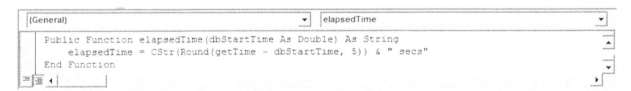

```
(General)                                      elapsedTime

Public Function elapsedTime(dbStartTime As Double) As String
    elapsedTime = CStr(Round(getTime - dbStartTime, 5)) & " secs"
End Function
```

Figure 6-10: The elapsedTime function (RecalcTimers module)

Figure 6-11 shows coding for the different type of calculations which could be timed. Each sub-routine calls the **getRecalcTime** sub-routine with an argument describing the task to perform (Figure 6-12).

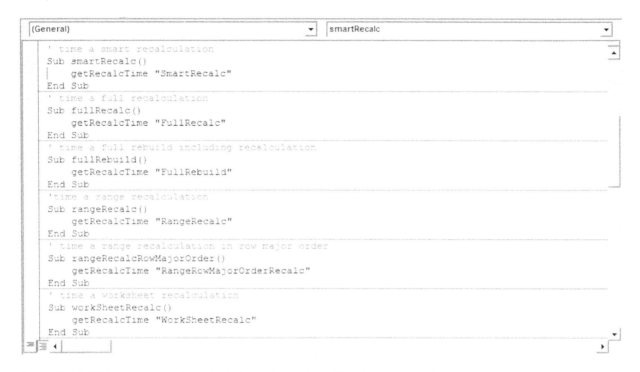

Figure 6-11: Different types of recalculation sub-routines (RecalcTimers module)

Note: The **rangeRecalc** and **rangeRecalcMajorOrderRecalc** routines require a range to be selected before executing. They will then time the calculations for the selected range.

The **worksheetRecalc** routine will time the calculations for the active worksheet.

The output is shown in a message box with the details of the type of calculation and the elapsed time in seconds (or decimal fraction thereof).

Whilst timing the calculation speed is useful, the figures provided may differ slightly for the same test when run multiple times. This is to be expected as the operating system will be running multiple services and applications simultaneously, all of which will require resources to be managed.

Note: Any timings should be compared on the basis of multiple tests both before and after any changes and averages taken to discount outside influences.

Figure 6-12 shows the **getRecalcTime** sub-routine which times the recalculation. The calculation mode is set to manual before proceeding with the routine and set back again at the end.

```
(General)                                    ▼   fullRecalc                                    ▼

    ' Recalculation timer routine.

Private Sub getRecalcTime(stCalcOption As String)
    Dim dbStartTime As Double, stMessage As String, lnCalcState As Long

    On Error GoTo ErrHandler

    ' Save calculation settings and set mode to manual.
    lnCalcState = Application.Calculation
    Application.Calculation = xlCalculationManual
    stMessage = stCalcOption & " "

    ' Get start time, then recalc based on option selected.
    dbStartTime = getTime

    ' Calculate based on selected option.
    Select Case stCalcOption
        Case "SmartRecalc"
            Application.Calculate
        Case "FullRecalc"
            Application.CalculateFull
        Case "FullRebuild"
            Application.CalculateFullRebuild
        Case "RangeRecalc"
            stMessage = stMessage & CStr(Selection.count) & " cells "
            Selection.Calculate
        Case "RangeRowMajorOrderRecalc"
            stMessage = stMessage & CStr(Selection.count) & " cells "
            Selection.CalculateRowMajorOrder
        Case "WorkSheetRecalc"
            stMessage = stMessage & ActiveSheet.Name & " "
            ActiveSheet.Calculate
    End Select
    ' Calculate time taken.
    MsgBox stMessage & "in " & elapsedTime(dbStartTime)
    GoTo Finish
ErrHandler:
    MsgBox "Cannot recalculate " & stMessage
Finish:
    ' Reset calculation settings.
    On Error GoTo 0
    Application.Calculation = lnCalcState
End Sub
```

Figure 6-12: The getRecalcTime sub-routine (RecalcTimers module)

7

BETTER DATA HANDLING

7 - BETTER DATA HANDLING

Whilst newer versions have worksheets capable of holding increasingly more rows and columns, this expansion also has inherent disadvantages.

When adding rows and columns to existing content try to design formulas that automatically refer to the new data area. Whilst large ranges in formulas can be used to achieve this, this can cause inefficient calculations and becomes difficult to maintain.

Most users logically create new worksheets (or even new workbooks) for different types of data and whilst this creates an organized business process, it may in itself introduce performance problems. It is not difficult to fathom that a single worksheet containing different types of data can actually be faster to process than other types of design.

One should be aware that whatever design is chosen, there is always a **used range** for every worksheet, the range perceived as that in use. It is this area that is saved as part of the workbook, so keeping this range to a minimum will help keep the file size as small as possible.

Another aspect is that some functions are **volatile** in that they and any other cells dependent on them are recalculated every time a recalculation takes place, even if no changes were made to the cells containing such functions. Other actions may trigger a recalculation, so it is not always obvious and some would say avoid them at all costs! Whilst, some volatile functions are fast, others are not, so it is important to take such factors into account in the design process.

There are also techniques one can employ to make the design process simpler, more flexible and improve performance.

Minimize the used range

Various editing and formatting operations may extend the **used range** beyond that currently considered to be in use which can also affect performance. **CTRL+END** can be used to check the visible **used range** and remedial action, such as deleting the extra rows and/or columns beyond the required range may be necessary.

VBA code can also be written to detect and provide remedial action to reduce the **used range** by removing unnecessary data and formatting.

Note: Whilst there are various methods available to check for the **used range**, some may provide inaccurate information. For example, a blank row may actually contain data which is not visible and therefore may be considered part of the **used range**, even if not actually being used.

Structured table references

Using **Structured Table References**, which automatically expand and contract has the advantage of:
- o Fewer performance issues.
- o Ability to have multiple tables on a single worksheet.
- o Embedded formulas in the table also expand and contract with the data.
- o Formulas use named references which are far easier to read and comprehend.
- o Automatic headers, filters and sorting features.
- o Slicers can easily be added for extra versatility.

7 - BETTER DATA HANDLING

Figure 7-1 shows a summing a column of sales figures using table referencing.

Figure 7-1: SUM example

The **=SUM(Table1[Sales]])** formula sums the **Sales** column of **Table1**.

A table is created (the default is to use table headers) by selecting a cell within the desired table range and then using the **CTRL+T** key combination or via the **Insert->Table** option from the ribbon menu. Both options display the **Create Table** dialog as shown in Figure 7-2.

Figure 7-2: Create Table dialog

Next, select the range and *click* the **OK** button to create the table. Once created the **Design** option (Figure 7-3) on the ribbon menu can be used to maintain the table including changing the **Table Name**.

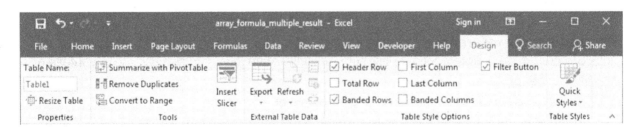

Figure 7-3: Design tab

Note: Using **Table Headers** during the creation process automatically provides a structured reference for each column which can then be used within worksheet functions.

The visual appearance and attributes of a table are configurable from the ribbon or via the *right-click* context sensitive menu.

From the *right-click* context sensitive menu are options particular to tables including:
- o Inserting table rows and columns.
- o Deleting table rows and columns.
- o Selecting table rows and columns.
- o Sorting.
- o Filtering.

On the ribbon there is an option in the **Table Style Options** group to create a **Total Row** which automates the process of providing this common requirement and some options which are ticked by default.

The **Design->Insert Slicer** option is particularly useful in providing the user with quick filtering and an indication of current filtering state.

Design->Resize Table activates a dialog where the table size can be changed (Figure 7-4).

Figure 7-4: Resize Table dialog

Table references and their use in formulas

The ability to use named table references when creating a formula is a very useful feature. It makes the formula easy to write and understand as well as being common across different rows in the same column.

Although the table name defaults to **Table{n}** where **n** is the next unused number in numerical sequence, the name can be changed, thus **Table1** could be renamed to something more meaningful.

Special areas (or ranges) of the table have their own references as follows:
- o [#Data] – data only
- o [#Headers] – column headers
- o [#Totals] - totals
- o [#All] – all areas
- o @ – this row

The column headings automatically become table references for the columns and can be used in formulas.

If the table named **Medals** was a sports medals table with columns for **Position**, **Country**, **Gold**, **Silver**, **Bronze** and **Points** the references could be used in formulas with relative ease as follows:

- o **=Medals[Gold]** would reference a single column and only include the data.
- o **=Medals[@]** would reference the full row.
- o **=Medals[@[Position]]** would reference a single cell in the data.
- o **=Medals[#Headers]** would reference only the header row.
- o **=Medals[[#Headers],[#Data]]** would reference both the header row and data.
- o **=Medals[#All]** would reference all areas including all rows; header, data and total.

In Figure 7-5 assuming that defined names for **Gold**, **Silver** and **Bronze** were created then the formula would become **=[@Gold]*Gold+[@Silver]*Silver+[@Bronze]*Bronze** and this would be copied to every data cell in the **Points** column.

A formula to show the correct **Position** requires considering the relative table position within the worksheet. There are two possible formulas:

1. =ROW()-ROW(Medals[#Headers])
2. =ROW()-ROW(Medals)+1

The chosen formula can be entered to the first **Position** cell and then copied down for all cells.

Note: Method 1 takes the current row less the row where the headers start whereas method 2 takes the current row less the position where the data in the table starts which requires an additional value of one being added to get the correct position.

=[@Gold]*Gold+[@Silver]*Silver+[@Bronze]*Bronze

F	G	H	I	J	K
				Gold	5
				Silver	3
				Bronze	1

Position ▾	Country ▾	Gold ↵	Silver ↵	Bronze ▾	Points ↵
1	USA	12	5	8	83
2	Russia	9	5	3	63
3	Germany	4	1	3	26
4	GB	2	3	4	23
5	Australia	2	1	3	16
6	Italy	1	3	2	16
7	Spain	0	2	1	7
8	Canada	0	1	4	7
9	France	0	1	2	5

Figure 7-5: Medals table (InternalReferencing worksheet)

In Figure 7-5 the **Medals** table requires sorting by the **Points** total (in descending order) and then for ties by number of **Gold**, **Silver** and **Bronze**. One method which could be used is to write code for the **Worksheet_Change** event as in Figure 7-6.

The code works as follows:

- o Create a range using the **Union** statement to combine the **Medals** table's **Gold**, **Silver** and **Bronze** columns with the defined names for points awarded for **Gold**, **Silver** and **Bronze**.
- o If the **Target** range (cell just changed) intersects with the **combined** range sort the **Medals** table by the columns in order; **Points**, **Gold**, **Silver** and **Bronze**.

```
Worksheet                                    ▼   Change                                              ▼

    Private Sub Worksheet_Change(ByVal Target As Range)
        Dim rg As Range
        Set rg = Union(Me.ListObjects("Medals").ListColumns(3).DataBodyRange.Resize(, 3), _
            Range("Gold"), Range("Silver"), Range("Bronze"))

        If Not Intersect(Target, rg) Is Nothing Then
            With Me.ListObjects("Medals").Sort
                .SortFields.Clear
                .SortFields.Add Key:=Range("Medals[[#All],[Points]]"), SortOn:= _
                    xlSortOnValues, Order:=xlDescending, DataOption:=xlSortNormal
                .SortFields.Add Key:=Range("Medals[[#All],[Gold]]"), SortOn:= _
                    xlSortOnValues, Order:=xlDescending, DataOption:=xlSortNormal
                .SortFields.Add Key:=Range("Medals[[#All],[Silver]]"), SortOn:= _
                    xlSortOnValues, Order:=xlDescending, DataOption:=xlSortNormal
                .SortFields.Add Key:=Range("Medals[[#All],[Bronze]]"), SortOn:= _
                    xlSortOnValues, Order:=xlDescending, DataOption:=xlSortNormal
                .Header = xlYes
                .Apply
            End With
        End If
    End Sub
```

Figure 7-6: Worksheet_Change event handler (InternalReferencing worksheet code)

Table references used in code

Structured table references are also available in code. In Figure 7-6, the **Medals** table is shown as a **ListObject** being one member of the **ListObjects** collection on the current worksheet.

With any collection the **count** property will indicate how many objects there are in the collection.

For example, in Figure 7-6 the **ListColumns** collection contains all the columns in a table, just one column being available via the **ListColumn** property of the **ListObject**. Similarly, there is the **ListRows** collection with one row being a **ListRow** object.

Since tables have distinctly identifiable areas these are also available as follows:

- o HeaderRowRange – the header row.
- o DataBodyRange - the data area.
- o TotalsRowRange – the totals row.

Tables or areas of a table can also be resized (Resize property), added to (Add property) and deleted (Delete property).

Defined names

Defined names are especially useful for creating a unique reference to an individual value although can be used for any kind or range.

A defined name can be added in the following ways:

- By inputting a reference in the Name box to the left of the formula bar (Figure 7-7).
- From the Defined Names group in the Formulas tab on the ribbon as follows:
  - Define Name option (Figure 7-8).
  - Name Manager dialog (Figure 7-9).
  - Create from Selection option.

To create a defined name with **global scope**, simply select a range and then type the defined name in the **Name** box to the left of the formula bar or via one of the **Defined Names** options available from the **Formulas** tab on the ribbon.

Note: Once the **scope** has been set for a defined name it cannot be amended. To change the scope requires deleting the defined name and re-creating it. However, the name itself can be changed.

The defined name **Region** is applied to the range **A2:A7** in Figure 7-7.

Region				f_x	Europe		
	A	B	C	D	E	F	G
1	Region	Area	Country	Code	Rate	Value (£)	Sterling (£)
2	Europe	1	UK	GBP	1.0000	352,156	352,156.00
3	Americas	1	US	USD	1.4065	250,321	177,974.40
4	Europe	2	Eurozone	EUR	1.1465	2,345,012	2,045,365.90
5	Americas	2	Brazil	BRL	4.6240	647,890	140,114.62
6	Americas	1	Canada	CAD	1.8224	403,343	221,325.18
7	Europe	3	Switzerland	CHF	1.3420	68,986	51,405.37

Figure 7-7: Defined name example (WorldwideSales worksheet)

The **scope** of a defined name can be set for the entire workbook or limited to a worksheet using the Define Name or Name Manager dialogs.

Note: When creating a formula, if unsure of the correct name to use, the **Formulas->Use in Formula** option from the ribbon displays a list of all defined names from where one can be selected.

When using **Defined Names** dependent ranges are automatically updated for insertions and deletions within the defined range. However, if a cell is appended after the last item in the range, this value is not included in any calculations. One method to avoid this issue is to always have a blank cell extending beyond the range as part of the defined name and inserting before this cell.

Another method is to use **OFFSET** and **COUNTA** functions in the definition of a named range so that the area that is referred to by the named range dynamically expands and contracts. The formula automatically includes new entries as they are appended.

Figure 7-8 shows the use of **OFFSET** and **COUNTA** functions in defining a dynamic range.

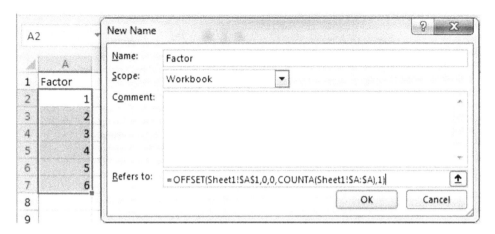

Figure 7-8: New Name dialog

OFFSET is a **volatile** function, so performance may be affected as it is always recalculated.   An alternative method would be to split the formula and have a separate cell to contain the dynamic range part of the formula or use a macro, which could be hidden if required.

To manage defined names, use the **Name Manager** dialog (Figure 7-9) from the **Formulas** tab on the ribbon.

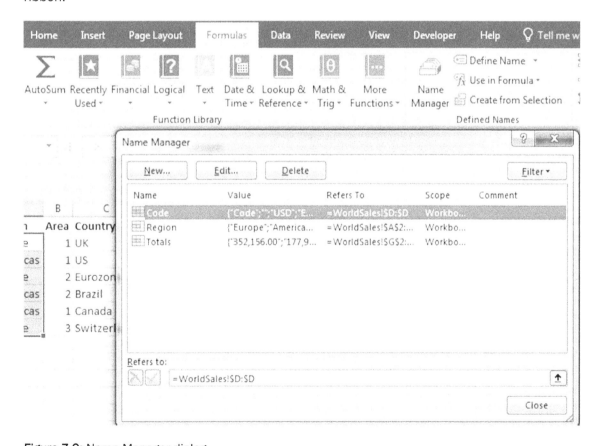

Figure 7-9: Name Manager dialog

The **Filter** dropdown option (Figure 7-10) in the Name Manager dialog is useful in checking the status of defined names.

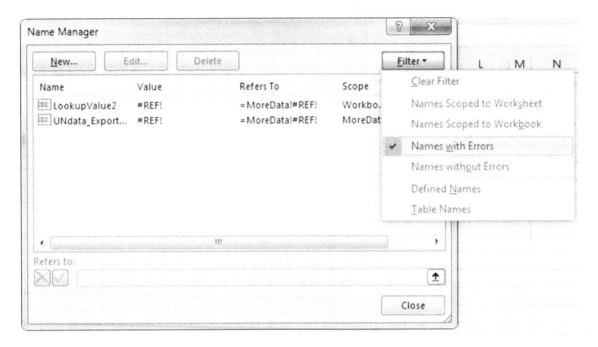

Figure 7-10: Filter dropdown list

Note: When copying a worksheet containing defined names to another worksheet, additional defined names are created with the new worksheet's scope.

The **Create from Selection** option for creating a defined name range is another method although it uses names based on labels designated in the range as follows:

- o Top row.
- o Left column.
- o Bottom row.
- o Right column.

Combining structured table references and defined names

Defined names can be used in conjunction with **Structured Table References** within formula, to make them easier to understand.

Note: Automating processes using VBA code may include calculations internally, so that additional cells, rows and/or columns might not be needed within the worksheet.

In Figure 7-11, **Margin** is a single cell defined name (percentage) and used within a formula to multiply by the row cell in the **Cost** column in a structured table to return the total margin. The same formula will appear in every cell for the same column.

=[@Cost]*Margin

Figure 7-11: Defined name and table reference formula

In Figure 7-12 the **Margin** column is not actually required unless the calculated figure for margin is actually required. Simply including **[@Cost]** to the formula in Figure 7-9 as an addition to the existing total would give the **Total** without the need for the "helper" column.

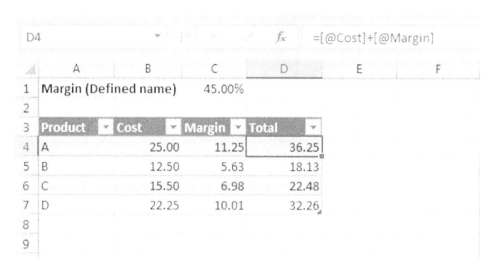

Figure 7-12: Defined name and table references example (InternalReferencing worksheet)

Whole column and row references

An alternative to **Structured Table Referencing** and **Defined Names** is the **Whole Column** or **Row Referencing** method, so in Figure 7-1 a formula for total sales might be **=SUM(B:B)**. Similarly, a whole row reference might look like **=SUM(2:2)** for the sum of all data in row 2.

Be aware that:

o Many built-in functions work efficiently via this method (**SUM**, **SUMIF**) but array calculations like **SUMPRODUCT** may not.

o UDFs should be designed so that they use the last "used" row/column reference to mitigate performance issues, although determining this location can in itself be an issue.

o It is not easy to mix whole row/column referencing techniques with structured table techniques.

o Whole row and column reference negate the use of multiple tables on the same worksheet and any sub-totalling required (as these would get included in any calculations).

8

ARRAY FORMULAS

8 - ARRAY FORMULAS

Referred to as **CTRL SHIFT ENTER** or **CSE** formulas because of the requirement to press **CTRL+SHIFT+ENTER** to input them in the worksheet, array formulas are very powerful formulas that can perform calculations which might not be feasible with basic worksheet functions.

Use an array formula to:
- o Simplify the formula required to calculate one or more results.
- o Remove the need for intermediate helper columns or rows which may be required to calculate the result(s).
- o Ensure consistency of formulas (only one formula required for multiple results) and less clutter in a worksheet.

Whilst array formulas can reduce the need for numerous helper rows and/or columns, they are like a volatile formula i.e. changes to dependent cells requires complete recalculation. Keeping the number of cells used as small as possible is key to optimizing speed.

Any expressions or range references used in array formulas may need moving to separate helper columns and rows to make better use of the smart recalculation processes, which in some respects may contradict the rationale for using them.

There are two types of array formula:
- o those that perform several calculations to generate a single result.
- o those that calculate multiple results.

Some worksheet functions return arrays of values or require an array of values as a parameter.

Array formulas use standard formula syntax with the exception that it is necessary to press **CTRL+SHIFT+ENTER** rather than just the **ENTER** key to automatically insert the formula between {} (a pair of opening and closing braces).

Note: Manually typing braces around a formula does not convert it into an array formula, it is necessary to press **CTRL+SHIFT+ENTER** to create an array formula. Any time an array formula is edited, the braces {} disappear from the array formula, and it is necessary to press **CTRL+SHIFT+ENTER** again to incorporate the changes into an array formula with the braces.

Create an array formula that calculates a single result

Calculating a single result using an array formula can simplify a worksheet model by not requiring intermediate calculations or complex formulas.

The process of creating an array formula is as follows:
- o *Click* the cell in for input of the array formula.
- o Enter the formula and then press CTRL+SHIFT+ENTER to create the array formula.

8 - ARRAY FORMULAS

In Figure 8-1 an array formula calculates the total value of an array of weights of different fruits and their respective quantities to give the overall combined weight.

D6				f_x	{=SUM(B2:C2*B3:C3)}		
	A	B	C	D	E	F	
1		Oranges	Apples	Total			
2	Weight (g)	100	150				
3	Quantity	2	3				
4	Sub-Total	200	450	650			
5							
6	Total			650			

Figure 8-1: Single result array formula example

In Figure 8-2, the formula is input to one cell and then the **CTRL+SHIFT+ENTER** key combination is used to complete the task, resulting in the creation of an array formula with the encompassing braces (curly brackets).

{=SUM(B2:C2*B3:C3)}

Figure 8-2: Array formula (ArrayFormulas worksheet)

When editing the formula remember to use the **CTRL+SHIFT+ENTER** key combination to re-save it.

Note: Sometimes helper columns or rows are required as part of the solution. In the example, separate totals for Oranges and Apples may be required, so a sub-total row would be meaningful. However, this results in three separate formulas, the total being the sum of the two sub-totals instead of the one array formula.

Create an array formula that calculates multiple results

To calculate multiple results by using an array formula, input the array formula into the range of cells required for the results.

In many cases the range will be cells in a single column which matches the number of rows in the raw data or conversely cells in a single row matching the number of columns.

Note: The range may also return results for duplicates when used in a lookup, so may be indeterminate in size.

The process of creating an array formula for multiple results is as follows:
- o Select the range of cells requiring input of the array formula.
- o Enter the formula and then use the **CTRL+SHIFT+ENTER** key combination to complete the task.

In Figure 8-3 given a series of sales figures (column B) for a series of quarters (column A), the TREND function determines the straight-line values for the sales figures.

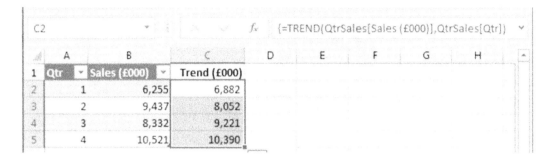

Figure 8-3: Multiple cell array formula

Inputting the formula (Figure 8-4) as an array formula, produces separate trend results based on the sales figures and quarters from the **QtrSales** table. To display all the results of the formula, it is entered into the cells in column C (C2:C5).

Figure 8-4: TREND formula example (ArrayFormulas worksheet)

When editing the formula remember to select the entire range used for the result, make the changes and then use the **CTRL+SHIFT+ENTER** key combination to save it.

Note: Try not to reference complete rows or columns but instead use **dynamic range names** or **structured table references** which whilst volatile, minimizes the size of ranges used in calculations.

Array and function calculation performance issues

Whilst the calculation engine is optimized to exploit array formulas and functions that reference ranges, there are some instances where performance issues may occur, for example:

- References which overlap.
- Array formulas and range functions that reference cell ranges used in another array formula or range function, such as in time series analysis.
- Row and column formulas used in the same calculations.

Note: Array formulas are very difficult to change once created, which may be an advantage when the data range does not change, only the data within it. Although it is possible to append a block of data and then expand the array formula it is not possible to insert or delete data without re-creating the array formula.

9

ALTERNATIVES TO ARRAY FORMULAS

9 - ALTERNATIVES TO ARRAY FORMULAS

An alternative way to achieve the same results as performed by an array formula is to use the worksheet function **SUMPRODUCT** which may be slightly faster in calculation speed and does not require the use of **CTRL+SHIFT+ENTER**.

In Figure 9-1, **SUMPRODUCT** is used instead of an array formula to produce the same result as that shown in Figure 8-1.

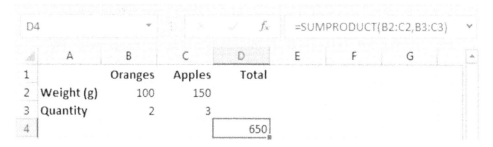

Figure 9-1: SUMPRODUCT example 1

The **SUMPRODUCT** formula used to produce the result in Figure 9-1 is shown in Figure 9-2.

Figure 9-2: SUMPRODUCT formula example 1 (ArrayFormulas worksheet)

In Figure 9-3, **defined names** for column A (**Region**) and column G (**Totals**) are used with **SUMPRODUCT** to determine total value for each **Region**.

G12					f_x	=SUMPRODUCT(--(Region="Americas"),Totals)	

	A	B	C	D	E	F	G	H
1	Region	Area	Country	Code	Rate	Value (£)	Sterling (£)	
2	Europe	1	UK		1.0000	352,156	352,156.00	
3	Americas	1	US	USD	1.4065	250,321	177,974.40	
4	Europe	2	Eurozone	EUR	1.1465	2,345,012	2,045,365.90	
5	Americas	2	Brazil	BRL	4.6240	647,890	140,114.62	
6	Americas	1	Canada	CAD	1.8224	403,343	221,325.18	
7	Europe	3	Switzerland	CHF	1.3420	68,986	51,405.37	
8								
9	Totals						2,988,341.46	
10								
11					Total Europe		2,448,927.26	
12					Total Americas		539,414.20	

Figure 9-3: SUMPRODUCT example 2

Note: In Figure 9-3, although the heading for column G is **Sterling (£)** the defined name has been set as **Totals**. In a **Structured Table** the column heading automatically is set as the reference.

Figure 9-4 shows the SUMPRODUCT formula used in the worksheet in Figure 9-3.

```
=SUMPRODUCT(--(Region="Americas"),Totals)                                    ⌄
```

Figure 9-4: SUMPRODUCT formula example 2 (WorldwideSales worksheet)

Note: The use of double negative (unary) in the formula coerces the true or false value from the conditional test into a 1 or 0, so that the values can be used to multiply by the sales value to get a numerical total.

An alternative method of using **SUMPRODUCT** is to **multiply** the terms inside the formula (Figure 9-5).

```
=SUMPRODUCT((Region="Americas")*Totals)                                      ⌄
```

Figure 9-5: Alternative SUMPRODUCT formula (WorldwideSales worksheet)

This method may be slightly slower than using the comma syntax and gives an error if the range to sum contains a text value. However, it is more flexible in that the range to sum may have, for example, multiple columns when the conditions have only one column.

Other worksheet functions in place of array formulas

It may be better to use **SUMIFS**, **COUNTIFS**, and **AVERAGEIFS** functions instead of array formulas where possible as their calculation speed is faster.

In the regional sales example the **SUMPRODUCT** formula for the Americas region could be re-written using **SUMIFS** (Figure 9-6).

```
=SUMIFS(Totals,Region,"Americas")                                           ⌄
```

Figure 9-6: SUMIFS formula (WorldwideSales worksheet)

The range to sum is **Totals**, the criteria range **Regions** and the criteria to test is **Americas**.

Multiple criteria can be used together from the same or different columns (Figure 9-7).

```
=SUMIFS(Totals,Region,"Americas",Area, 1)                                   ⌄
```

Figure 9-7: SUMIFS multiple criteria (WorldwideSales worksheet)

The formula (Figure 9-7) would calculate the total value for area **1** in the **Americas** region.

Using SUMPRODUCT for multiple conditions

Always use the **SUMIFS**, **COUNTIFS**, and **AVERAGEIFS** functions instead of **SUMPRODUCT** formulas where possible.

However, an alternative **SUMPRODUCT** expression for two conditions can be used as follows:

=SUMPRODUCT(-(Condition1),-(Condition2),RangetoSum)

The **SUMIFS** example (Figure 9-7) could be re-written using a **SUMPRODUCT** equivalent (Figure 9-8).

=SUMPRODUCT(-(Region="Americas"),-(Area=1),Totals)

Figure 9-8: SUMPRODUCT formula instead of SUMIFS equivalent (WorldwideSales worksheet)

Note: The size and shape of the ranges or arrays that are used in the conditional expressions and range to sum must be the same, and they cannot contain entire columns.

As noted earlier, it is possible to multiply conditions with the range to sum rather than use the comma format, albeit slower in calculation speed.

When additional conditions are added use the double negative style for the first item in an odd number of conditions (Figure 9-9).

=SUMPRODUCT(--(Region="Americas"),-(Area=1),-(Code="USD"),Totals)

Figure 9-9: SUMPRODUCT formula with double negatives (WorldwideSales worksheet)

Converting a range to a structured table

A range such as that in Figure 9-10 can be converted to a structured table by placing the cursor inside the range and using the **CTRL+T** keyboard shortcut. The range is automatically detected and added to the **Create Table** dialog. Click **OK** to create.

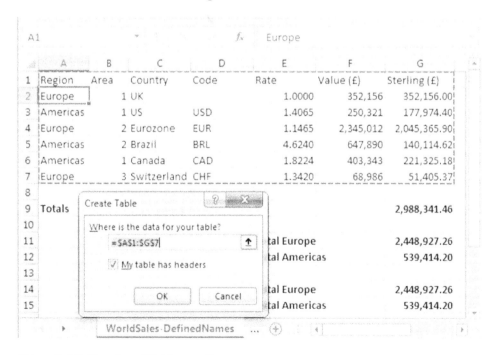

Figure 9-10: Structured Table creation

9 - ALTERNATIVES TO ARRAY FORMULAS

Once the table has been created the table name can be changed to **Sales** using the **Design->Table Name** option on the ribbon. The column headings are automatically available as structured defined names for use in formulas.

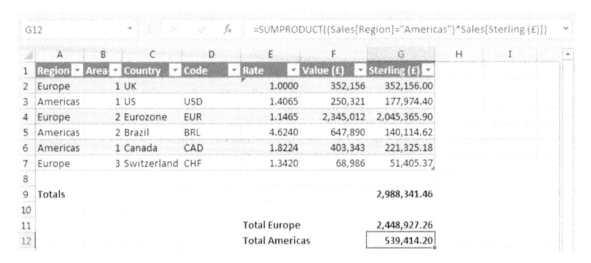

Figure 9-11: Structured Table Sales example

The formula from the named **Sales** table for the totals in the **Americas** region can be written using structured table references (Figure 9-12).

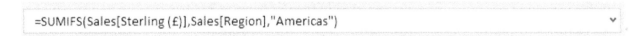

Figure 9-12: SUMPRODUCT formula with table references (WorldwideSales worksheet)

The formula in Figure 9-12 may appear more complicated than the **defined names** version, but it gives no doubt as to where the columns come from i.e. part of a **named structured table**. Other benefits include:

- o Insertions and deletions do not affect the formula.
- o Column dropdown options to sort, filter and select data are automatically added.
- o A totals row, slicers or other features can be added at the touch of a button.
- o Table helper list when entering references and additional referencing features.

SUMIFS can be used instead of **SUMPRODUCT** (Figure 9-13).

```
=SUMIFS(Sales[Sterling (£)],Sales[Region],"Americas")
```

Figure 9-13: SUMIFS formula using structured table references (WorldwideSales worksheet)

10

LOOKUPS

10 - LOOKUPS

Traditionally **VLOOKUP** and **HLOOKUP** have been the "go to" functions for lookups, as they are simple to use, easy to understand and work well, so long as the data is arranged in the correct way.

However, alternative methods can have the following advantages:
- Improved performance on larger worksheets.
- More flexible.
- One method for both vertical and horizontal lookups.
- One method for both ascending and descending data.
- No requirement for the data to be sorted in a particular way to work reliably.

Alternatives to using VLOOKUP and HLOOKUP

The **INDEX** function is fast and non-volatile which speeds up recalculation, so using this in conjunction with **MATCH** can be faster than other types of lookup function.

For example, formulas can be created (Figure 10-1 and Figure 10-2) using different lookup functions to return the same result.

```
=VLOOKUP(LookupValue,Tyres,9,FALSE)
```

Figure 10-1: Lookup formula using VLOOKUP (Tyres worksheet)

```
=INDEX(Tyres,MATCH(LookupValue,Tyres[Code],0),9)
```

Figure 10-2: Lookup formula using INDEX and MATCH combination (Tyres worksheet)

The formula in Figure 10-2 uses the **MATCH** function with an **exact match** search (the zero value in the **MATCH** function) for a **LookupValue** (stored as a Defined Name) of **1556514** in the **Code** column (A) of a **Structured Table Definition** named **Tyres** to return the row number **40** in Figure 10-3.

The **INDEX** function returns **£52.00** which is in the **Price** column, being the 9th i.e. results column in Figure 10-3. The data has been sorted by **Code** and only the first value which matches its returned, although there are a few potential matches.

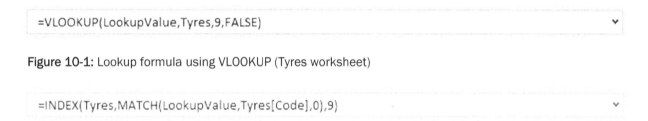

	A	B	C	D	E	F	G	H	I
38	Code	Width	Profile	Diameter	Rating	Seasons	Make	Name	Price
39	1457013	145	70	13	71T	Summer	Dunlop	Streetresponse 2	£ 49.50
40	1556514	155	65	14	73T	Summer	Dunlop	Streetresponse 3	£ 52.00
41	1556514	155	65	14	75T	All Season	Goodyear	Vector 4Seasons Gen-2	£ 63.50
42	1556514	155	65	14	75T	Summer	Kumho	ES31	£ 44.00
43	1556514	155	65	14	75T	Summer	Dunlop	Streetresponse 2	£ 52.50
44	1556514	155	65	14	75T	Summer	Continental	Eco Contact 3	£ 54.50
45	1556514	155	65	14	75T	Summer	Goodyear	Efficientgrip Compact	£ 57.50

Figure 10-3: Tyres structured table (Tyres worksheet)

Note: Always use relative references where possible, so that changes are automatically updated. In Figure 10-2 the formula can be changed so that the column number is inferred as in Figure 10-4. The method only works, if the first column is column A i.e. the very first column.

```
=INDEX(Tyres,MATCH(LookupValue,Tyres[Code],0),COLUMN(Tyres[Price]))
```

Figure 10-4: Inferred column number formula using COLUMN (Tyres worksheet)

Retrieving column numbers in a structured table

Whilst the **COLUMN** function is useful in retrieving a column number it refers to the worksheet column numbers and not necessarily column numbers within a structured table, unless the first column also starts at column A (1).

To ensure that the correct column number is returned in all scenarios use the **MATCH** function instead.

In Figure 10-5, the value **9** is returned by using an exact match lookup for the **Price** column header within the **Header** row of the **Tyres** table in Figure 10-3.

```
=MATCH("Price",Tyres[#Headers],0)
```

Figure 10-5: Inferred column number formula using MATCH (Tyres worksheet)

Note: The MATCH function returns the index value rather than column number, so always returns the correct value within a structured table.

Simplifying the lookup formula

When using **INDEX** and **MATCH** functions together in a formula, if the results column from a structured table is used as the **INDEX** array there is only one column, so the row number returned from the **MATCH** function lookup is all that is required to complete the formula.

In Figure 10-6, the array used in the INDEX function is **Tyres[Price]**, the results column, so the **MATCH** function returns the row number which is used to return the **Price** as there is only the one column.

```
=INDEX(Tyres[Price],MATCH(LookupValue,Tyres[Code],0))
```

Figure 10-6: Simplified lookup formula (Tyres worksheet)

Note: The simplified method is the "go to" formula style recommended for most scenarios.

Speeding up lookups

Ways to help improve lookup performance:

- Make sure data is sorted to ensure reliability and speed of lookup.
- Use one worksheet where possible, as it is faster when both the lookup and data are on the same sheet.
- Use defined ranges/structured table references rather than whole column/row references.

Lookups with missing values

Where it is not certain that the lookup value exists in the lookup range, an **Exact** match formula with error checking (Figure 10-7) can be used.

```
=IFERROR(INDEX(Tyres[Price],MATCH(LookupValue,Tyres[Code],0)),"NoMatch")
```

Figure 10-7: Exact match with error checking (Tyres worksheet)

In Figure 10-7, "NoMatch" is returned if an error occurs. The error message or value should be appropriate. Sometimes a value such as a zero may be applicable, where this value is then used in calculations to give a nil result. However, it can also cause errors such as a division by zero. A blank message may confuse the user, so messages indicating that there is no match may be more useful in communicating the type of error.

The **IFERROR** function can be used for the following error types:
- #N/A
- #VALUE!
- #REF!
- #DIV/0!
- #NUM!
- #NAME?
- #NULL

Note: The formula in Figure 10-7 does not require data to be sorted, although where possible data should always be sorted for best performance. Where data is sorted an approximate match can be used, the type of which depends on the sort order i.e. **Less than** for **Ascending** and **Greater than** for **Descending**.

Lookups on multiple columns

INDEX and **MATCH** can be used to create a lookup on multiple columns by using the **&** symbol to combine the columns and inputting as an **array formula**.

Figure 10-8 shows such a formula. **Defined Names** called **Width**, **Profile** and **Diameter** are used to look up in the corresponding columns from the **Tyres** table (Figure 10-3) i.e. **Tyres[Width]**, **Tyres[Profile]** and **Tyres[Diameter]** returning the **Price**.

```
{=INDEX(Tyres[Price],MATCH(Width&Profile&Diameter,Tyres[Width]&Tyres[Profile]&
  Tyres[Diameter],0))}
```

Figure 10-8: Multiple column lookup formula (Tyres worksheet)

Note: Remember to use **CTRL+SHIFT+ENTER** to complete the formula.

Figure 10-9 shows the result of the lookup from formula in Figure 10-8.

B	C	D	E	F	G	H	I
Width	**Profile**	**Diameter**					
155	65	14					
£52.00	£52.00						

Figure 10-9: Array formula result 1 (Tyres worksheet)

The array formula can be refined to work in cases where data is not sorted and give a meaningful message (instead of #N/A) when the lookup data does not exist such as in Figure 10-10.

```
{=IFERROR(INDEX(Tyres[Price],MATCH(Width&Profile&Diameter,Tyres[Width]&Tyres[Profile]&
  Tyres[Diameter],0)),"")}
```

Figure 10-10: Array formula with error checking (Tyres worksheet)

In Figure 10-10 the **IFERROR** function uses the **INDEX** and **MATCH** functions to return a result, which if in error returns an empty string, although a more meaningful message such as "Not Found" or "No Match" could be returned instead.

Lookup duplicates to return results to multiple columns

The **SMALL** function can be used within an array formula to retrieve multiple results for duplicate lookups as in Figure 10-11.

```
{=IFERROR(INDEX(Tyres[Price],SMALL(IF(Tyres[Code]=LookupValue,ROW(Tyres[Price])-MIN(ROW(
  Tyres[Price]))+1),COLUMNS($A$1:A1))),"")}
```

Figure 10-11: Duplicate lookup multiple results formula (Tyres worksheet)

Note: Remember to use **CTRL+SHIFT+ENTER** to complete the formula.

Figure 10-12 uses column cells to hold each of the matching values. The formula is created in the first cell where the first result should appear. Then, **COPY** this formula across as many columns as required.

```
{=IFERROR(INDEX(Tyres[Price],SMALL(IF(Tyres[Code]=LookupValue,ROW(Tyres[Price])-MIN(ROW(
  Tyres[Price]))+1),COLUMNS($A$1:A1))),"")}
```

B	C	D	E	F	G	H	I
Duplicates	1	2	3				
1556514	£52.00	£63.50	£44.00				

Figure 10-12: Multiple results from array formula (Tyres worksheet)

10 - LOOKUPS

The **Price** is returned for any duplicate codes found in the **Code** column of the **Tyres** table, otherwise an empty string is returned as determined by the **IFERROR** function. The formula is automatically changed in each cell to reference the offset from the first column in the **COLUMNS** function.

In the example **COLUMNS($A$1:A1)** will return a value of **1**. In the adjacent cell, the formula it returns a value of **2** i.e. **COLUMNS($A$1:B1)**. The initial range reference used in the **COLUMNS** function is immaterial as it merely helps generate the required sequence i.e. 1, 2, 3 and so on.

The **COLUMNS** function is used to return the nth value from the **SMALL** function. The **SMALL/IF** function combination in conjunction with **ROW(Tyres[Price]) - MIN(ROW(Tyres[Price])) +1** is used to create an array containing the position of any **LookupValue** which matches the **Code** column value (otherwise it implicitly returns a **FALSE** – as no value has been specified).

Note: The **SMALL** function ignores all but **numerical** values when determining the nth value, so explicitly returning a non-numerical value would not change the result.

Lookup duplicates to return results to multiple rows

For returning multiple results by row instead of by column change the **array formula** using **SMALL** but with the **ROWS** function, instead of **COLUMNS** (Figure 10-13).

```
{=IFERROR(INDEX(Tyres[Price],SMALL(IF(Tyres[Code]=LookupValue,ROW(Tyres[Price])-MIN(ROW(
Tyres[Price]))+1),ROWS($A$1:A1))),"")}
```

Figure 10-13: Multiple row results from single array formula (Tyres worksheet)

Note: Remember to use **CTRL+SHIFT+ENTER** to complete the formula.

When copying down the formula the **ROWS** function changes to **ROWS($A$1:A2)** in the second cell, ROWS($A$1:A3) in the third cell and so on. The initial range reference used in the **ROWS** function is immaterial as it is only used to help generate the sequence i.e. 1, 2, 3 etc.

Figure 10-14 shows the results of using the formula in Figure 10-13.

F34					f_x	{=IFERROR(INDEX(Tyres[Seasons],SMALL(IF(Tyres[Code]=LookupValue,ROW(Tyres[Seasons])-MIN(ROW(Tyres[Seasons]))+1),ROWS($A$1:A1))),"")}			
	A	B	C	D	E	F	G	H	I
34						Summer	Dunlop	Streetresponse 3	£52.00
35						All Season	Goodyear	Vector 4Seasons Gen-2	£63.50
36						Summer	Kumho	ES31	£44.00
39									
43	Code	Width	Profile	Diameter	Rating	Seasons	Make	Name	Price
44	1457013	145	70	13	71T	Summer	Dunlop	Streetresponse 2	£ 49.50
45	1556514	155	65	14	73T	Summer	Dunlop	Streetresponse 3	£ 52.00
46	1556514	155	65	14	75T	All Season	Goodyear	Vector 4Seasons Gen-2	£ 63.50
47	1556514	155	65	14	75T	Summer	Kumho	ES31	£ 44.00

Figure 10-14: Multiple results from array formula to row and column (Tyres worksheet)

123

The example could be expanded by returning as many rows as are required for each of the columns using this technique. If more rows are specified than there are duplicates, the additional ones are left empty. In Figure 10-14, there are four different formulas, one for each column, copied down for as many rows as are required i.e. row 34 to row 36 returning values from rows 45 to 47.

Each column array formula in Figure 10-14 differs only by referencing of the column name to which it refers, so the first one created can be copied and then amended accordingly.

Return a lookup row for a series of columns
MATCH can be used with the OFFSET function to return a block of cells using an array formula. OFFSET is **volatile**, so may be slower than other methods. However, the advantage is that one formula can be used to return the entire block of cells required.

The entire range is selected and then the array formula is entered and CTRL+SHIFT+ENTER used to complete the task. This returns all the cells required as a single result.

The cell to be used for the offset is the intersection of the **Header Row** and the **Code Column** i.e. Tyres[[#Headers],[Code]].

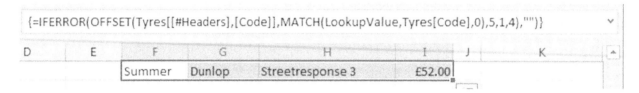

Figure 10-15: Multiple columns from array formula using offset (Tyres worksheet)

In Figure 10-15, column F is 5 columns offset from the Code lookup column, with the result being 1 row high (the height parameter) and 4 columns wide (the width parameter).

The IFERROR function either returns the desired result or an empty string.

Note: This technique is useful for a lookup where only one row is required as the output result.

Return a lookup row beginning at the first column
To return several contiguous columns (from the first column), the INDEX function can be used in an array formula by using **0** as the column number. Select, the number of columns required and then enter the formula, remembering to use CTRL+SHIFT+ENTER to complete the task (Figure 10-16).

Figure 10-16: Formula to return all columns from a lookup row (Tyres worksheet)

In Figure 10-17 all columns are returned (including the lookup value) from the **Tyres** table for the first row found via the **LookupValue** when entered as an array formula across as many columns as are required to fill with the resulting data.

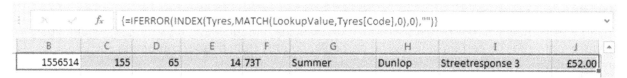

```
fx    {=IFERROR(INDEX{Tyres,MATCH(LookupValue,Tyres[Code],0),0),"")}
```

B	C	D	E	F	G	H	I	J
1556514	155	65	14 73T	Summer	Dunlop	Streetresponse 3	£52.00

Figure 10-17: Multiple results from array formula (Tyres worksheet)

Two-way lookups

Two-way table lookups are possible using separate lookups on the rows and columns of a table by using an **INDEX** function with two embedded **MATCH** functions, one for the row and one for the column.

Figure 10-18, shows the formula required to look up the pass mark required to achieve a specified **Grade** in a particular **Subject** from a **Passmarks** table.

```
=IFERROR(INDEX(Passmarks[#Data],MATCH(Subject,Passmarks[Subject],0),MATCH(Grade,
Passmarks[#Headers],0)),"")
```

Figure 10-18: Two-way lookup formula (PassMarks worksheet)

In Figure 10-19, the **INDEX** function is used with the row and column number intersection point to return the pass mark from the **#Data** area in the **Passmarks** table.

```
=IFERROR(INDEX(Passmarks[#Data],MATCH(Subject,Passmarks[Subject],0),MATCH(Grade,
Passmarks[#Headers],0)),"")
```

Subject	1	2	3	4	5
Math	85	65	55	45	35
English	75	60	50	40	30
Science	79	65	55	45	35
Geography	75	60	50	40	30
History	75	59	50	40	30
Languages	80	65	50	40	30
Religion	75	60	50	40	30

Subject	Grade			Pass mark
history	2			59

Figure 10-19: Result of two-way lookup (PassMarks worksheet)

The defined name **Subject** (value of "History") is used to lookup the **Subject** column in the **Passmarks** table, returning the row number. The defined name **Grade** (value of "2") is used to lookup the **Passmarks [#Headers]** row, returning the column number.

The **IFERROR** returns an empty string if the lookup fails, although this could be a warning message such as "No Match" or similar.

Multiple key lookup

In large worksheets, it may be necessary to look up using multiple keys, for example, to look up how many people speak a certain language in particular country from a table containing such information.

A look up can be performed by using concatenated lookup values. However, this may be inefficient due to:

- o Concatenating strings is a calculation-intensive operation.
- o The lookup may cover a large range.

It is often more efficient to calculate a subset range for the lookup (for example, by finding the first and last row for the country in the table sorted by country, and then looking up the language within that range and returning the population value).

```
=IFERROR(INDEX(OFFSET(Both[[#Headers],[Country]],MATCH(Country,Both[Country],0),2,MATCH(
Country,Both[Country],1),2),MATCH(Language,OFFSET(Both[[#Headers],[Country]],MATCH(Country,
Both[Country],0),2,MATCH(Country,Both[Country],1),1),0),2),0)
```

Figure 10-20: Multiple key lookup formula (LanguageByGender worksheet)

In Figure 10-20, the **OFFSET** functions are used to return the same range of cells from the **Language** column being 2 columns offset from the first column (Figure 10-21).

MATCH functions within each **OFFSET** function return the first and last matching row numbers which are used to return the range using the **Country** (Anguilla). There is a further **MATCH** function which looks up the **Language** defined name (English) in the offset column (**Language**) to determine the row number within the resultant range.

The **INDEX** function is then used to return the result from the **Value** column or a value of zero if no language data was found.

In Figure 10-21, the result from the table named **Both** is shown (left most table).

B	C	D	E	F	G	H	I	J	K	L	M
Country	Gender	Language	Value								
anguilla		2 english	11,329		<- CSE finds only the first matching item in Both table (Both Sexe						
			5,749		<- CSE choose based on Gender defined name						

Country	Sex	Language	Value		Country	Sex	Language	Value		Country	Sex
Anguilla	Both Sexes	Chinese	7		Anguilla	Female	Chinese	1		Anguilla	Male
Anguilla	Both Sexes	Dutch	2		Anguilla	Female	Dutch	0		Anguilla	Male
Anguilla	Both Sexes	English	11,329		Anguilla	Female	English	5749		Anguilla	Male
Anguilla	Both Sexes	Other	8		Anguilla	Female	Other	5		Anguilla	Male
Anguilla	Both Sexes	Spanish	84		Anguilla	Female	Spanish	47		Anguilla	Male
Anguilla	Both Sexes	Total	11,430		Anguilla	Female	Total	5,802		Anguilla	Male
Armenia	Both Sexes	Armenian	3,139,152		Armenia	Female	Armenian	535,783		Armenia	Male

Figure 10-21: Result of multiple key lookup (LanguageByGender worksheet)

Three-Dimensional Lookup

There may be occasions when it is necessary to look up a value which may be in more than one table, range or other type of array.

The **CHOOSE** function can be one way of selecting where to look up and can work efficiently where there is a relatively small number of tables.

The three language tables (Figure 10-22) are based on gender i.e. both sexes, female and male. These tables can be used to facilitate the choosing of a table to look up based on gender (Figure 10-23).

The **CHOOSE** function selects the table name based on the **Gender** defined name (1 = Both, 2 = Female, 3 = Male).

A multi-column exact match lookup for the **Country** and **Language** defined names has been used within a **MATCH** function, so the array formula must be entered using **CTRL+SHIFT+ENTER**.

The resultant **Value** is returned from the **table** column **4**.

IFERROR returns **zero** where the lookup is unsuccessful.

Country	Gender	Language	Value				
anguilla		2 english	11,329	<- CSE finds only the first matching item in Both table (Both Sexes			
			5,749	<- CSE choose based on Gender defined name			

Country	Sex	Language	Value		Country	Sex	Language	Value		Country	Sex
Anguilla	Both Sexes	Chinese	7		Anguilla	Female	Chinese	1		Anguilla	Male
Anguilla	Both Sexes	Dutch	2		Anguilla	Female	Dutch	0		Anguilla	Male
Anguilla	Both Sexes	English	11,329		Anguilla	Female	English	5,749		Anguilla	Male
Anguilla	Both Sexes	Other	8		Anguilla	Female	Other	5		Anguilla	Male
Anguilla	Both Sexes	Spanish	84		Anguilla	Female	Spanish	47		Anguilla	Male
Anguilla	Both Sexes	Total	11,430		Anguilla	Female	Total	5,802		Anguilla	Male
Armenia	Both Sexes	Armenian	3,139,152		Armenia	Female	Armenian	535,783		Armenia	Male

Figure 10-22: Three-dimensional lookup result (LanguageByGender worksheet)

The formula in Figure 20-23 uses the value **2** (**Gender** defined name) in the **CHOOSE** function to return the **Female** table, which is then used to lookup the **Country** and **Language**.

```
{=IFERROR(INDEX(CHOOSE(Gender,Both,Female,Male),MATCH(Country&Language,CHOOSE(Gender,
Both[Country]&Both[Language],Female[Country]&Female[Language],Male[Country]&
Male[Language]),0),4),0)}
```

Figure 10-23: Three-dimensional lookup array formula (LanguageByGender worksheet)

Using a lookup instead of multiple IFs

In some circumstances a lookup can be used to good effect instead of multiple **IF** tests but only where a table can be created such that it conforms to the required pattern.

For example, assuming scores are allocated to staff according to time spent helping customers at a call centre, where 0 to 15 minutes is 5, 16-30 minutes is 3, 31-60 minutes is 1 and over 60 minutes is 0, a lookup can be used to work out the score.

A structured table named **CallScore** (Figure 10-24) can be created with the lower bands of the time spent and equivalent scores.

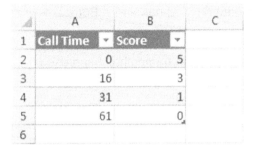

Figure 10-24: CallScore structured table (CallTime worksheet)

The advantage of this method is that the formula remains the same, no matter how many categories there are. In Figure 10-24 there are only four possible results but there could be situations where there are tens or even hundreds of possibilities.

A lookup formula (Figure 10-25) can be used with **INDEX** and **MATCH** functions to locate the correct row (column 2) in the **CallScore** lookup table.

The **MATCH** function uses a less than match to determine the correct row.

Thus, in the example (Figure 10-25) assuming the cell reference B9 has a call time of **12** minutes, the result will be 5.

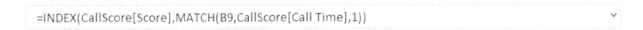

```
=INDEX(CallScore[Score],MATCH(B9,CallScore[Call Time],1))
```

Figure 10-25: Lookup score formula (CallTime worksheet)

Note: For the lookup method to work for multiple IF's there must be a row which can be matched against, generally there will always be a zero band. For example, if a lookup table of road fuel scale charges was being used where 120 was the lowest band (anything less using the 120 band) for O2 emissions, then setting another band at 0 with the same figures as the 120 band would solve the issue of emissions being below the 120 level.

11

REFERENCES AND LINKS

11 - REFERENCES AND LINKS

Whilst references to other worksheets and workbooks can degrade performance there are instances where there is no option but to use them. **Pre-defined references** can make the design much more flexible and less prone to error when changes are made.

Creating external references

External referencing works in much the same way as internal referencing, except that the workbook and worksheet names are added to the reference.

To help with the referencing task the **View->View Side by Side** (with **Synchronous Scrolling** disabled) option on the ribbon can be used.

When the source workbook is open, the external reference includes the workbook name in square brackets ([]), followed by the worksheet name, an exclamation point (!), and the cells that the formula depends on.

Figure 11-1 shows an external reference to an **opened** workbook, where the exchange rate is being referenced from the worksheet **RatesSheet** directly from the workbook named **ExchangeRates.xlsx** to the absolute cell location D4.

=[ExchangeRates.xlsx]RatesSheet!$D$4

Figure 11-1: External reference to a cell in an open workbook (ExternalReferences worksheet)

If the source workbook were closed the same reference might then display as in Figure 11-2.

='C:\Examples\[ExchangeRates.xlsx]RatesSheet'!$D$4

Figure 11-2: External reference to a cell in a closed workbook (ExternalReferences worksheet)

Figure 11-2 shows the additional information of the full path to the external workbook.

Note: If the name (or path) of the other worksheet or workbook contains non-alphabetical characters, it must be enclosed within single quotation marks ('). Formulas that link to a defined name in another workbook use the workbook name followed by an exclamation point (!) and the name.

Using direct cell references to external worksheets is not recommended. Any changes to the source workbook such as an insertion, deletion or sorting of data may render the reference invalid, if the destination workbook is closed when such changes occur. Use a named reference instead.

Figure 11-3 shows an exact match lookup formula to ensure that the correct value is used (assuming the external workbook is open):

```
=IFERROR(INDEX(ExchangeRates.xlsx!Rates[Rate],MATCH(Country,ExchangeRates.xlsx!
Rates[Country],0)),0)
```

Figure 11-3: External exact match lookup formula (ExternalReferences worksheet)

Note: To return zero from a formula (Figure 11-3) may be counterintuitive. Instead it may be better to return the standard or other error message and then deal with the issue directly within the external workbook.

In Figure 11-4, the **Country** is set as a defined name with the value "Dubai" and the result returned is **5.1662**.

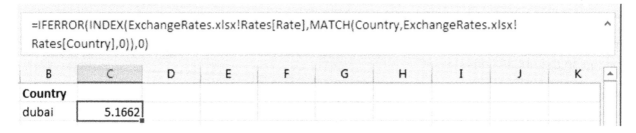

=IFERROR(INDEX(ExchangeRates.xlsx!Rates[Rate],MATCH(Country,ExchangeRates.xlsx!Rates[Country],0)),0)

B	C	D	E	F	G	H	I	J	K
Country									
dubai	5.1662								

Figure 11-4: Result of exact match lookup formula (ExternalReferences worksheet)

The formula in Figure 11-3 assumes that the value from the defined name **Country** cell exists in the **Country** column of the **Rates** table from the **RatesSheet** of the **ExchangeRates** workbook (Figure 11-5) otherwise the result from the error check is zero.

Although error checking can be added to ensure a result is returned from the formula, it is sometimes difficult to return a value which is meaningful.

B	C	D	E	F	G
Country	Currency	Currency code	Rate	Start date	End date
Abu Dhabi	Dirham	AED	5.1662	01/04/2018	30/04/2018
Dubai	Dirham	AED	5.1662	01/04/2018	30/04/2018
UAE	Dirham	AED	5.1662	01/04/2018	30/04/2018
Albania	Lek	ALL	148.17	01/04/2018	30/04/2018
Armenia	Dram	AMD	674.61	01/04/2018	30/04/2018
Angola	Readj Kwanza	AOA	301.97	01/04/2018	30/04/2018

Figure 11-5: RatesSheet in ExchangeRates workbook

Where there are many rows to reference, creating a lookup formula using a structured table makes the task that much easier both to create and understand.

It is recommended that all workbooks are open when using external references, although this is not compulsory, otherwise the task on entering the formula becomes more cumbersome (Figure 11-6).

=IFERROR(INDEX('C:\Examples\ExchangeRates.xlsx'!Rates[Rate],MATCH(Country,'C:\Examples\ExchangeRates.xlsx'!Rates[Country],0)),0)

Figure 11-6: Formula using references in closed workbook (ExternalReferences worksheet)

Open and close linked workbooks with VBA code

VBA code can be used to automate the process of opening and closing workbooks which are linked. Such code can be placed in the correct method for the **ThisWorkbook** object.

The methods available are shown in the right dropdown list for the **Workbook** (when it has been selected from the left dropdown list of options) as shown in Figure 11-7.

Once a method has been created for one of the workbook events it is shown in **bold** in the dropdown list.

Note: Event methods available from the dropdown list directly relate to the selected object.

```
Workbook                              ▼   Open                              ▼

    Private Sub Workbook_Open()           Open
                                          PivotTableCloseConnection
        ' Initialize the with events event handle  PivotTableOpenConnection
        initializeAppWithEvents           RowsetComplete
                                          SheetActivate
        ' Redirect the F9 recalc key.     SheetBeforeDelete
        Application.OnKey "{F9}", "recalc"  SheetBeforeDoubleClick
                                          SheetBeforeRightClick
        ' Open the Exchange Rates workbook when t  SheetCalculate
        Workbooks.Open fileName:="C:\Examples\Exc  SheetChange
            ReadOnly:=True                SheetDeactivate
        ThisWorkbook.Activate             SheetFollowHyperlink

    End Sub
```

Figure 11-7: Workbook methods dropdown list

In Figure 11-8, a **Workbook Open** event method automatically opens the linked workbook in read-only mode and then makes sure that the host workbook is activated immediately thereafter.

```
Workbook                              ▼   Open                              ▼

    Private Sub Workbook_Open()
        ' open the Exchange Rates workbook when we open this workbook
        Workbooks.Open fileName:="C:\Examples\ExchangeRates.xlsx", _
            ReadOnly:=True
        ThisWorkbook.Activate

    End Sub
```

Figure 11-8: Opening an external workbook via code from ThisWorkbook

---

Note: Other tasks could be executed within the **Workbook Open** event such as the initializing of the **WithEvents** event handler and re-directing the **F9** key for recalculations such as in Figure 11-7.

When the workbook is closed, the **Workbook BeforeClose** event could be used to automatically close the external workbook. Such code may need error trapping, just in case the user has closed the external workbook manually.

The **Workbook WindowActivate** event method could show both workbooks in a side by side comparison for easier viewing, with synchronized scrolling turned off. This method will only work if both workbooks have separate windows available at the time the event takes place, otherwise an error will occur.

Figure 11-9 shows example code for the **Workbook BeforeClose** and **WindowActivate** event handlers for controlling an opened external workbook.

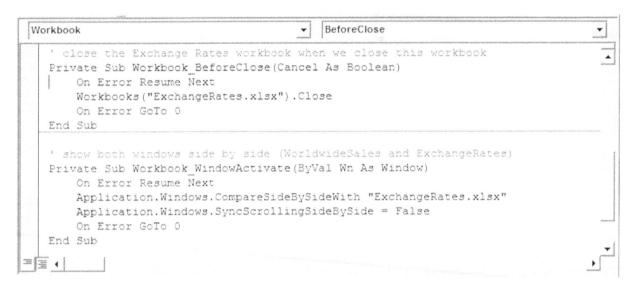

```
Workbook                                      ▼   BeforeClose                                    ▼

    ' close the Exchange Rates workbook when we close this workbook
    Private Sub Workbook_BeforeClose(Cancel As Boolean)
        On Error Resume Next
        Workbooks("ExchangeRates.xlsx").Close
        On Error GoTo 0
    End Sub

    ' show both windows side by side (WorldwideSales and ExchangeRates)
    Private Sub Workbook_WindowActivate(ByVal Wn As Window)
        On Error Resume Next
        Application.Windows.CompareSideBySideWith "ExchangeRates.xlsx"
        Application.Windows.SyncScrollingSideBySide = False
        On Error GoTo 0
    End Sub
```

Figure 11-9: BeforeClose and WindowActivate event methods

Note: A quick (and some might say dirty way) to ignore errors is to add an **On Error Resume Next** statement beforehand and then at the end of the routine return error handling to the default via the **On Error Goto 0** statement.

Referencing between cells in different workbooks

To create an external reference between cells in different workbooks requires both workbooks to be open and the procedure is as follows:

1. Open both workbooks and then select the one (destination) where the link is to be created.

2. Select the cell or cells in which the external reference is to be created.

3. Type the = (equal sign). To perform calculations or functions on the external reference's value, type the operator or function preceding the external reference.

4. Switch to the source workbook, and then click the worksheet that contains the cells to link to.

5. Select the cell or cells to link to.

6. Press **ENTER** to return to the destination workbook.

Note: Press **ENTER** for a simple link or **CTRL+SHIFT+ENTER** for an array formula link which surrounds the link in curly braces {}.

Referencing a defined name in another workbook

Open both the destination and source workbooks, then:

1. Select the cell or cells in which the external reference is to be created.

2. Type the = (equal sign). To perform calculations or functions on the external reference's value, type the operator or function preceding the external reference.

3. On the **View** tab, in the **Window** group, *click* **Switch Windows**, *click* the source workbook, and then *click* the worksheet that contains the cells to link to.

4. Press **F3**, and then select the name to link to, *click* **OK** then press **Enter**.

Define a name with a reference to cells in another workbook

Open both the destination and source workbooks, then:

1. In the destination workbook, on the **Formulas** tab, in the **Defined Names** group, *click* **Define Name**.

2. In the **New Name** dialog box, in the **Name** box, type a name for the range.

3. In the **Refers to** box, delete the contents and keep the cursor in the box.

4. If the name contains a formula, input the formula and then position the cursor where the external reference is required. For example, type **=SUM()**, and then position the cursor between the parentheses.

5. On the **View** tab, in the **Window** group, *click* **Switch Windows**, *click* the source workbook, and then *click* the worksheet that contains the cells to link to.

6. Select the cell or range of cells to link to.

7. In the **New Name** dialog box, *click* **OK**.

Note: Defining a name in the above manner only creates the link, it does not place it on the destination workbook, although it is available to use in formulas.

A **Currency** defined name can be created (Figure 11-10) within the **ExternalReferences** sheet of the current workbook which refers to the **Currency** column in the **Rates** table of the **ExchangeRates.xlsx** workbook.

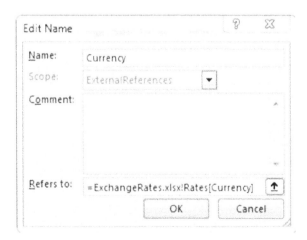

Figure 11-10: Defining a name to an external workbook range

Check that links are working correctly

The links to other workbooks is configured from the **Edit Links** dialog which is available from the **Data**->**Edit Links** option in the **Connections** group on the ribbon.

Note: The Edit Links option is unavailable if no links exist.

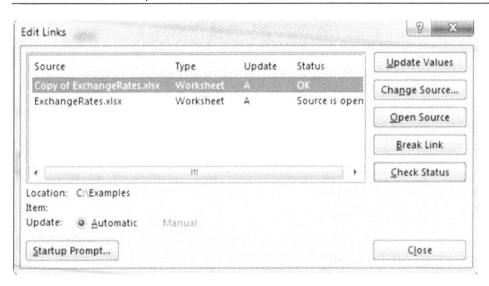

Figure 11-11: Edit Links dialog

The list presented in the **Edit Links** dialog (Figure 11-11) shows the following columns:

- o Source.
- o Type.
- o Update.
- o Status.

Source refers to the linked filename, **Type** normally shows Worksheet, **Update** indicates whether the links are updated automatically or manually and **Status** shows Unknown, OK or Error: Source not found.

The **Update Values** button will make sure that the latest values are pushed from the linked worksheet to the host worksheet.

The **Change Source** option allows for changes to the source file name, in case it has been renamed for any reason.

The **Open Source** option will open the workbook containing the link and position the cursor to the actual source link.

The **Startup Prompt** controls how links are updated as follows:

- o Let the user choose.
- o Don't update automatic links.
- o Update the links.

Break a link

In the **Source** list, *click* the link to break.

To select multiple linked objects, hold down **Ctrl**, and then *click* each linked object.

To select all links, press **CTRL+A**. *click* **Break Link.**

A prompt will display asking for confirmation to **Break Links** or **Cancel** to abort operation.

Check Status

The **Check Status** button will perform a check on the links to determine those that may have changed such as when the file has been removed.

Delete the name of a defined link

If the link used a defined name, the name is not automatically removed. To delete the name as well, on the **Formulas** tab, in the **Defined Names** group, *click* **Name Manager.**

In the **Name Manager** dialog box, *click* the name to select it, *click* **Delete**, then *click* **OK** to confirm the deletion.

When a link is broken to the source workbook of an external reference, all formulas that use the value in the source workbook are converted to their current values.

Figure 11-12 shows the result of breaking the link to the external reference.

```
=SUM('C:\Examples\[Costs.xlsx]Costs'!$C$6:$C$12)
```

Figure 11-12: Broken link to external reference

In Figure 11-12, the SUM formula is replaced by the calculated value, whatever that may be.

Also, because this action cannot be undone, it may be prudent to save a version of the destination workbook as a backup.

When using an external data range, a parameter of the query may also use data from another workbook. It may be prudent to check for and remove any of these types of links.

Avoid forward referencing

Avoid designing formulas which refer forward (to the right and below) to other formulas and cells.

At the start of a calculation sequence it might take longer to establish a calculation sequence if there are numerous formulas requiring deferred calculations.

Avoid circular references with iteration

Circular reference calculation with iterations is slow because multiple calculations are needed.

Try to design so that iterative calculations are not needed. Place all calculations on the same sheet and if necessary use extra columns to hold intermediate calculations.

Avoid links between workbooks

Avoid inter-workbook links as they can be slow, easily broken and not always easy to find and fix.

Using fewer larger workbooks may be better than using many smaller workbooks except in cases where there is a lack of RAM or front-end calculations are rarely needed.

Try to use simple direct references that work on closed workbooks, so avoiding recalculation. This also makes it easier to diagnose and audit workbooks.

Open workbooks which are linked to first and then open the master workbook, so that calculation performance does not rely on "opening" a linked workbook before starting calculations.

It may be possible to automate this process via VBA code providing the linked workbook is not used to link to other workbooks.

Unless linked workbooks are used to link to other workbooks, it is better to combine the two or more workbooks into one larger workbook.

Avoid links between worksheets

Using many worksheets may make a workbook easier to use but re-calculation performance is generally slower than inter-worksheet calculations.

It may be better to have linked data as separate tables on the same worksheet, if performance is the primary concern.

Output links information to an html file

Sometimes it is necessary to know where the links are located within a workbook. VBA code can be used to output the information such as to a text or HTML file. Tabs are used to format text in a text or HTML file for readability.

In Figure 11-13 variables are declared for use throughout the module and include tab settings, symbol constants used in HTML files for converting illegal characters and the file handle object.

```
(General)                                          (Declarations)

' Links Module

' Public Routine: createLinksFile

' ROUTINES TO OUTPUT LINKS TO HTML FILE

' Copyright 1997-2018, Simon A. Towell

Option Explicit

' HTML file handle.
Private m_obHTML As Object

' Tab constant.
Private Const mc_lnTabs As Long = 5
' Tab declarations.
Private m_stArrTab(0 To mc_lnTabs) As String
```

Figure 11-13: Declarations at module level (Links module)

The **createLinkFile** sub-routine shown in Figure 11-14 works as follows:
- o A declaration made and the **getInFileName** function is used to return the name of the input file name (**stInFileName**) i.e. a workbook.
- o If a valid file name is returned, a declaration is made and the **setOutFileName** function is used to return the name of the HTML output file.
- o If a valid output HTML file name is set, the **setTabs** sub-routine is called to set up the tabs for display purposes.
- o Finally, the **outputLinksToHTML** sub-routine is called to output the links to the HTML file.
- o Error messages are displayed if the input or output file names are not chosen.

```
(General)                                      createLinksFile

' Create an HTML file with all links.

Public Sub createLinksFile()

    ' Declare and get input file name (workbook).
    Dim stInFileName As String: stInFileName = getInFileName()

    ' Only proceed if a workbook has been selected to open.
    If stInFileName <> vbNullString Then

        ' Set output file name to match workbook file name but as .html.
        Dim stOutFileName As String: stOutFileName = setOutFileName(stInFileName)

        ' Only proceed if a filename has been set as output file.
        If stOutFileName <> vbNullString Then
            ' Configure tab settings for formatting document.
            setTabs
            ' Now process workbook and output to html file.
            outputLinksToHTML stInFileName, stOutFileName
        Else
            MsgBox "Please select an HTML file to save to"
        End If
    Else
        MsgBox "Please select a workbook to open"
    End If
End Sub
```

Figure 11-14: The creatLinksFile sub-routine (Links module)

The **getInFileName** function in Figure 11-15 works as follows:
- o The open file dialog is used to choose the workbook and return the result as a variant.
- o The **getStringFileName** function is used to convert the variant result to a string.
- o Finally, the result is returned back to the **createLinksFile** sub-routine (Figure 11-14).

```
(General)                                      getInFileName

' Get input file name.
' Use file dialog to get workbook and then make sure it is returned as string.

Private Function getInFileName() As String
    Dim vtFileName As Variant: vtFileName = Application.GetOpenFilename("Workbook, *.xl*")
    getInFileName = getStringFileName(vtFileName)
End Function
```

Figure 11-15: The getInFileName function (Links module)

The **getStringFileName** function in Figure 11-16 works as follows:

- o If the variant file name argument does not have a value of **False** it is returned as a string version.
- o Otherwise, the returned result is the **vbNullString**.

```
(General)                                                  getStringFileName

' Get string file name from a possible variant file name.
' Result is either the actual file name or the vbNullString.

Private Function getStringFileName(vtFileName As Variant) As String
    Select Case vtFileName
        Case Is <> False
            getStringFileName = vtFileName
        Case Else
            getStringFileName = vbNullString
    End Select
End Function
```

Figure 11-16: The getStringFileName function (Links module)

In Figure 11-17 the **setOutFileName** function works as follows:

- o The sting file name argument (**stFileName**) is amended to have the **.htm** file extension.
- o The new version of the argument is then used within the **Save As** dialog and the result stored as a variant.
- o The variant file name is passed as an argument of the **getStringFileName** function (Figure 11-16) and the result returned as a string value.
- o Finally, the result is returned back to the **createLinksFile** sub-routine (Figure 11-14).

```
(General)                                                  setOutFileName

' Set output file name.
' Use input file name to make up matching name with .htm file extension.
' Use the Save As dialog to set it up and return result as string file name.
' Argument stFileName passed ByVal so original does not get altered.

Private Function setOutFileName(ByVal stFileName As String) As String
    Dim vtFileName As Variant
    stFileName = Left$(stFileName, InStr(stFileName, ".") - 1) & ".htm"
    vtFileName = Application.GetSaveAsFilename _
        (stFileName, "HTML (*.htm), *.htm,XML only (*.xml), *.xml", 1, _
        "Create iXBRL Output File:")
    setOutFileName = getStringFileName(vtFileName)
End Function
```

Figure 11-17: The setOutFileName function (Links module)

Providing both the input file name (workbook) and output file name (HTML file) have been selected correctly the **createLinksFile** sub-routine can continue to the next stage.

The next step is to configure the tab settings to be used in the output, since an HTML source file is formatted with indentation for each element in a nested fashion, very much like VBA code for readability. Tabs can also be used to format the final output in conjunction with styling.

Figure 11-18 shows the **setTabs** sub-routine which sets module level tab variables with incremental tabs and is called by the **createLinksFile** sub-routine (Figure 11-14). In combination with module level declarations five-tab settings are created and stored in a string array (**m_stArrTab**).

```
(General)                              ▼   setTabs                              ▼

' Create a series of tab settings for formatting purposes in HTML file.

Private Sub setTabs()
    Dim lnCount As Long
    For lnCount = 0 To mc_lnTabs
        m_stArrTab(lnCount) = String$(lnCount, Chr(9))
    Next lnCount
End Sub
```

Figure 11-18: The setTabs sub-routine (Links module)

In Figure 11-19 the **outputLinksToHTML** sub-routine works as follows:
- o The string versions of the input and output file names are used as arguments.
- o A reference is set to the open workbook with the string input file name argument.
- o The **getHTMLFile** function is used to set a reference to the output file handle.
- o The first few required elements of an HTML document are output including the **html** element and then the **outputHeadElement** sub-routine is called to add the HTML **head** element.
- o Next, the start of the Body element is output and the **getAllLinks** sub-routine called to add any links to the HTML **body** element.
- o Finally, the **body** and **html** element close tags are output before closing the HTML file handle.

```
(General)                              ▼   outputLinksToHTML                    ▼

' Output links to the HTML file using the chosen input and output file names.

Private Sub outputLinksToHTML(stInFileName As String, stOutFileName As String)
    'Declare and set a reference to the open workbook.
    Dim wb As Workbook: Set wb = Workbooks.Open(stInFileName)

    ' Set module level file handle to HTML output file.
    Set m_obHTML = getHTMLFile(stOutFileName)

    ' *** BEGIN HTML DOCUMENT OUTPUT ***
    writeIt m_stArrTab(0), "<?xml version='1.0' encoding='UTF-8'?>"
    writeIt m_stArrTab(0), _
        "<html xmlns='http://www.w3.org/1999/xhtml'" _
        & " xmlns:xlink='http://www.w3.org/1999/xlink'>"
    ' *** HEADER INFORMATION ***
    outputHeadElement
    ' *** BODY OF XHTML DOCUMENT ***
    writeIt m_stArrTab(1), "<body xml:lang='en'>"

    ' output link results to html file
    getAllLinks wb

    ' *** FOOTER INFORMATION FOR HTML document to close correctly
    writeIt m_stArrTab(1), "</body>"     ' End of BODY
    writeIt m_stArrTab(0), "</html>"     ' End of HTML
    m_obHTML.Close       ' close file
End Sub
```

Figure 11-19: The outputLinksToHTML sub-routine (Links module)

In Figure 11-20 the **getHTMLFile** function is used to create a reference to the file handle object for the output file.

```
(General)                                      ▼   getHTMLFile                                        ▼
    ' Return a file handle to HTML output file.                                                        ▲

    Private Function getHTMLFile(stFileName As String) As Object
        Dim obFileSys As Object: Set obFileSys = CreateObject("Scripting.FileSystemObject")
        Set getHTMLFile = obFileSys.createtextfile(stFileName, True)
    End Function                                                                                        ▼
```

Figure 11-20: The getHTMLFile function (Links module)

In Figure 11-21 the **writeIt** sub-routine outputs one line of data (**stOutString** parameter) using the appropriate tab setting (parameter **stTab**) and is called as required.

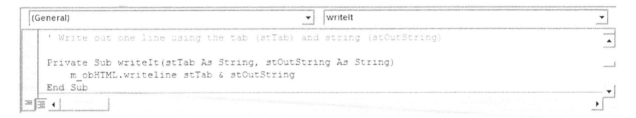

```
(General)                                      ▼   writeIt                                            ▼
    ' Write out one line using the tab (stTab) and string (stOutString)                               ▲

    Private Sub writeIt(stTab As String, stOutString As String)
        m_obHTML.writeline stTab & stOutString
    End Sub                                                                                             ▼
```

Figure 11-21: The writeIt sub-routine (Links module)

In Figure 11-22 the **outputHeadElement** sub-routine is used to output the HTML **head** element information including **CSS** styling of **h1** to **h5**.

```
(General)                                      ▼   outputHeadElement                                  ▼
    ' Output the Head element of an HTML document.                                                     ▲

    Private Sub outputHeadElement()
        writeIt m_stArrTab(1), "<head>"
        writeIt m_stArrTab(2), _
            "<meta content='application/xhtml+xml; charset=UTF-8'" _
                & " http-equiv='Content-Type' />"
        writeIt m_stArrTab(1), "<style>"
        writeIt m_stArrTab(2), "h1 {text-indent: 0em;}"
        writeIt m_stArrTab(2), "h2 {text-indent: 2em;}"
        writeIt m_stArrTab(2), "h3 {text-indent: 4em;}"
        writeIt m_stArrTab(2), "h4 {text-indent: 6em;}"
        writeIt m_stArrTab(2), "h5 {text-indent: 8em;}"
        writeIt m_stArrTab(1), "</style>"
        writeIt m_stArrTab(1), "</head>"
    End Sub                                                                                             ▼
```

Figure 11-22: The outputHeadElement sub-routine (Links module)

After the head element has been output, the **body** element is output ready for the links information.

Next the **getAllLinks** sub-routine, Figure 11-23 is run to find different types of links including hyperlinks, links on worksheets and names for all workbooks and worksheets currently open.

Each links sub-routine is called in turn as follows:

- o listHyperLinks.
- o listLinks.
- o listNames.

```
(General)                              ▼   getAllLinks                              ▼

' Process each worksheet in collection of worksheets and find the different types of links.

Private Sub getAllLinks(wb As Workbook)
    Dim ws As Worksheet
    writeIt m_stArrTab(2), "<h1>Workbook: <span style='color:blue'>" & wb.Name & "</span></h1>

    For Each ws In wb.Worksheets
        writeIt m_stArrTab(3), "<h2>Worksheet name:<span style='color:green'>" _
            & ws.Name & "  [Code name: " & ws.CodeName & "]</span></h2>"
        ' List hyperlinks
        listHyperlinks ws
        ' List links in formulas.
        listLinks ws
        ' List links in defined names.
        listNames ws
    Next ws
End Sub
```

Figure 11-23: The getAllLinks sub-routine (Links module)

The **listHyperLinks** sub-routine in Figure 11-24 lists all hyperlinks showing name and address, including the total number of links found. If no hyperlinks are found the routine ends immediately.

```
(General)                              ▼   listHyperlinks                           ▼

' List Hyperlinks for this worksheet (if any exist).

Private Sub listHyperlinks(ws As Worksheet)
    ' Continue if any hyperlinks found.
    If ws.Hyperlinks.count > 0 Then

        writeIt m_stArrTab(4), "<h3>HYPERLINKS</h3>"

        ' Output each hyperlink in the collection of hyperlinks.
        Dim hl As Hyperlink
        For Each hl In ws.Hyperlinks
            writeIt m_stArrTab(5), "<h4>Hyperlink Name: <span style='color:purple'>" _
                & hl.Name & "</span></h4>"
            writeIt m_stArrTab(5), "<h4>Address: <span style='color:red'>" _
                & hl.Address & "</span></h4>"
            writeIt m_stArrTab(5), "<br/>"
        Next hl
        ' Finish by outputting the number of hyperlinks.
        writeIt m_stArrTab(5), "<h4>No of Hyperlinks: " & CStr(ws.Hyperlinks.count) _
            & "</h4>"
    End If
End Sub
```

Figure 11-24: The listHyperLinks sub-routine (Links module)

The **listLinks** sub-routine in Figure 11-25 displays links for each worksheet including address and formula, including the total number of links found. It works as follows:

- o An attempt is made to set a reference to a range (**rg**) for all cells on the worksheet with formulas.
- o If the range exists, each cell within the range is checked for an external link within its formula.
- o For the first link found a title is output and a flag set, so that it only occurs once.
- o A counter is kept for the total number of links found.
- o If an external link exists, the details are output to the HTML file.
- o On completion the totals are output.

```
(General)                                                    listLinks

' List links in formula for this worksheet.

Private Sub listLinks(ws As Worksheet)

    ' Attempt to find a range of formulas on the worksheet.
    On Error Resume Next
        Dim rg As Range: Set rg = ws.UsedRange.SpecialCells(xlCellTypeFormulas)
    On Error GoTo 0

    ' Continue if a range of formulas has been found.
    If Not (rg Is Nothing) Then
        Dim rgCell As Range
        Dim boLink As Boolean: boLink = False
        Dim lnCount As Long
        For Each rgCell In rg
            If InStr(1, rgCell.Formula, ".xl") > 0 Then
                If Not boLink Then
                    boLink = True
                    writeIt m_stArrTab(4), "<h3>LINKS</h3>"
                End If
                lnCount = lnCount + 1
                writeIt m_stArrTab(5), _
                    "<h4>Address: <span style='color:purple'>" _
                    & rgCell.Address(, , , True) & "</span></h4>"
                writeIt m_stArrTab(5), _
                    "<h4>Formula: <span style='color:red'>" _
                    & symbolTranslate(rgCell.Formula) & "</span></h4>"
                writeIt m_stArrTab(5), "<br/>"
            End If
        Next
        ' Output totals if any links were found.
        If boLink Then writeIt m_stArrTab(5), "<h4>No of Links: " & CStr(lnCount) & "</h4>"
    End If
End Sub
```

Figure 11-25: The listLinks sub-routine (Links module)

The **listNames** sub-routine in Figure 11-20 displays the defined names for each worksheet including name, refers to and number of names counted. It works as follows:

- o If no names exist the routine ends immediately.
- o For each name in the Names collection, the reference to an external link is checked.
- o If this is the first link found, a title is output.
- o A counter is kept for the total number of links found.
- o For each link found, its details are output to the HTML file.
- o On completion the total number of links is output.

```
(General)                                          listNames

    ' List links within defined names for worksheet.

Private Sub listNames(ws As Worksheet)
    ' Continue if there are any defined names.
    If ws.Names.count > 0 Then
        Dim boLink As Boolean: boLink = False
        Dim nm As Name
        Dim lnCount As Long

        ' Traverse Names collection and process each name.
        For Each nm In ws.Names
            If InStr(nm.RefersTo, ".xl") > 0 Then
                If Not boLink Then
                    boLink = True
                    writeIt m_stArrTab(4), "<h3>NAMES</h3>"
                End If
                lnCount = lnCount + 1
                writeIt m_stArrTab(5), "<h4>Name: <span style='color:purple'>" _
                    & nm.Name & "</span></h4>"
                writeIt m_stArrTab(5), "<h4>Refers: <span style='color:red'>" _
                    & nm.RefersTo & "</span></h4>"
                writeIt m_stArrTab(5), "<br/>"
            End If
        Next nm
        ' Output totals if any links were found.
        If boLink Then writeIt m_stArrTab(5), "<h4>No of Names: " & CStr(lnCount) & "</h4>"
    End If
End Sub
```

Figure 11-26: The listNames sub-routine (Links module)

11 - REFERENCES AND LINKS

The **symbolTranslate** function (Figure 11-27) is used to make sure that illegal XML/HTML characters are converted into compatible versions for display in the HTML file and works as follows:

- A text string is passed as an argument for checking.
- An empty replacement string is declared and set to receive the new version.
- Each character is checked by storing and then using against a list of known illegal characters.
- If an illegal character is found it is replaced with the correct version and this converted string is appended to the current replacement string.
- Special characters used for defining HTML elements have a beginning and end tag, so these are checked against, so that they are not converted, if being used as part of a tag definition.

```
(General)                              symbolTranslate

' Translate text string and convert illegal characters in XML/HTML to valid format.

Private Function symbolTranslate(stText)
    ' Declare counter and string to hold converted text.
    Dim lnItem As Long, stConverted As String
    ' Declare and set new text as null.
    Dim stNewText As String: stNewText = vbNullString
    ' Declare flag for tag with false indicating NOT inside tag definition.
    Dim boTag As Boolean
    ' Check each character of input string.
    For lnItem = 1 To Len(stText)
        ' Store one character ready to test.
        stConverted = Mid$(stText, lnItem, 1)
        Select Case stConverted
            Case """"
                If Not boTag Then stConverted = "&quot;"
            Case "#"
                If Not boTag Then stConverted = "&#35;"
            Case "'"
                If Not boTag Then stConverted = "&#39;"
            Case "<"
                If Mid$(stText, lnItem, 4) <> "<ix:"
                    And Mid$(stText, lnItem, 2) <> "</" Then
                    stConverted = "&lt;"
                    boTag = False
                Else
                    boTag = True
                End If
            Case ">"
                If Mid$(stText, lnItem, 1) <> ">" And Not boTag Then
                    stConverted = "&gt;"
                    boTag = False
                Else
                    boTag = True
                End If
            Case "&"
                stConverted = "&amp;"
            Case "£"
                stConverted = "&#163;"
            Case "€"
                stConverted = "&#8364;"
        End Select
        ' Append converted character to new text string.
        stNewText = stNewText & stConverted
    Next lnItem
    symbolTranslate = stNewText
End Function
```

Figure 11-27: The symbolTranslate UDF (Links module)

12

USING FUNCTIONS EFFICIENTLY

12 - USING FUNCTIONS EFFICIENTLY

Whilst functions can extend features, the way they are used can often affect calculation time, so being aware of the pitfalls can aid in finding the optimum solution.

Functions requiring a subscription

With the advent of on-line versions some newer worksheet functions may only be available for those with an **Office 365** subscription.

The **IFS** worksheet function is one such example.

Functions that process ranges

For functions like **SUM**, **SUMIF** and **SUMIFS** that handle ranges, the calculation time is proportional to the number of used cells being summed. Unused cells and non-numerical data are ignored, so whole column references are relatively efficient, but it is better not to include more used cells than needed.

Using tables, subset ranges or dynamic ranges can improve performance.

Volatile functions

Volatile functions can slow recalculation because they increase the number of formulas that must be recalculated at each calculation. These types of functions are those where the value cannot be assumed to be the same from one instance to another, thus requiring a complete recalculation.

Whilst function such as **RANDBETWEEN, NOW** and **TODAY** are obviously volatile, others are less obvious such as **OFFSET** and **INDIRECT**, whilst others are only volatile depending on the arguments being used such as **CELL**, **SUMIF** and **INFO**.

Often the number of volatile functions can be reduced by using **INDEX** instead of **OFFSET** and **CHOOSE** instead of **INDIRECT**.

Note: Some volatile functions such as **OFFSET** may outperform a formula with non-volatile functions used to return the same result.

User defined functions

UDFs can be programmed directly within **VBA** as well as other programming languages (the earliest versions provided the **XLM macro language** which was the basis for the **C API**).

Those programmed as **XLLs** and using the **C API** whilst more complex to create than using the built-in VBA language are regarded as the ideal choice for writing high performance worksheet functions.

The UDF can also link to **System Functions** to return information directly related to the operating system or hardware.

With the introduction of more features and other newer technologies such as those working across multiple platforms, UDFs may have a less important role to play in future releases of the product. For example, the newer worksheet functions **CONCAT** and **TEXTJOIN** allow the combining of text strings, whilst **MAXIFS** and **MINIFS** extend the "IFS" type of functions.

Custom functions

Newer features include the **Office Add-ins** platform (not to be confused with **COM** and **VSTO** add-ins designed to work only on **Office for Windows**) which harnesses the power of web-based technologies such as **JavaScript**, **HTML** and **CSS**.

Custom functions can be created to extend the functionality across multiple platforms and can be used for:

- o Read/Write data and interact with objects.
- o Web based task or content panes.
- o Custom ribbon buttons or contextual menu items.
- o Dialog window with rich interactive features.

An Office Add-in can be published to any of the following locations:

- o Via the Office 365 admin centre for cloud or hybrid deployment.
- o Sharepoint catalogue for on-premises environments.
- o AppSource for public distribution.
- o Network share for on-premises hosting.

Faster user defined functions

Worksheet functions tend to be faster than equivalent UDFs, as there are overheads in calling and transferring data to and from a UDF. Of course, there are always going to be exceptions.

If the UDF requires recalculation whenever cells change it must be made **volatile** by use of the **Application.Volatile** statement within the routine.

Where there are many formulas using these types of functions, it is sometimes prudent to use **Manual calculation** mode.

It is also better to pass references to worksheet cells as input parameters instead of in the body of the UDF, so that adding **Application.Volatile** can be avoided.

UDFs calculate much more slowly if the calculation is not called from VBA (for example, in automatic mode or when the **F9** key is pressed in manual mode). This is particularly true when the **VBE** (**ALT+F11**) is open or has been opened in the current session.

To take control of the **F9** recalculation option it can be redirected by placing a line in an appropriate event handler. In Figure 12-1 the **Workbook Open** event in the **ThisWorkbook** object code is used so that whenever the **F9** key is pressed the **recalc** sub-routine is executed.

Figure 12-1: F9 redirection via code

The **recalc** sub-routine (Figure 12-2) can then be added to a standard module.

```
(General)                                    ▼   recalc                              ▼

      ' Intercepted via ThisWorkbook.Workbook_Open event.

      Public Sub recalc()
          Application.Calculate
          MsgBox "Recalc complete."
      End Sub
```

Figure 12-2: The recalc routine (EventHandling module)

UDFs in **Automation add-ins** do not incur the VBE overhead because they do not use the integrated editor. Other performance characteristics of Visual Basic UDFs in Automation add-ins are similar to functions.

Sometimes a UDF can be used to combine multiple worksheet functions into a new single function.

The previous lookup examples with error checking using the **IFERROR**, **INDEX** and **MATCH** functions can be combined into a new UDF called **ufLOOKUP**. Figure 12-3 shows a formula using this new UDF.

The parameters required in the example **ufLOOKUP** function are:
   o   The lookup value - (**LookupValue**).
   o   The lookup array – (**Lookup** array in the **Lookups** table)
   o   The result array - (**Result** array in the **Lookups** table)
   o   Value to return if an error occurs - ("Not Found" string in the example).

```
=ufLOOKUP(LookupValue,Lookups[Lookup],Lookups[Result],"Not Found")
```

Figure 12-3: The ufLOOKUP UDF formula (UDFs worksheet)

Figure 12-4 shows the result of looking up the value **4** in the **Lookups** table on the **Lookup** column and returning the result of **four** from the **Result** column.

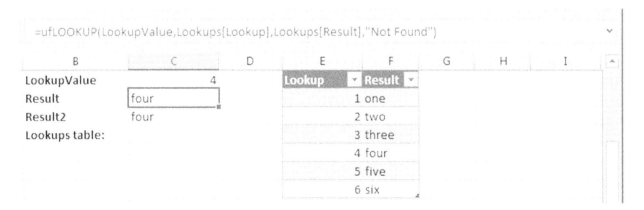

Figure 12-4: The ufLOOKUP UDF example (UDFs worksheet)

The **ufLOOKUP** function code is shown in Figure 12-5. The processes are:

- o Declare **vtResult** as a **Variant** data type to accept any other data type.
- o Use the **MATCH** function to lookup the value (**vtLkUp**) in the lookup array (**vtLkUpArr**) and return the item number.
- o Use the **INDEX** function to return the result from the results array (**vtResultArr**) using the item number returned from the **MATCH** function and store the result to **vtResult**.
- o Check to see if **vtResult** is in error and if not return the result otherwise return the **vtNotFound** argument passed into the UDF.

```
(General)                                          ufLOOKUP

' ufLOOKUP using INDEX and MATCH with error checking.
' MUST be only ONE row or column for lookup and result variant arrays.
' Using variant ensures it works for common data types.

Public Function ufLOOKUP(vtLkUp As Variant, vtLkUpArr As Variant, _
            vtResultArr As Variant, vtNotFound As Variant)

    ' Declare the result as a variant and use the INDEX and MATCH functions
    ' to return the result.
    Dim vtResult As Variant
    vtResult = Application.Index(vtResultArr, Application.Match(vtLkUp, vtLkUpArr, 0))

    If Not IsError(vtResult) Then
        ' Return the result if the INDEX and MATCH worked without error.
        ufLOOKUP = vtResult
    Else
        ' Return the vtNotFound result, passed as the last argument (message, value etc).
        ufLOOKUP = vtNotFound
    End If
End Function
```

Figure 12-5: The ufLOOKUP UDF code (UDFs module)

Note: The **ufLOOKUP** UDF is designed to use one dimension for each of the lookup and result arrays. Error checking could be added to check both arrays. The UDF is added to the list of other worksheet functions, although has the disadvantage of not having automatic intellisense to help in the creation of the formula.

If the UDF is using worksheet functions or object model methods to process a range, it may be more efficient to keep the range as an object variable, rather than transfer the data from the worksheet to the UDF. It may also be possible to replace a worksheet function used within code with an equivalent UDF, or write a specific UDF to combine all the required tasks. For example, a lookup using the worksheet functions INDEX and MATCH might be replaced with one UDF to mimic both functions as in Figure 12-6.

When a UDF is called early in the calculation chain, it can be passed un-calculated arguments which can be detected by testing using **IsEmpty** function and the **HasFormula** property of the cell. If both are **True** then the formula has not yet been calculated and corrective action can be taken.

Each call to a UDF and each transfer of data to and from the worksheet incurs a time overhead. One multiple cell array formula UDF, for example can help minimize this overhead.

Figure 12-6 shows the code for the **ufLOOKUP2** UDF without using any worksheet functions. Using the same arguments as the **ufLOOKUP** UDF the process is as follows:

o Declare and set a counter **InItem** to 1.
o Loop through **vtLkUpArr** until either a match is found for the lookup value (**vtLkUp**) or the item counter (**InItem**) exceeds the number of items in the list.
o Next return the **vtNotFound** argument value if the counter value is greater than the number of items in the list otherwise return the result from the item number in the **vtResultArr**.

```
(General)                                            ufLOOKUP2

' ufLOOKUP2 is WITHOUT the INDEX or MATCH functions.
' Only ONE row or column for lookup and result variant arrays.
' Using variant ensures it works for common data types.

Public Function ufLOOKUP2(vtLkUp As Variant, vtLkUpArr As Variant, _
            vtResultArr As Variant, vtNotFound As Variant)

    ' Start at lower bound of vtLkUpArr (normally 1).
    Dim lnItem As Long: lnItem = 1

    ' Traverse each item in vtLkUpArr until vtLkUp matches value
    ' or end when we run out of items to check.
    Do Until lnItem > vtLkUpArr.count Or vtLkUp = vtLkUpArr(lnItem)
        lnItem = lnItem + 1
    Loop

    ' If too many items then nothing found
    If lnItem > vtLkUpArr.count Then
        ufLOOKUP2 = vtNotFound
    Else
        ' Return result from vtLkUpArr
        ufLOOKUP2 = vtResultArr(lnItem)
    End If
End Function
```

Figure 12-6: The ufLOOKUP2 UDF code (UDFs module)

Subtotals
Use the **SUBTOTAL** function to **SUM** filtered lists.

The **SUBTOTAL** function is useful because, unlike **SUM**, it ignores the following:
o Hidden rows that result from filtering a list. **SUBTOTAL** can also be used to ignore all hidden rows, not just filtered rows.
o Other **SUBTOTAL** functions.

The **SUBTOTAL** has a function number; numbers 1 to 11 includes manually hidden rows, while 101 to 111 excludes them.

In Figure 12-7, 109 is the equivalent **SUM** function and the reference is a column from a structured table. The first and subsequent references must be data columns or vertical ranges.

```
=SUBTOTAL(109,[Sterling (£)])
```

Figure 12-7: SUBTOTAL formula (WorldwideSales worksheet)

Cumulative summing
There are various methods of cumulative summing, for example in Figure 12-8:

1. Create a formula (=B29) which equals the first cell in the **Values** column and place this in the **Results1** column on the same row (C29). Then in the next row of the **Results1** column (C30) create a formula to add the next value to the previous result (=C29+B30). This new formula can then be copied down for the rest of the rows in the **Results1** column to complete the task.

2. Create a formula for the first value as per method 1. Next, SUM the rows in the **Values** column (B) from the start row (29) to the next result row and place this formula in the **Results** column (D). The second row (30) result would thus have the formula =SUM(B29:B20), the third row (31) result would have the formula =SUM(B29:B31) and so on.

Note: The first example of cumulative summing has fewer calculations, so will be faster.

C29				f_x	=B29		
	A		B		C	D	E
28			Values		Results1	Results2	
29				10	10	10	
30				15	25	25	
31				30	55	55	
32				5	60	60	
33				20	80	80	
34				20	100	100	
35							
36			**100**				

Figure 12-8: Cumulative sum example (UDFs worksheet)

Subset summing

Calculation time is normally dependent on the size of a range being calculated, so it can be advantageous to use a dynamically created subset range of rows (or columns) where data is sorted into a specific order.

By combining **MATCH** lookup functions, a subset range can be calculated and used in the **SUM** or **SUMIF** function, although this could be simplified further by creating a **UDF** specifically for the purpose. The formulas then become much easier to read and understand.

In Figure 12-9 a **UDF** named **uf2COLLOOKUP** is used with the following parameters:

- o the first lookup value.
- o the second lookup value.
- o the first lookup array.
- o the second lookup array.
- o the results array.

In Figure 12-9, the defined names **Region** and **Language** are used as lookups to return the **SUM** of the **Population** range (Male and Female totals).

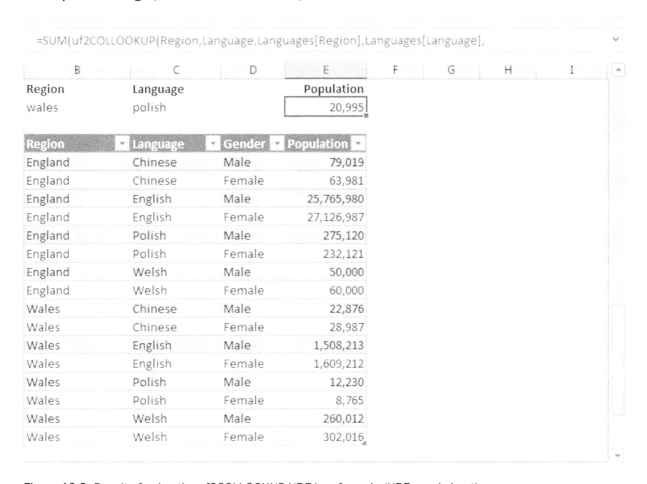

Figure 12-9: Result of using the uf2COLLOOKUP UDF in a formula (UDFs worksheet)

Note: The **uf2COLLOOKUP** UDF only works with columns. The data must be sorted by the first lookup column and then sorted within this range by the second lookup column, so that the results are in adjoining rows.

Figure 12-10 shows the code for the uf2COLLOOKUP UDF.

```
(General)                                      ▼   uf2COLLOOKUP                              ▼

' uf2COLLOOKUP creates a subset range based on a lookup within another lookup.
Public Function uf2COLLOOKUP(vtLkUp1 As Variant, vtLkUp2 As Variant, _
            vtLkUpArr1 As Variant, vtLkUpArr2 As Variant, vtResultArr As Variant)

    On Error Resume Next    ' resume to next line when an error occurs

    ' Find the offset row (as references are relative to table).
    Dim lnOffsetRow As Long
    lnOffsetRow = vtLkUpArr1.row - 1

    ' Return the column number for our second lookup column
    ' to help make up second lookup range.
    Dim lnColLkUp As Long: lnColLkUp = vtLkUpArr2.Column

    ' return first row number or zero if not found (error condition)
    Dim lnBegRow As Long: lnBegRow = Application.Match(vtLkUp1, vtLkUpArr1, 0)

    If lnBegRow > 0 Then
        ' Make up second lookup range using
        ' Range(Cells(start row,lookup lnCol),Cells(end row,lookup lnCol)).
        Dim vtLkUpCol As Range
        Set vtLkUpCol = Range(Cells(lnBegRow + lnOffsetRow, lnColLkUp), _
                    Cells(Application.Match(vtLkUp1, vtLkUpArr1, 1) _
                    + lnOffsetRow, lnColLkUp))

        ' Return item number of results array for final result range.
        Dim lnColResult As Long: lnColResult = vtResultArr.Column

        ' Return offset row for range based on previous lookup.
        lnOffsetRow = vtLkUpCol.row - 1

        ' return our results range to use in SUM or other function
        Dim rgResult As Range
        Set rgResult = Range(Cells(Application.Match(vtLkUp2, vtLkUpCol, 0) _
                    + lnOffsetRow, lnColResult), _
                    Cells(Application.Match(vtLkUp2, vtLkUpCol, 1) _
                    + lnOffsetRow, lnColResult))

        ' Check that a good result was returned.
        If Not IsError(rgResult) Then
            uf2COLLOOKUP = rgResult
        Else
            uf2COLLOOKUP = Nothing
        End If
    Else
        uf2COLLOOKUP = Nothing
    End If
    On Error GoTo 0
End Function
```

Figure 12-10: The uf2COLLOOKUP UDF code (UDFs module)

The methodology used in the UDF in Figure 12-10 is to use the **MATCH** function to find the first row and last row for the first lookup value, then create a lookup range for the second lookup column and again find the first and last row which matches the second lookup value. The row numbers can then be used to return the relevant subset range for the results column.

If the first lookup value does not exist an error occurs, so using **On Error Resume Next** ensures the code continues to the next line where a check is made for the first row being greater than zero, otherwise the range result can be set to nothing and the routine ended.

At both lookup stages it is necessary to calculate the offset from the first actual data row, as the range will be a subset of the whole i.e. starting back at row one again. The offset row value is added to the end result to locate the actual position within the original range.

Our second lookup value might not exist, in which case another error will occur, which can be handled as before.

DFunctions

DFunctions such as **DSUM**, **DCOUNT** and **DAVERAGE** are significantly faster than equivalent array formulas.

Figure 12-11 shows an equivalent formula to that in Figure 12-9 replacing the **SUM** and **uf2COLLOOKUP** UDF with a **DSUM**. The entire array (**UKLang[#All]**) is looked up using the defined name range (**RegionLangCriteria**) with the results being returned from the **Population** column. The **RegionLangCriteria** range includes column heading descriptions and values (B1:C2). Cell B1 has the criteria "Region" and cell C1 the criteria "Language", the values to lookup "wales" being in cell B2 and "polish" being in cell C2. The criteria must match the column headings.

```
=DSUM(UKLang[#All],"Population",RegionLangCriteria)
```

Figure 12-11: DSUM formula (DFunctions worksheet)

DFunctions may also be faster than using a subset range depending on size of range being calculated and the equivalent **SUMIFS**, **COUNTIFS** and **AVERAGEIFS** functions. Figure 12-12 shows a **SUMIFS** formula equivalent to the **DSUM** formula in Figure 12-11.

```
=SUMIFS(UKLang[Population],UKLang[Region],RegionCriteria,UKLang[Language],LangCriteria)
```

Figure 12-12: Equivalent SUMIFS formula example (DFunctions worksheet)

Note: With the equivalent example **SUMIFS** each set of criteria has to be defined separately whereas with a **DSUM** the criteria are specified as a range of cells, which may be a potential disadvantage (Figure 12-12).

Passing data between workbook and VBA code

Reading and writing data between a workbook and code should be minimized but when necessary there are methods which can be employed to make the task easier and with the minimum of overhead.

If the necessity arises, copy the entire range into a variant array variable in VBA code and then back again after the task is completed.

In Figure 12-13, a **selected range** containing columns with the **Name** and **Age** of some people is passed to a VBA routine (**sortRange**) which sorts the data by column number **2** (**Age**) in **Ascending** order and then passes it back to the worksheet.

	A	B	C
1	Name	Age	
2	Steve	58	
3	Roger	78	
4	Lindsey	62	
5	Jane	76	
6	Doug	43	
7	Dave	43	
8	Bob	62	
9	Babs	57	

Figure 12-13: Sorting example (Sorting worksheet)

Note: **sortRange** is a special macro example in that it uses parameters, so is not displayed in the Macro dialog. To execute it is necessary to enter the macro name enclosed in single quotation marks (') followed by a space and the arguments separated by commas (,) matching the required parameters; the column number to sort by and whether the data is sorted in ascending order.

Figure 12-14 shows the **Run Macro** dialog with the **sortRange** macro input to sort the **selected range** by column 2 in descending order (**false** value). To sort in ascending order the last argument would be set as a **true** value.

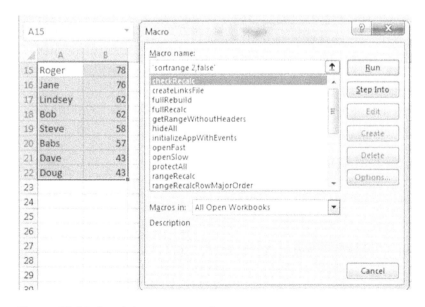

Figure 12-14: Special macro example

To run the macro input into the Macro name box, *click* the **Run** button (Figure 12-14).

Note: The **selected range** should not include the headers otherwise they will be included in the sort.

Although not a UDF the **sortRange** sub-routine (Figure 12-15) shows one method of transferring data to and from the worksheet.

The **sortRange** sub-routine handles the reading and writing of the range data, with the sorting being handled by the appropriate quicksort routine.

The **selected range** is read into a variant array variable **then** passed to the sorting routine with parameters to sort by the specified column and whether in ascending or descending order and then replaced with the newly sorted array.

The **selected range** is stored as a transposed variant array within the routine prior to processing by the appropriate quicksort routine.

Note: Transposing a range reverses the dimensions so that the variable dimension (typically the rows) is the last one in the array. When re-dimensioning a dynamic array it is only the last dimension which can be changed. This makes a routine more flexible when used with other routines which need to re-dimension an array and then sort the contents.

On completion the selected range is replaced by the newly sorted array once transposed back into its original state.

```
(General)                                        sortRange

   Public Sub sortRange(lnCol As Long, boAsc As Boolean)

       Dim vtArr() As Variant
       If IsArray(Selection.Value) Then
           vtArr = Application.Transpose(Selection.Value)
       Else
           Exit Sub
       End If

       ' Sort vtArr array on column lnCol from item 1 to the last item
       ' either in ascending or descending order based on boAsc.
       If boAsc Then
           quickSortAsc vtArr, lnCol, 1, UBound(vtArr, 2)
       Else
           quickSortDsc vtArr, lnCol, 1, UBound(vtArr, 2)
       End If
       Selection.Value = Application.Transpose(vtArr)
   End Sub
```

Figure 12-15: The sortRange sub-routine (Sorting module)

Note: The quicksort routines also require the value of the first and last row as arguments which are passed by value (**ByVal**) not by reference (**ByRef**). This is due to the fact that they are recursive i.e. call themselves using different values for these two parameters.

Figure 12-16 shows the **quickSortAsc** sub-routine which sorts an array in Ascending order. Although the routine looks at first glance quick complex, the fundamentals are fairly simple (as with most sorting routines). It works by moving an item to its final position in the list being sorted and whilst performing this task rearranging other items before and after the original item, so that the list is partitioned into two smaller sub-lists. In turn this task is repeated until there are no more items to sort. The sub-routine is called recursively that is by itself to achieve the task of sorting the sub-lists.

This type of routine is one of the best for sorting as it optimises the process in most if not all cases.

```
(General)                                        ▼   quickSortAsc                                          ▼

Public Sub quickSortAsc(ByRef vtArrItem() As Variant, ByRef lnCol As Long, _
    ByVal lnLPart As Long, ByVal lnRPart As Long)
    Dim lnPosHolder As Long, lnPointer As Long, lnLTmp As Long, lnRTmp As Long
    Dim lnColumns As Long: lnColumns = UBound(vtArrItem, 1)
    If lnRPart - lnLPart > 1 Then
        lnPosHolder = lnLPart
        lnLTmp = lnLPart
        lnRTmp = lnRPart + 1
Lbl1:
        lnRTmp = lnRTmp - 1
        If vtArrItem(lnCol, lnRTmp) > vtArrItem(lnCol, lnPosHolder) Then GoTo Lbl1
        If lnRTmp = lnPosHolder Then GoTo Lbl3
Lbl2:
        lnLTmp = lnLTmp + 1
        If lnLTmp < lnRTmp Then
            If vtArrItem(lnCol, lnLTmp) <= vtArrItem(lnCol, lnPosHolder) Then GoTo Lbl2
            swapArrayRows vtArrItem, lnColumns, lnLTmp, lnRTmp: GoTo Lbl1
        End If
        If lnLTmp = lnRTmp _
            And vtArrItem(lnCol, lnRTmp) >= vtArrItem(lnCol, lnPosHolder) Then
            lnRTmp = lnRTmp - 1
        End If
        swapArrayRows vtArrItem, lnColumns, lnRTmp, lnPosHolder
Lbl3:
        lnPointer = lnRTmp
        If lnPointer = lnLPart Then
            Call quickSortAsc(vtArrItem, lnCol, lnLPart + 1, lnRPart)
        Else
            If lnPointer = lnRPart Then
                Call quickSortAsc(vtArrItem, lnCol, lnLPart, lnRPart - 1)
            Else
                If 2 * lnPointer - lnLPart > lnRPart Then
                    Call quickSortAsc(vtArrItem, lnCol, lnPointer + 1, lnRPart)
                    Call quickSortAsc(vtArrItem, lnCol, lnLPart, lnPointer - 1)
                Else
                    Call quickSortAsc(vtArrItem, lnCol, lnLPart, lnPointer - 1)
                    Call quickSortAsc(vtArrItem, lnCol, lnPointer + 1, lnRPart)
                End If
            End If
        End If
    Else
        ' Final swap if last two elements are out of sequence
        If lnRPart - lnLPart = 1 And _
                vtArrItem(lnCol, lnLPart) > vtArrItem(lnCol, lnRPart) Then
            swapArrayRows vtArrItem, lnColumns, lnLPart, lnRPart
        End If
    End If
End Sub
```

Figure 12-16: The quickSortAsc sub-routine (Sorting module)

Figure 12-17 shows the **quickSortDsc** routine for sorting in a Descending order.

```
(General)                                                quickSortDsc

    Public Sub quickSortDsc(ByRef vtArrItem() As Variant, ByVal lnCol As Long, _
        ByVal lnLPart As Long, ByVal lnRPart As Long)
        Dim lnPosHolder As Long, lnPointer As Long, lnLTmp As Long, lnRTmp As Long
        Dim lnColumns As Long: lnColumns = UBound(vtArrItem, 1)
        If lnRPart - lnLPart > 1 Then
            lnPosHolder = lnLPart
            lnLTmp = lnLPart
            lnRTmp = lnRPart + 1
    Lbl1:
            lnRTmp = lnRTmp - 1
            If vtArrItem(lnCol, lnRTmp) < vtArrItem(lnCol, lnPosHolder) Then GoTo Lbl1
            If lnRTmp = lnPosHolder Then GoTo Lbl3
    Lbl2:
            lnLTmp = lnLTmp + 1
            If lnLTmp < lnRTmp Then
                If vtArrItem(lnCol, lnLTmp) > vtArrItem(lnCol, lnPosHolder) Then GoTo Lbl2
                swapArrayRows vtArrItem, lnColumns, lnLTmp, lnRTmp: GoTo Lbl1
            End If
            If lnLTmp = lnRTmp _
                And vtArrItem(lnCol, lnRTmp) < vtArrItem(lnCol, lnPosHolder) Then
                lnRTmp = lnRTmp - 1
            End If
            swapArrayRows vtArrItem, lnColumns, lnRTmp, lnPosHolder
    Lbl3:
            lnPointer = lnRTmp
            If lnPointer = lnLPart Then
                Call quickSortDsc(vtArrItem, lnCol, lnLPart + 1, lnRPart)
            Else
                If lnPointer = lnRPart Then
                    Call quickSortDsc(vtArrItem, lnCol, lnLPart, lnRPart - 1)
                Else
                    If 2 * lnPointer - lnLPart > lnRPart Then
                        Call quickSortDsc(vtArrItem, lnCol, lnPointer + 1, lnRPart)
                        Call quickSortDsc(vtArrItem, lnCol, lnLPart, lnPointer - 1)
                    Else
                        Call quickSortDsc(vtArrItem, lnCol, lnLPart, lnPointer - 1)
                        Call quickSortDsc(vtArrItem, lnCol, lnPointer + 1, lnRPart)
                    End If
                End If
            End If
        Else
            ' Final swap if last two elements are out of sequence
            If lnRPart - lnLPart = 1 _
                And vtArrItem(lnCol, lnLPart) <= vtArrItem(lnCol, lnRPart) Then
                swapArrayRows vtArrItem, lnColumns, lnLPart, lnRPart
            End If
        End If
    End Sub
```

Figure 12-17: The quickSortDsc sub-routine (Sorting module)

Note: The quick sort routines in Figures 12-16 and 12-17 are based on a version originally coded by the author of this guide (circa 1979 in the Algol language) for improved performance and based on the work of C.A.R. Hoare and his theories on partition-exchange sorting.

In the quick sort routines, a further sub-routine **swapArrayRows** is used to swap array rows which are out of sequence (Figure 12-18).

```
(General)                                          swapArrayRows

    Private Sub swapArrayRows(vtArrItem() As Variant, _
            lnColumns As Long, lnLPart As Long, lnRPart As Long)

        ' Create a temporary dumping ground array for the no of columns.
        Dim vtDump() As Variant
        ReDim vtDump(lnColumns)

        ' Swap each column.
        Dim lnCol As Long
        For lnCol = 1 To lnColumns
            vtDump(lnCol) = vtArrItem(lnCol, lnLPart)
            vtArrItem(lnCol, lnLPart) = vtArrItem(lnCol, lnRPart)
            vtArrItem(lnCol, lnRPart) = vtDump(lnCol)
        Next lnCol

    End Sub
```

Figure 12-18: The swapArrayRows sub-routine (Sorting module)

In Figure 12-18, the first of the two array rows to be swapped is stored column by column in a temporary variable, so that it can be replaced with its new value. The temporary stored row then replaces the second of the two rows, to complete the swapping process.

To copy the sorted array to another worksheet location a UDF could be written and used in an **array formula**. The result of such a formula is shown in Figure 12-19 using the **ufSORT** UDF which has three parameters:

- o Range to sort.
- o Which column in range to use to sort on.
- o Sort Ascending (TRUE) or Descending (FALSE).

D2				f_x {=ufSORT(A2:B9,2,FALSE)}						
	A	B	C	D	E	F	G	H	I	J
1	Name	Age								
2	Steve	58		Roger	78					
3	Roger	78		Jane	76					
4	Lindsey	62		Bob	62					
5	Jane	76		Lindsey	62					
6	Doug	43		Steve	58					
7	Dave	43		Babs	57					
8	Bob	62		Dave	43					
9	Babs	57		Doug	43					

Figure 12-19: Example ufSORT UDF CSE formula result

In Figure 12-20, the sort range **"A2:B9"** is sorted by column **2** in descending order (the **FALSE** value). The **array formula** is entered into an equivalent selected range to that being sorted (without the header row, otherwise it would be included in the sort).

```
{=ufSORT(A2:B9,2,FALSE)}
```

Figure 12-20: Sorting function example (Sorting worksheet)

The **ufSORT** UDF code is shown in Figure 12-21 and works as follows:

- o The range is passed as **rgData** and checked to make sure it is an array (not just a single cell otherwise the "No array" message is returned).
- o The range is then stored as a transposed array (**vtArr**) since the range will be supplied in **column-row** order rather than **row-column** order. The transposed array is passed to the appropriate quicksort routine as determined by the **boAsc** argument (Ascending by default).
- o Once the array has been sorted it is transposed back to its original format and returned as the result.

```
(General)                                    ▼    ufSORT                              ▼

Public Function ufSORT(rgData As Range, lnCol As Long, boAsc As Boolean)
    ' Check that the range passed as an argument is an array.
    If Not IsArray(rgData) Then
        ufSORT = "No array"
        Exit Function
    End If

    ' Declare an array to hold the data range to be sorted and transpose it
    ' as the range will be column/row rather than row/column order.
    Dim vtArr() As Variant
    vtArr = Application.Transpose(rgData)

    If boAsc Then
        quickSortAsc vtArr, lnCol, 1, UBound(vtArr, 2)
    Else
        quickSortDsc vtArr, lnCol, 1, UBound(vtArr, 2)
    End If
    ' Transpose the sorted array.
    ufSORT = Application.Transpose(vtArr)
End Function
```

Figure 12-21: The ufSORT UDF (Sorting module)

Note: Since a UDF requires the input of an array formula and copying of the original data to another location, it may be more useful to use a sub-routine to process a range in situ for most cases.

Wildcards in functions

Many functions allow the use of the wildcard characters which can also be used in combination with the **Like** operator to compare strings:

- o ? (any single character)
- o * (none or any number of characters)
- o # (any single digit)
- o [*charlist*] (any single character in *charlist*)
- o [!*charlist*] (any single character not in *charlist*)

as part of the criteria on alphabetical ranges and string comparisons.

The special characters:

- o exclamation point (!) at the beginning of a character list to indicate any character *except* those in the list.
- o hyphen (-) at the beginning or end of a list to match itself or between characters to indicate a range of characters.
- o Brackets ([ ]) surrounding a valid pattern which must be in ascending order i.e. [A-Z] not [Z-A] to match to a single character.

For example,

- o [A-Z] matches any single alphabetic upper-case character.
- o [a-zA-Z0-9] matches any single alphanumeric character.
- o [!A-Z] matches to any single non-alphabetic upper-case character.
- o "a*" matches to any string beginning with the letter a.
- o "a#" matches to a string beginning with the letter a followed by a numeric digit i.e. **"a2a" Like "a#a"** returns **True**.
- o "a[*]b" matches to the exact string a*b.
- o "a?" matches to a two-character string beginning with the letter a i.e. **"a2" Like "a?"** returns **True** but **"abc" Like "a?"** returns **False**.

13

PERFORMANCE OPTIMISATION

13 - PERFORMANCE OPTIMISATION

Sometimes opening, closing, and saving workbooks is much slower than expected. This may simply because the workbook is large, but there may also be other causes.

There are many methods which may be employed to improve workbook performance from changing the hardware and operating system configuration to saving in a different file format or making design changes on the workbook itself.

Use enough memory

Although the majority of personal computers today use 64-bit operating systems, many applications are still only 32-bit. In fact, many manufacturers may recommend using the 32-bit version of their application even where they have both available. One of the issues moving from 32-bit to 64-bit is that of compatibility as third-party software might not work with the 64-bit version.

Originally 32-bit versions were only capable of using up to 2 GB of RAM. With the introduction of the **Large Address Aware** (LAA) feature this increased to 3gb on 32-bit Windows (providing the PC has 4gb of RAM installed and the "/3gb" boot switch enabled) and 4gb on 64-bit Windows (providing the machine has 4gb of free memory for the application to use).

Expert users may benefit more from the 64-bit versions especially if they require the extra resources which may be available with more RAM and/or larger file sizes.

Save workbooks in xlsb format

Most users are unaware of the pros and cons of the **.xlsb** Binary Workbook Format.

Binary Workbook files store information in binary format instead of the XML format like with most other files. Since XLSB files are binary, they can be read from and written to much faster, making them extremely useful for very large spreadsheets. This also implies that with XLSB files calculations will be faster and workbooks much smaller.

XLSX can take up to four times longer to load, twice as long to save and can be one and a half times the file size of XLSB, so well worth considering.

In addition, from a security point of view, since data is in binary format and not in XML, XLSB files will display unreadable contents if a user tries to change the extension of the file.

Other advantages of XLSB file format include:
- o Saving in binary allows formulas to be saved properly if they are longer than the standard limit.
- o Macros i.e. VBA code is fully supported.

Disadvantages of XLSB files:
- o No Ribbon modification allowed for XLSB formats. Convert back to XLSM, make the Ribbon changes and then convert back to XLSB.
- o A potential lack of interoperability with OpenOffice.
- o Not compatible with the 2003 and earlier versions.
- o Compatibility in using the data with software that wants XML instead of binary (web server for instance). Linking between layers of an XML based system will no longer work.

Minimizing the used range

Used ranges larger than those actually being used can cause slow opening and increased file size.

The cell location for the perceived last row and column can be found by using the shortcut key combination **CTRL+END**. Removing any "invisible" rows and columns may help improve performance.

Remove add-ins which slow down startup

Add-ins can increase loading time, so removing those not used can be of benefit.

To disable one or more Add-ins, use the appropriate dialog for the type of add-in.

There is an **Add-ins** group from the **Developer** tab on the ribbon (if enabled) where the different types of add-in can be selected.

Alternatively, choose **File**->**Options** then *click the* **Add-ins** tab from the **Excel Options** dialog.

Next, on the **Manage** drop-down menu *click* the type of **Add-in** required and then *click* the **Go...** button.

Within the presented **Add-ins** dialog untick all add-ins not used and *click* **OK** to finish.

Control calculation mode to improve processing

In complex workbooks, changing one value in a cell can affect numerous reiterative calculations, so every time a change is made it is necessary to wait for the calculations to finish. Setting calculation mode to manual before data input and then setting back again afterwards will alleviate bottlenecks.

Control calculation mode to speed up open and save

When a workbook is recalculated on opening or saving, this process may take longer than expected. Controlling when calculations take place can help improve performance.

Other reasons for slow open and close

If one or more workbooks open and close more slowly than is reasonable, it might be caused by interference from concurrent applications or higher levels of processing than normal within the operating system.

Other contributory factors may need investigating to determine the exact cause.

Open externally referenced workbooks beforehand

Opening externally referenced workbooks before those that link to them is to be encouraged as this can improve performance. It is possible to automate the process of opening all required workbooks. One method would be to create a master workbook with the VBA code, which then opens the workbooks in the order required to ensure the best performance.

For example, when the **Workbook Calculation** option in the **Excel Options** dialog is set to **Manual**, the **Recalculate workbook** before **saving** is enabled by default. The process of saving may be much slower than expected but the opening process may be much quicker as a result. As an alternative, the workbook can be set to manual calculation mode only, without any recalculation on saving. The downside of this option is that the user must manage recalculation manually via the **Calculate Now** (**F9** shortcut) option.

Use defined names wisely

Defined names are one of the most powerful features, but they do take additional calculation time. Using names that refer to other worksheets adds an additional level of complexity to the calculation process. Also, try to avoid nested names (names that refer to other names).

Because names are calculated every time a formula that refers to them is calculated, avoid putting calculation-intensive formulas or functions in defined names. In these cases, it can be significantly faster to put calculation-intensive formula or function in a spare cell somewhere and refer to that cell instead, either directly or by using a name.

Reduce the amount of formatting

A workbook doesn't have to be pretty, so use as little formatting as required to keep it legible.

To test for formatting issues, make a copy of the workbook and remove formatting to test it. To select formatting press **CTRL+A** to select one worksheet, then whilst holding down the **SHIFT** key *click* the last worksheet tab to select all worksheets.

Then, in the **Home** Ribbon's **Editing** group, *click* the drop-down arrow next to the **Clear** icon and select **Clear Formats**. Save the file. Now reload to see the difference.

Reduce the number of formulas that are used only occasionally

Many workbooks contain a significant number of formulas and lookups that are concerned with getting the input data into the appropriate shape for the calculations or are being used as defensive measures against changes in the size or shape of the data. When blocks of formulas are used only occasionally, copy and paste special values to temporarily eliminate the formulas, or put them in a separate, rarely opened workbook. Because worksheet errors are often caused by not noticing that formulas have been converted to values, the separate workbook method may be preferable.

Limit hidden rows or columns with non-standard formatting

Hidden rows or columns that have non-standard height or width can also affect the performance of the workbook.

Limit the use of conditional formats and data validation

Conditional formats and data validation are useful but excessive use can significantly slow down calculation. If the cell is displayed, every conditional format formula is evaluated at each calculation and also when the display of the cell that contains the conditional format is refreshed. The object model has a **Worksheet.EnableFormatConditionsCalculation** property for enabling or disabling the calculation of conditional formats.

Remove temporary files

Temporary files can accumulate. These files are created for the workbook, and in particular, for controls that are used by open workbooks. Software installation programs also create temporary files. If the application stops responding for any reason, it may be necessary to delete these files.

Too many temporary files can cause problems, requiring an occasional clean up. However, if software is installed that requires a restart of the computer it should be restarted before deleting the temporary files.

Reduce the number of controls on worksheets

Whilst worksheet controls can be used to improve the design of a workbook, an excessive number can slow down the speed of opening a workbook because of the number of temporary files that are used.

Improve workbook efficiency

There are numerous ways to improve the efficiency of workbook calculations such as:

- o Minimizing the number of actual calculations.
- o Improving formulas.
- o Using helper columns and rows to reduce complexity.
- o Reducing volatility.
- o Minimizing the size of ranges used in calculations.
- o Avoiding single-threaded functions.
- o Using efficient worksheet functions in preference to UDFs and array formulas.
- o Sorting data for improving lookup performance.

Use workbook protection only if actually required

A workbook that is protected may open and close much slower than one without protection.

In some case protection may be a necessity, such as with workbooks containing company payroll information. Various protection methods are available.

For encryption of the workbook with a password use the **File->Info->Protect Workbook->Encrypt with Password** option.

To protect the structure with a password, use the **File->Info->Protect Workbook->Protect Workbook Structure** option. This prevents adding, removing or renaming sheets and can be useful when VBA uses specific sheets in the code.

The structure can be protected without a password but this can be overridden by selecting the same option again (without adding a password again) to remove the protected status.

A workbook may be marked as **Final** and saved as **read-only**, this being a method to discourage editing. When opening such a workbook a prompt is displayed to indicate this status with a button to **Edit Anyway**.

Individual sheets in a workbook may be protected with or without a password. The **File->Info->Protect Workbook->Protect Current Sheet** option works in the same fashion as the protection of the workbook structure.

Sheet protection options are also available from the ribbon. *Click* the **Home** tab, then the **Format** option in the **Cells** group and lastly either the **Protect Sheet** option or the **Unprotect Sheet** option depending on the status of the current sheet.

The **Protect Sheet** dialog (Figure 13-1) can be used not only to password protect the sheet (or not) but also controls which elements can be protected.

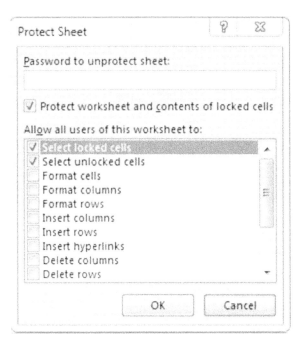

Figure 13-1: Protect sheet dialog

When saving a workbook using the **File**->**Save As** option there is a further option for password protecting the file. In the **Save As** dialog *click* the **Tools** button and then from the dropdown menu *click* the **General Options...** option. In the **General Options** dialog (Figure 13-2) a password can be entered both to **Open** and to **Modify** the file and a checkbox to set the workbook as **Read-only** (this is recommended). Finally *click* the **OK** button to complete the task.

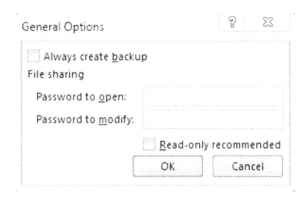

Figure 13-2: General options dialog

The **read-only** status can be overridden when the workbook is opened, if necessary when the password to **Modify** has been input.

The **Save As** option should be used with the **General Options** dialog to remove all passwords (simply by deleting the characters shown).

Disable the tracking changes in a shared workbook feature

The older method of tracking changes in a Shared Workbook has many limitations and has been replaced by co-authoring, a feature of Office 365 and available by subscription.

Whilst the tracking changes option may still be available it is prone to increased file size, so can slow down workbook processing.

Check that the toolbar file is not an issue

Each user has a unique XLB file comprising their customized toolbar which is typically between 10 KB and 20 KB in size.

Renaming it, will cause a new one to be created without any customizations which can reveal if there is any kind of slowdown on loading the application.

Note: The new version can be removed and the old renamed one restored if necessary.

Use pivot tables to report data

PivotTables provide an efficient way to summaries large amounts of data.

Totals as Final Results

To produce totals and subtotals as part of the final results of the workbook, try using PivotTables.

Totals as Intermediate Results

PivotTables are a great way to produce summary reports, but try to avoid creating formulas that use PivotTable results as intermediate totals and subtotals in the calculation chain unless they meet the following conditions:

- The PivotTable has been refreshed correctly during the calculation.
- The PivotTable has not been changed so that the information is still visible.

If PivotTables are required for intermediate results, try using the **GETPIVOTDATA** function.

Defragment the disk

Be sure that any operating system swap files are located on a disk that has a plenty of free space and that the disk is defragmented.

Check that virus scanner does not interfere with file operations

Some virus scanner settings can cause issues with file operations. Exceptions can normally be added to the virus scanner for those workbooks known to be safe. The virus scanner can be disabled temporarily when testing their effects on file operations.

14

USEFUL FORMALAS, MACROS AND UDFS

14 - USEFUL FORMULAS, MACROS AND UDFS

This section contains some potentially useful worksheet formulas.

Functions used in these examples include:

CLEAN

Removes the first 32 non-printing characters in the 7-bit ASCII code (values 0 to 31) from text.

CODE

Returns the ANSI code of the first character of a specified text string, which may be required to determine codes for hidden or non-printable characters.

IFERROR

Returns the value specified if a formula evaluates to an error, otherwise return the result of the formula.

LEN

Returns the number of characters in a text string.

SUBSTITUTE

Replaces specified text within a text string with a different text string and optionally specify just one occurrence of the specified text rather than all occurrences.

Note: This function can be used to replace higher value Unicode characters which CLEAN does not remove.

TEXT

Convert a numeric value into a text string and formats according to the specified format code.

TRIM

Removes the 7-bit ASCII code value 32 (space characters) from text.

TYPE

Returns the type of value as follows:
- o 1 – Number
- o 2 – Text
- o 4 – Logical value
- o 16 – Error value
- o 64 - Array

VALUE

Converts a numeric string into a numeric value.

Data cleaning

Sometimes data in cells contain unwanted characters, either at the beginning, in between characters or at the end. There are a number of useful worksheet functions which can be used within formulas to clean data such as that imported from other systems or incorrectly entered during data input.

TRIM removes spaces from the start and end of a text value (Figure 14-1).

```
=TRIM(A2)
```

Figure 14-1: Using the TRIM function (UsefulFormulas worksheet)

SUBSTITUTE replaces one string with another such as replacing any space character from a string with an empty text string (Figure 14-2).

```
=SUBSTITUTE(A3," ","")
```

Figure 14-2: Using the SUBSTITUTE function (UsefulFormulas worksheet)

VALUE returns the numeric value of a text string and can be used in conjunction with **TRIM** and **CLEAN** to convert a numeric text string with leading zeroes which may also contain unwanted characters to a numeric value (Figure 14-3).

```
=VALUE(TRIM(CLEAN(A4)))
```

Figure 14-3: Using the VALUE function (UsefulFormulas worksheet)

TEXT can be used to convert a value into a text string which in combination with **TRIM** and **CLEAN** can convert a numeric text string which may contain unwanted characters to a numeric value and then reformat as a text string (Figure 14-4).

```
=TEXT(VALUE(TRIM(CLEAN(A5))),"#")
```

Figure 14-4: Using the TEXT function (UsefulFormulas worksheet)

In Figure 14-5 the **ufREMOVE** UDF can be used to trim and then remove all occurrences of an unwanted character only from the start or end of the string, finally using **CLEAN** to remove any other unwanted characters.

```
=CLEAN(ufREMOVE(A6,0,TRUE))
```

Figure 14-5: Using the ufREMOVE UDF (UsefulFormulas worksheet)

The **ufREMOVE** UDF in Figure 14-6 takes the arguments of the original text string, text string to remove and whether to start search from the beginning (TRUE) or end (FALSE).

```
(General)                                              ▼    ufREMOVE                                              ▼

Function ufREMOVE(stText As String, stTextToRemove As String, _
        boForwardDirection As Boolean) As String

    ' Use to determine if character found in string.
    Dim boFound As Boolean: boFound = False

    ' Set up direction of looping.
    Dim lnItem As Long, lnBeg As Long, lnEnd As Long, lnDirection As Long
    If boForwardDirection Then
        lnDirection = 1
        lnBeg = 1
        lnEnd = Len(stText)
    Else
        lnDirection = -1
        lnBeg = Len(stText)
        lnEnd = 1
    End If

    ' Remove spaces surrounding string.
    stText = Trim(stText)

    ' Check string and locate first position past unwanted character.
    For lnItem = lnBeg To lnEnd Step lnDirection
        If Mid(stText, lnItem, 1) <> stTextToRemove Then
            ' Return result.
            boFound = True
            If lnDirection = 1 Then
                ufREMOVE = Mid(stText, lnItem)
            Else
                ufREMOVE = Mid(stText, 1, lnItem)
            End If
            Exit For
        End If
    Next lnItem
    ' Return trimmed string only if unwanted character missing.
    If Not boFound Then ufREMOVE = stText
End Function
```

Figure 14-6: The ufREMOVE UDF (UDFs module)

Splitting text values into two parts

Sometimes there is a requirement to split a value into separate parts such as splitting first name from surname and storing in separate cells.

Figure 14-7 shows a formula for retrieving just the **left** part of a **text** value which has two words separated by a space or nothing if there is only one word.

```
=IFERROR(LEFT(A7,FIND(" ",A7)-1),"")
```

Figure 14-7: Using the LEFT function (UsefulFormulas worksheet)

Figure 14-8 shows a formula for retrieving the **right** part of the **text** value or the value itself if there is only one word.

```
=IFERROR(RIGHT(A7,LEN(A7)-FIND(" ",A7)),A7)
```

Figure 14-8: Using the RIGHT function (UsefulFormulas worksheet)

Figure 14-9, shows examples of data cleaning. The columns are **Before** and **After** with the **Length** of the string and **Type** value.

| E2 | | | | | f_x | =TYPE(C2) | |

	A	B	C	D	E	
1	Before	Len	After	Len	Type	
2	abcdef	9	abcdef	6	2	
3	ab cd ef	11	abcdef	6	2	
4	00012344	12	12344	5	1	
5	00012344	12	12344	5	2	
6	0000abc256	10	abc256	6	2	
7	Simon Towell	12	Simon	5		
8			Towell	6		

Figure 14-9: Examples of data cleaning (UsefulFormulas worksheet)

Note: Where multiple rows or columns require data cleaning it may be advantageous to write a sub-routine to process the entire range in and replace with the result or add to a new worksheet.

Functions used in combination with others

LEN is used to return the number of characters (including spaces and other characters) in a text string (Figure 14-10).

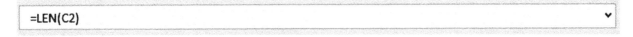

```
=LEN(C2)
```

Figure 14-10: Using the LEN function (UsefulFormulas worksheet)

TYPE is used to return the type of a value (Figure 14-11).

```
=TYPE(C2)
```

Figure 14-11: Using the TYPE function (UsefulFormulas worksheet)

Worksheet protection and visibility

Automating commonly used workbook features can be a way of saving time when processing workbooks, such as worksheet protection and visibility (Figure 14-12).

```
(General)                                    protectionAndVisibility

    Option Explicit
Public Sub protectAll()
    protectionAndVisibility "protect"
End Sub
Public Sub unProtectAll()
    protectionAndVisibility "unprotect"
End Sub
Public Sub hideAll()
    protectionAndVisibility "hide"
End Sub
Public Sub unhideAll()
    protectionAndVisibility "unhide"
End Sub
Public Sub veryHide()
    protectionAndVisibility "veryhide"
End Sub
```

Figure 14-12: Protection and visibility macro examples (ProtectionAndVisibility module)

```
(General)                                    protectionAndVisibility

    ' Action for all sheets in this workbook.
Private Sub protectionAndVisibility(stAction As String)
    On Error Resume Next
    Dim ws As Worksheet
    Dim wb As Workbook: Set wb = ThisWorkbook
    ' Apply protection for every worksheet in worksheets collection.
    For Each ws In wb.Worksheets
        Select Case LCase(stAction)
            Case "protect"
                ws.Protect
            Case "unprotect"
                ws.Unprotect
            Case "hide"
                ws.Visible = xlSheetHidden
            Case "unhide"
                ws.Visible = xlSheetVisible
            Case "veryhide"
                ws.Visible = xlSheetVeryHidden
        End Select
    Next ws
    On Error GoTo 0
End Sub
```

Figure 14-13: The protectionAndVisibility sub-routine (ProtectionAndVisibility module)

The examples in Figure 14-12 and Figure 14-13 could be extended to work on individual sheets.

Note: The error checking in Figure 14-13 could be changed to provide further information on causes of errors and possible solutions for individual worksheets. The routine shown is purely for the sake of an example.

Check digit validation

Sometimes it is necessary to validate cell values which conform to standard formats. For example, the ISBN code printed on a book uses a check digit to verify that the code is correctly formatted. Until the end of 2006 the ISBN code comprised 10 digits but since then it has been 13 digits.

Figure 14-14 shows two UDFs, **ufCHECKISBN13** and **ufCHECKISBN10** which could be used to validate these codes.

```
(General)                                        ▼   ufCHECKISBN10                                ▼

    Function ufCHECKISBN13(vtISBN As Variant)                                                     ▲

        Dim stText As String: stText = Left(vtISBN, 12)
        Dim stCheckDigit As String: stCheckDigit = Right(vtISBN, 1)
        Dim lnTotal As Long: lnTotal = 0
        Dim lnItem As Long
        For lnItem = 1 To Len(stText)
            lnTotal = lnTotal + Val(Mid(stText, lnItem, 1)) * IIf((lnItem Mod 2) = 0, 3, 1)
        Next lnItem

        lnTotal = lnTotal Mod 10

        If lnTotal <> 0 Then lnTotal = 10 - lnTotal

        If Trim(Str(lnTotal)) = stCheckDigit Then
            ufCHECKISBN13 = "OK"
        Else
            ufCHECKISBN13 = "INVALID"
        End If
    End Function

    Function ufCHECKISBN10(vtISBN As Variant)

        Dim stText As String: stText = Left(vtISBN, 9)
        Dim stCheckDigit As String: stCheckDigit = Right(vtISBN, 1)
        Dim lnTotal As Long: lnTotal = 0
        Dim lnItem As Long
        For lnItem = 1 To Len(stText)
            lnTotal = lnTotal + Val(Mid(stText, lnItem, 1)) * (11 - lnItem)
        Next lnItem

        lnTotal = lnTotal Mod 11

        If lnTotal <> 0 Then lnTotal = 11 - lnTotal

        If Trim(Str(lnTotal)) = stCheckDigit Then
            ufCHECKISBN10 = "OK"
        Else
            ufCHECKISBN10 = "INVALID"
        End If
    End Function                                                                                  ▼
```

Figure 14-14: The ufCHECKISBN13 and ufCHECKISBN10 UDFs (UDFs module)

Note: The methods for checking ISBN codes with 13 digits and 10 digits are slightly different.

15

FASTER MACROS

15 - FASTER MACROS

The following section introduces some basic tips for creating faster macros.

Turn off state settings while code is running

Macro performance can be improved by turning off the functionality that is not required while code executes.

Often, one recalculation or one redraw after code runs is all that is necessary and can improve performance. Once code executes, functionality can then be restored to its original state.

Functionality which can be turned off while code executes may include the following:

- **Application.ScreenUpdating** when set to **False** turns off screen updating which stops the flicker associated with multiple re-draws.
- **Application.DisplayStatusBar** when set to **False** turns off the status bar which normally shows the status of operations and may not be required as there are other means in code of displaying the status.
- **Application.Calculation** when set to **xlCalculationManual** (manual calculation mode) will not re-calculate. In code at the very end of a task, it is possible to initiate a recalculation, if required.
- **Application.EnableEvents** when set to **False t**urns off events. In many cases event handling may not be required during code execution, so can be safely turned off.
- **ActiveSheet.DisplayPageBreaks** when set to False turns off page breaks. The calculating of page breaks is not normally required during code execution.

Note: Some features must be enabled for functionality to work as intended, whilst others may interfere with proper code execution. Using the **With...End With** construct to change multiple properties of an object may improve performance and readability of code.

The disabling and enabling of the state settings are one of the easiest methods to implement and can provide significant performance improvements. However, care has to be taken when changing state settings in nested routines.

Sometimes it may be necessary for a state setting to be turned on in one routine but turned off in another, so passing arguments by value (**ByVal**) may be necessary to keep multiple copies of a setting to use from one routine to another, rather than by reference (**ByRef**) the default, which may change the underlying value.

Another situation to be wary of is the handling of events. Changes within code may require a particular event to be handled, at other times events may interfere with the correct processing of a routine.

In some scenarios, settings such as a status bar may need to be on during processing. In such cases, another set of routines could be written to handle this individual case, or parameters may be used to determine which settings to switch off/on.

In Figure 15-1 state settings are declared **Public** (global) so that they are available throughout the system, although there are other potentially better ways to manage this. There is a sub-routine **turnOffStateSettings** to use at the start of a routine and another **resetStateSettings** which can be used at the end of the same routine to reset the settings. The current state of the settings is stored in the corresponding global variable, so that it is available when required in the reset process.

```
' StateSettings Module
'
' Public Routines: turnOffStateSettings, resetStateSettings
'
' ROUTINES TO MEMORIZE, TURN OFF AND RESET STATE SETTINGS
'
Option Private Module
Option Explicit
' Make public state settings so that they can be used anywhere in project.
Public g_boAlertState As Boolean
Public g_itCalcState As Integer
Public g_boEventState As Boolean
Public g_boScreenUpdatingState As Boolean
Public g_boStatusBarState As Boolean
Public g_boPageBreakState As Boolean

' Remember state settings and then turn them off to improve code performance.

Public Sub turnOffStateSettings()
    g_boAlertState = Application.DisplayAlerts
    g_itCalcState = Application.Calculation
    g_boEventState = Application.EnableEvents
    g_boScreenUpdatingState = Application.ScreenUpdating
    g_boStatusBarState = Application.DisplayStatusBar
    g_boPageBreakState = ActiveSheet.DisplayPageBreaks
    With Application
        .DisplayAlerts = False
        .Calculation = xlCalculationManual
        .EnableEvents = False
        .DisplayStatusBar = False
        .ScreenUpdating = False
    End With
    ActiveSheet.DisplayPageBreaks = False
End Sub

' Reset state settings back to remembered state.

Public Sub resetStateSettings()
    With Application
        .DisplayAlerts = g_boAlertState
        .Calculation = g_itCalcState
        .EnableEvents = g_boEventState
        .ScreenUpdating = g_boScreenUpdatingState
        .DisplayStatusBar = g_boStatusBarState
    End With
    ActiveSheet.DisplayPageBreaks = g_boPageBreakState
End Sub
```

Figure 15-1: Routines to handle state settings (StateSettings module)

Note: Remember to restore functionality to its original state after code executes and only turn off events when appropriate to do so.

Figure 15-2 shows code for the opening of a workbook through automation:

- o The **openSlow** sub-routine opens a chosen workbook on an as is basis.
- o The **openFast** sub-routine uses the **turnOffStateSettings** sub-routine prior to opening the workbook and then the **resetStateSettings** sub-routine once it is open and ready to use.
- o Both routines use the same routines, the **getWorkbookName** function to retrieve the name of the workbook and then the **openWorkbook** sub-routine to open the workbook (which also times the opening process and outputs the results to the **Immediate Window**).

```
(General)                                          (Declarations)

    ' Test opening workbook without trying improve performance.

    Public Sub openSlow()
        ' Declare and attempt to get workbook name.
        Dim stWorkbookName As String: stWorkbookName = getWorkbookName()
        If Len(stWorkbookName) > 0 Then
            ' Success so open workbook.
            openWorkbook stWorkbookName
        End If
    End Sub


    ' Attempt to improve opening speed.

    Public Sub openFast()
        ' Declare and attempt to get workbook name.
        Dim stWorkbookName As String: stWorkbookName = getWorkbookName()
        If Len(stWorkbookName) > 0 Then
            ' Success so open workbook, controlling settings before and after.
            turnOffStateSettings
            openWorkbook stWorkbookName
            resetStateSettings
        End If
    End Sub


    ' Get workbook to open.

    Private Function getWorkbookName() As String
        ' Use variant for workbook name and get file name.
        Dim vtWorkbookName As Variant
        vtWorkbookName = Application.GetOpenFilename(FileFilter:="Excel Files,*.xl*;*.xm*")
        ' Return value of file name as a string or null string.
        If VarType(vtWorkbookName) = vbString Then
            getWorkbookName = vtWorkbookName
        Else
            getWorkbookName = vbNullString
        End If
    End Function


    ' Open workbook.

    Private Sub openWorkbook(stWorkbookName)
        ' Declare and set a simple timing mechanism.
        Dim dtStartTime As Date: dtStartTime = Now()
        ' Open workbook, then wait until it is ready to use before printing time taken.
        Dim wb As Workbook: Set wb = Application.Workbooks.Open(stWorkbookName)
        Do Until wb.ReadOnly = False
        Loop
        Debug.Print Int(CSng((Now() - dtStartTime) * 24 * 3600)) & " Seconds"
    End Sub
```

Figure 15-2: Automating the opening of a workbook (OpenWorkbook module)

Create a combined range and process as one unit

Repeating the same task on multiple ranges is much quicker when applied to one single combined range rather than one range at a time.

Figure 15-3 shows a method of creating one range for a series of columns which have no title in row 1 and then hide them all in one pass. There is an associated worksheet in the **Examples** workbook (available for download) with a worksheet named **oneRange** to show this working.

The code works as follows:
- o The **oneRangeHide** sub-routine calls the **findColumnsWithNoTitle** to create a single range for all empty columns on the worksheet. It then uses the range to **hide** the columns.
- o The **oneRangeUnHide** sub-routine likewise calls the **findColumnsWithNoTitle** and uses the range to **unhide** the empty columns.

```vba
(General)                                          oneRangeUnHide

' Handle columns with no title and store in a module level range object variable.
Option Private Module
Option Explicit
Private m_rgOneRange As Range

' Find columns with no title in row 1 and create a single range.
Private Sub findColumnsWithNoTitle()
    Set m_rgOneRange = Nothing

    Dim ws As Worksheet: Set ws = Worksheets("oneRange")

    ' find last column using Ctrl + Shift + End
    Dim lnCol As Long, lnLastCol As Long
    lnLastCol = ws.Cells(1, ws.Columns.count).End(xlToLeft).Column

    For lnCol = 1 To lnLastCol
        ' Check for blank column title and then create range combining any new columns.
        If ws.Cells(1, lnCol).Value = vbNullString Then
            If m_rgOneRange Is Nothing Then
                Set m_rgOneRange = ws.Columns(lnCol)
            Else
                Set m_rgOneRange = Union(m_rgOneRange, ws.Columns(lnCol))
            End If
        End If
    Next lnCol
End Sub

' Hide columns referenced by module level range object.
Public Sub oneRangeHide()
    findColumnsWithNoTitle
    m_rgOneRange.Columns.Hidden = True
End Sub

' Unhide columns referenced by module level range object.
Public Sub oneRangeUnHide()
    findColumnsWithNoTitle
    m_rgOneRange.Columns.Hidden = False
End Sub
```

Figure 15-3: Combining ranges example (OneRange module)

Note: The **m_rgOneRange** range uses the **Union** statement to combine each column with no title into a single range.

Other methods to improve performance

There are many other ways performance of macro code may be improved including:

- o Avoid using **Copy** and **Paste** instead copy an array direct to the **Value2** property of a range object.
- o Use the **With...End With** construct to apply multiple properties in one go.
- o Avoid complex **If...Else...Endif** and favour toggling Boolean values where possible or use **Select...Case** instead if more appropriate.
- o Release memory when no longer required.
- o Use **For Each...Next** and **For...Next** loops appropriate to circumstances.
- o Manipulate collections and arrays rather than ranges.
- o Use specific variable types where possible.
- o Use **vbNullString** rather than an empty string.
- o Reduce the number of lines using colon (:) as a line separator.
- o Direct coding is always better than recording a macro.

The following are examples of coding using some of the methods outlined above:

```
(General)                                    forEachLoopMethod

Private Sub forEachLoopMethod()
    ' Declare and create reference for this workbook.
    Dim wb As Workbook: Set wb = ThisWorkbook
    ' Declare and create a new collection.
    Dim cnExample As collection: Set cnExample = New collection
    ' Declare a worksheet object.
    Dim ws As Worksheet
    ' Declare and set start time.
    Dim dbStartTime As Double: dbStartTime = getTime
    ' The For Each..Next loop.
    For Each ws In wb.Worksheets
        ' Create new item in collection.
        addClassItem cnExample, ws
    Next ws
    ' Remove all items in collection.
    Set cnExample = New collection
    Debug.Print "For Each loop collection: " & elapsedTime(dbStartTime)
End Sub
```

Figure 15-4: The forEachLoopMethod sub-routine (Techniques module)

In Figure 15-4 there are examples of placing code together on one line using the ":" separator i.e. the declaration and setting of the **cnExample**, **wb** and **dbStartTime** variables.

Note: Whilst, some developers may not recommend the use of the ":" line separator, in the examples shown it keeps the declaration and setting together, so in such cases may actually be of benefit, such as when moving the code to another location, it remains as one unit.

The **getTime** function in Figure 6-9 is used to return the start time and the **elapsedTime** function in Figure 6-10 for the elapsed time.

In Figure 15-4 the new collection is emptied at the end of the routine (before the time elapsed is calculated), simply to show one quick method of releasing the memory by removing all items from the collection. This can be achieved by setting the collection to a new collection.

The **For...Each...Next** loop in Figure 15-4 traverses all worksheets in the worksheets collection for this workbook and then calls the **addClassItem** sub-routine (Figure 15-5) to add some of the sheet information to a new collection.

```
(General)                                        addClassItem

    Private Sub addClassItem(cnExample As collection, ws As Worksheet)
        ' Declare/create class (as per class module clsSheetInfo).
        Dim clsSheetInfoTemp As New clsSheetInfo

        ' use [With...End With] to set up details of class item
        With clsSheetInfoTemp
            .Name = ws.Name
            .CodeName = ws.CodeName
            .UsedRows = ws.UsedRange.Rows.count
            .UsedCols = ws.UsedRange.Columns.count
            .NoOfNames = ws.Names.count
        End With
        ' Add this new class item to the the collection.
        cnExample.Add item:=clsSheetInfoTemp, Key:=ws.Name
    End Sub
```

Figure 15-5: The addClassItem sub-routine (Techniques module)

The **With...End With** construct is used in Figure 15-5 to set the properties of the **clsSheetInfoTemp** object to the sheet properties declared in the **clsSheetInfo** class (Figure 15-6) so that the newly created object can then be added to the collection.

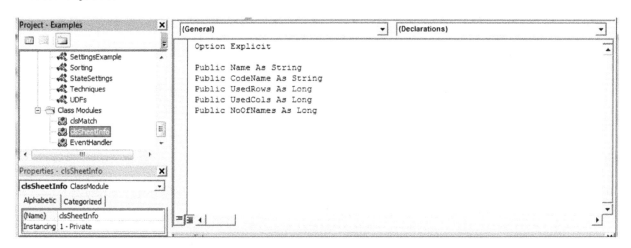

Figure 15-6: The clsSheetInfo class module property declarations

Although the example of a creating another worksheet collection which mimics a built-in collection may seem a redundant, one advantage is that extra properties can be added to the **clsSheetInfo** class, so that in this way the new collection can be extended beyond the original.

Classes are very useful in creating "building blocks" of information which can be handled as a single unit. In addition to the properties, methods can be added to work with the properties in the class.

The **For...Next** loop in Figure 15-7 uses the count of worksheets in the worksheets collection as the upper bound and sets the variable **ws** to the current worksheet in the collection, so that it matches the information required for the **addClassItem** (Figure 15-5) to add items to the new collection.

```
(General)                                    ▼  forLoopMethod                          ▼

    Private Sub forLoopMethod()
        ' Declare & set this workbook.
        Dim wb As Workbook: Set wb = ThisWorkbook
        ' Declare & set collection.
        Dim cnExample As collection: Set cnExample = New collection
        ' Declare the worksheet object.
        Dim ws As Worksheet              ' declare worksheet
        ' Declare & set start time.
        Dim dbStartTime As Double: dbStartTime = getTime
        ' Declare an item counter to use in loop.
        Dim lnItem As Long
        ' The For...Next loop.
        For lnItem = 1 To wb.Worksheets.count
            ' Set ws to worksheet object from collection of worksheets.
            Set ws = wb.Worksheets(lnItem)
            ' Create a new item in the collection.
            addClassItem cnExample, ws
        Next lnItem
        ' Remove all items in the collection.|
        Set cnExample = New collection
        Debug.Print "For loop collection: " & elapsedTime(dbStartTime)
    End Sub
```

Figure 15-7: The forLoopMethod sub-routine (Techniques module)

Figure 15-8 shows the **forLoopArrayMethod** sub-routine, an alternative to using a collection.

```
(General)                                    ▼  forLoopArrayMethod                     ▼

    Private Sub forLoopArrayMethod()
        ' Declare and create reference for this workbook.
        Dim wb As Workbook: Set wb = ThisWorkbook
        ' Declare array for 5 properties and worksheets count.
        ReDim vtArr(1 To 5, 1 To wb.Worksheets.count) As Variant
        ' Declare worksheet.
        Dim ws As Worksheet
        ' Declare and set start time.
        Dim dbStartTime As Double: dbStartTime = getTime
        ' Declare an item counter.
        Dim lnItem As Long
        ' The For...Next loop
        For lnItem = 1 To wb.Worksheets.count
            ' Set ws to worksheet object from collection of worksheets.
            Set ws = wb.Worksheets(lnItem)
            ' Create a new item in array.
            addArrayItem lnItem, vtArr, ws
        Next lnItem
        Debug.Print "For loop array: " & elapsedTime(dbStartTime)
    End Sub
```

Figure 15-8: The forLoopArrayMethod sub-routine (Techniques module)

15 - FASTER MACROS

In Figure 15-8 the routine works by storing the data in the two-dimensional array named **vtArr** which is declared with 5 properties for the first dimension and the number of worksheets in the worksheets collection as the second dimension. The routine calls the **addArrayItem** sub-routine to add the worksheet information to the array **vtArr**.

The **addArrayItem** sub-routine in Figure 15-9 sets each property in the array to the sheet information required for the worksheet item.

```
(General)                                          addArrayItem

    Private Sub addArrayItem(lnItem As Long, vtArr As Variant, ws As Worksheet)
        vtArr(1, lnItem) = ws.Name
        vtArr(2, lnItem) = ws.CodeName
        vtArr(3, lnItem) = ws.UsedRange.Rows.count
        vtArr(4, lnItem) = ws.UsedRange.Columns.count
        vtArr(5, lnItem) = ws.Names.count
    End Sub
```

Figure 15-9: The addArrayItem sub-routine (Techniques module)

16

CONNECTING TO EXTERNAL DATA

16 - CONNECTING TO EXTERNAL DATA

There are many ways to get external data into a worksheet, available from the **Data** tab on the ribbon interface. The newest methods are to be found in the **Get & Transform** group. Older methods are still available but may lack the power of the newer options.

The **Data** tab on the ribbon menu has various groups as follows:
- o Get External Data
- o Get & Transform
- o Connections
- o Sort & Filter
- o Data Tools
- o Forecast
- o Outline

The **Get External Data** group as shown in Figure 16-1 is primarily used for importing data from external data sources and some features are included for backward compatibility with previous versions.

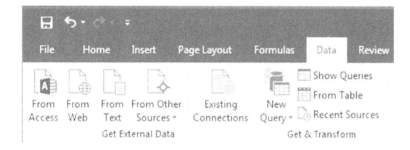

Figure 16-1: Data tab

Using Get & Transform

The **Get & Transform** group, also shown in Figure 16-1 provides a more powerful set of features for connecting to data and may be referred to as **Power Query**, the same features as used in the **Power BI**, and the **Power Query Add-In** available in previous versions.

When creating and managing a connection to an external data source the **Query Editor** is used to record and modify each step as required.

The four steps to can be categorized as follows:
- o Make connections to one or more data sources.
- o Transform the data to meet the requirements (the original sources are not changed).
- o Combine data from sources to get a unique view into the data.
- o Save the query and share or use it for reporting.

Once created the query automatically resizes the data view as the data changes.

The **New Query** option in the **Get & Transform** group is used to connect to data from a variety of sources.

In Figure 16-2, a connection is being made to an external CSV file.

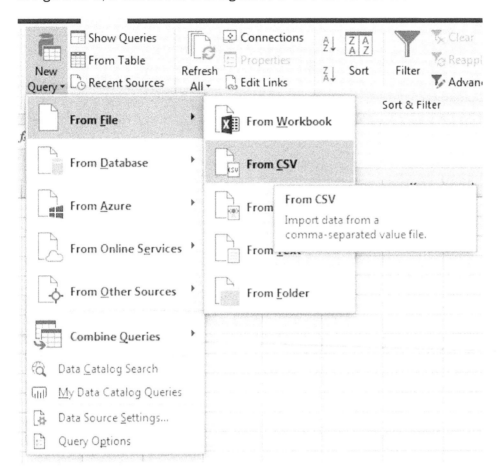

Figure 16-2: New Query option

The **Import** file dialog is used to make a connection to a file such as the **From CSV** example in Figure 16-2.

Note: The connection type chosen will present the dialog appropriate for the corresponding data source. Some data sources may require information to be added to a series of dialogs to initiate the loading process.

In example 16-3 the **scores.csv**, a collection of match results from the games of the 2017/18 English Football Premiership season is opened as a data connection.

Prior to importing the data options available via the data connections dialog are:
- o Load (or Load To via the dropdown list)
- o Edit
- o Cancel

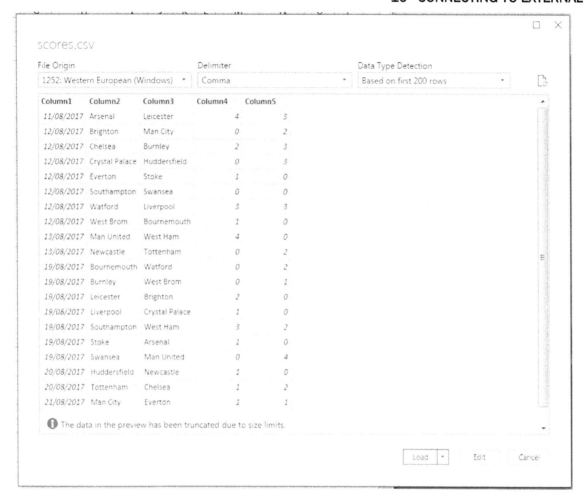

Figure 16-3: Data connection dialog

Click the **Load** button to load the data to a new worksheet or alternatively, click the dropdown list option and *click* the **Load To** button to display the dialog (Figure 16-4).

Loading to a **Table** (recommended) and on a **New worksheet** are the default settings.

Note: Once a table has been created, refreshing the data will automatically re-size the rows to match the data.

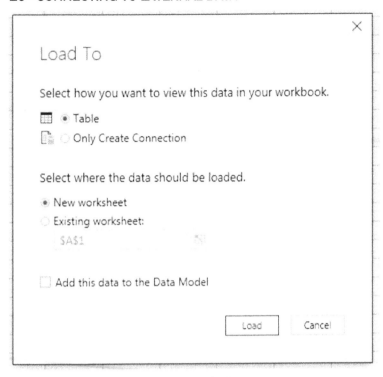

Figure 16-4: Load To dialog

The **Edit** button displays the **Power Query Editor** (Figure 16-5) where the data can be transformed. For example, the column headings can be changed to something more meaningful such as **Date**, **HomeTeam, AwayTeam, HomeScore** and **AwayScore**. Just *double-click* on a column heading to make the change.

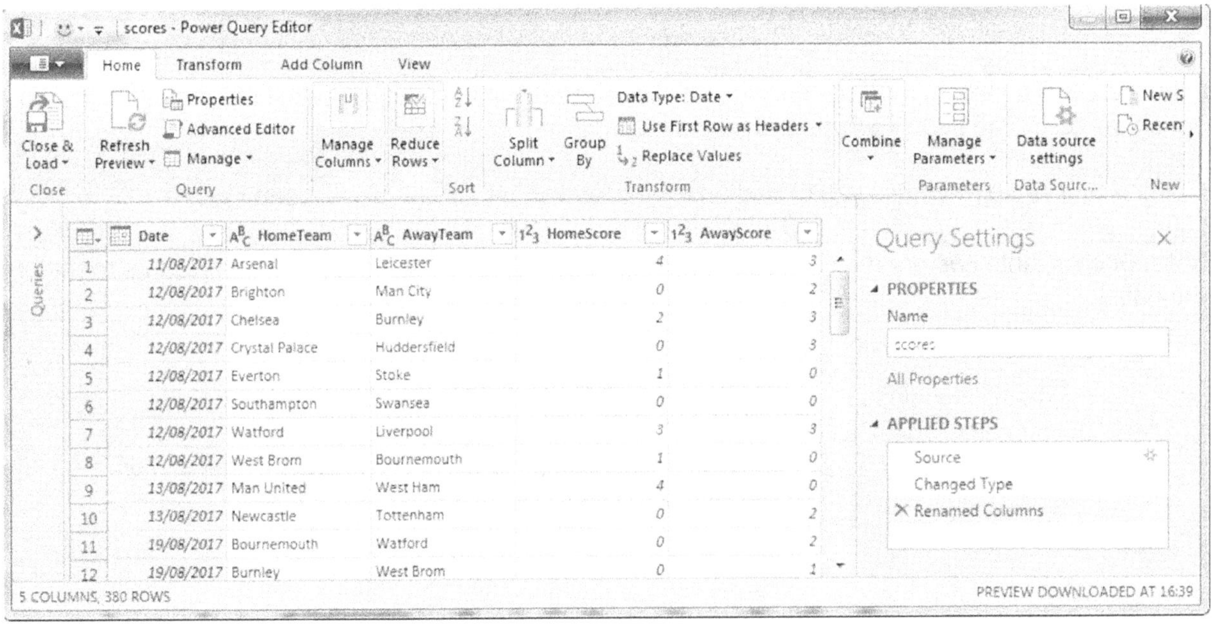

Figure 16-5: Power Query Editor

The **Close & Load** button within the Power Query Editor will refresh the data with any changed settings.

The data can now be used, in this example, to create a premiership league table based on the scores imported to date.

A structured table can be used which contains a list of teams and associated formulas to calculate a team's position in the league, matches played, wins, draws, losses, goals for and against, goal difference and points.

A **Refresh** button can be added to the worksheet with some background VBA code to update the data and Premiership League tables including sorting into points order and showing the position of each team in the league.

Figure 16-6 shows the various elements once created.

	A	B	C	D	E	F	G	H	I	J	K	L	M	N	O	P
1	Date	HomeTeam	AwayTeam	HomeScore	AwayScore		Pos	Team	MP	W	D	L	GF	GA	GD	Pts
2	11/08/2017	Arsenal	Leicester	4	3		1	Man City	38	32	4	2	106	27	79	100
3	12/08/2017	Brighton	Man City	0	2		2	Man United	38	25	6	7	68	28	40	81
4	12/08/2017	Chelsea	Burnley	2	3		3	Tottenham	38	23	8	7	74	36	38	77
5	12/08/2017	Crystal Palace	Huddersfield	0	3		4	Liverpool	38	21	12	5	84	38	46	75
6	12/08/2017	Everton	Stoke	1	0		5	Chelsea	38	21	7	10	62	38	24	70
7	12/08/2017	Southampton	Swansea	0	0		6	Arsenal	38	19	6	13	74	51	23	63
8	12/08/2017	Watford	Liverpool	3	3		7	Burnley	38	14	12	12	36	39	-3	54
9	12/08/2017	West Brom	Bournemouth	1	0		8	Everton	38	13	10	15	44	58	-14	49
10	13/08/2017	Man United	West Ham	4	0		9	Leicester	38	12	11	15	56	60	-4	47
11	13/08/2017	Newcastle	Tottenham	0	2		10	Newcastle	38	12	8	18	39	47	-8	44
12	19/08/2017	Bournemouth	Watford	0	2		11	Crystal Palace	38	11	11	16	45	55	-10	44
13	19/08/2017	Burnley	West Brom	0	1		12	Bournemouth	38	11	11	16	45	61	-16	44
14	19/08/2017	Leicester	Brighton	2	0		13	West Ham	38	10	12	16	48	68	-20	42
15	19/08/2017	Liverpool	Crystal Palace	1	0		14	West Ham	38	10	12	16	48	68	-20	42
16	19/08/2017	Southampton	West Ham	3	2		15	Watford	38	11	8	19	44	64	-20	41
17	19/08/2017	Stoke	Arsenal	1	0		16	Brighton	38	9	13	16	34	54	-20	40
18	19/08/2017	Swansea	Man United	0	4		17	Huddersfield	38	9	10	19	28	58	-30	37
19	20/08/2017	Huddersfield	Newcastle	1	0		18	Southampton	38	7	15	16	37	56	-19	36
20	20/08/2017	Tottenham	Chelsea	1	2		19	Swansea	38	8	9	21	28	56	-28	33
21	21/08/2017	Man City	Everton	1	1		20	West Brom	38	6	13	19	31	56	-25	31
22	26/08/2017	Bournemouth	Man City	1	2											
23	26/08/2017	Crystal Palace	Swansea	0	2											
24	26/08/2017	Huddersfield	Southampton	0	0											
25	26/08/2017	Man United	Leicester	2	0											
26	26/08/2017	Newcastle	West Ham	3	0				REFRESH							
27	26/08/2017	Watford	Brighton	0	0											

Figure 16-6: Premiership League table 2017/18 season

197

The team's league position can be calculated using a formula similar to that shown in Figure 16-7. The **ROW** function can be used to determine the position taking off one row to take account of the header row. A Structured Table is used with the **[@Pos]** reference to get the current row for the **Pos** column.

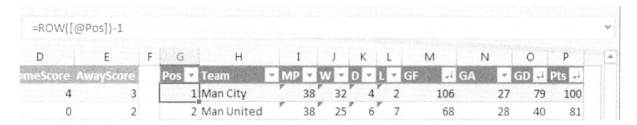

Figure 16-7: League position formula

Each team name is entered in the column headed **Team**.

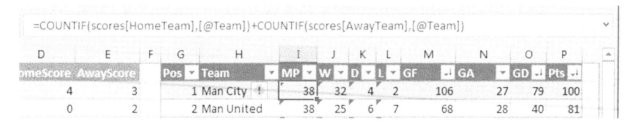

Figure 16-8: Matches Played formula

The formula in Figure 16-8 uses the **COUNTIF** function to count matches played for the team on the current row for both home and away columns (heading of **MP**).

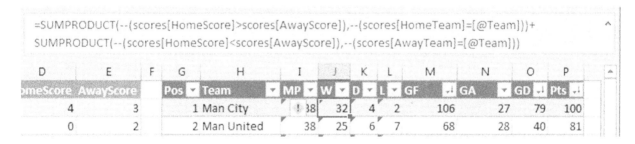

Figure 16-9: Matches Won formula

The formula in Figure 16-9 uses the **SUMPRODUCT** function to calculate the number of matches won based on the home score being greater than the away score where the current row team is the home team and that the away score is greater than the home score where the current row team is the away team (heading of **W**).

The formula in Figure 16-10 uses the **SUMPRODUCT** function to calculate the number of matches drawn based on both home and away scores being equal for the team on the current row being either the home or away team (heading of **D**).

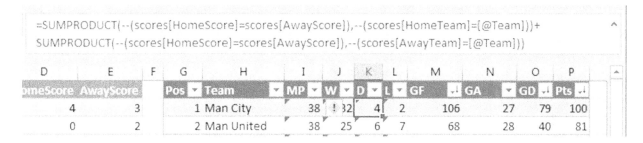

Figure 16-10: Matches Drawn formula

The matches lost formula is the reverse of the matches won formula (heading of **L**).

```
=SUMIFS(scores[HomeScore],scores[HomeTeam],[@Team])+SUMIFS(scores[AwayScore],
scores[AwayTeam],[@Team])
```

D	E	F	G	H	I	J	K	L	M	N	O	P
omeScore	AwayScore		Pos	Team	MP	W	D	L	GF	GA	GD	Pts
4	3			1 Man City	38	32	4	2	106	27	79	100
0	2			2 Man United	38	25	6	7	68	28	40	81

Figure 16-11: Goals For formula

The formula in Figure 16-11 uses the **SUMIFS** function to calculate the number of goals scored by the team in the home and away columns where that team is the same as the one on the current row (heading of **GF**).

Similarly, the goals against are calculated for the opposing teams from the home and away columns where the team is the same as the one on the current row (heading of **GA**).

The goal difference formula is thus, the goals for minus the goals against as shown in the goal difference column (heading of **GD**).

The points are calculated where a win is worth 3 points and a draw is worth 1 point. Thus, the total matches won is multiplied by 3 and this is added to the number of matches drawn to give a total points value (column heading of **Pts**).

The **Refresh** button is added as an Active-X worksheet control (CommandButton) named **RefreshButton** and the **Click** method is coded as per Figure 16-12.

```
RefreshButton                          ▼   Click                                          ▼

    Option Explicit
    Private Sub RefreshButton_Click()
        ' declare and set this workbook
        Dim wb As Workbook: Set wb = ThisWorkbook

        ' declare and set this worksheet
        Dim ws As Worksheet: Set ws = wb.Worksheets("DataImport")

        ' declare and set scores data table
        Dim loScores As ListObject: Set loScores = ws.ListObjects("scores")

        ' declare and set league table
        Dim loTable As ListObject: Set loTable = ws.ListObjects("Table")

        loScores.QueryTable.Refresh BackgroundQuery:=False   ' refresh data

        Application.Calculate    ' re-calculate (autocalc may be off)

        ' set league table to sort by Pts, GD & GF
        With loTable.Sort
            .SortFields.Clear
            .SortFields.Add Key:=Range("Table[[#All],[Pts]]"), SortOn:= _
                xlSortOnValues, Order:=xlDescending, DataOption:=xlSortNormal
            .SortFields.Add Key:=Range("Table[[#All],[GD]]"), SortOn:= _
                xlSortOnValues, Order:=xlDescending, DataOption:=xlSortNormal
            .SortFields.Add Key:=Range("Table[[#All],[GF]]"), SortOn:= _
                xlSortOnValues, Order:=xlDescending, DataOption:=xlSortNormal
            .Header = xlYes
            .MatchCase = False
            .Orientation = xlTopToBottom
            .SortMethod = xlPinYin
            .Apply
        End With
    End Sub
```

Figure 16-12: RefreshButton Click method (DataImport worksheet code)

The VBA code creates references to the scores data table and the league table and then the data table is refreshed.

Finally, the league table uses the Sort method to clear any existing sort keys and then creates a new sort order based on total points (Pts) then goal difference (GD) and then goals for (GF) which is then applied.

Import data from a text file using VBA code

It is possible to import data and store it in memory rather than to a worksheet using VBA code.

The fundamental processes required to code entirely in VBA the Premiership League Table might be:

- o Open the scores.csv file as a new workbook.
- o Load the matches data into a new collection.
- o Create a dictionary of teams used to make up the rows.
- o Close the scores.csv workbook (without saving).
- o Calculate the values for each team on a column by column basis.
- o Post the results to the worksheet sorted in correct league position.

Figure 16-13 shows the **Premiership League Table** results where everything is achieved within VBA code linked to the **Click** method of the Active-X worksheet control (**CommandButton**) with the caption "Update League Table". The code is stored as part of the **DataImport2** worksheet object. In the example, the defined name **ToDate** is used to limit the results up to and including the date entered. Teams are sorted first on Points, with Goal Difference and finally Goals For used in case of ties.

⊿	A	B	C	D	E	F	G	H	I	J	K	L	M	N	O
1						Pos	Team	MP	W	D	L	GF	GA	GD	Pts
2						1	Man City	21	19	2	0	61	12	49	59
3						2	Chelsea	21	14	3	4	39	14	25	45
4		Update League Table				3	Man United	21	13	5	3	43	16	27	44
5						4	Liverpool	21	11	8	2	48	24	24	41
6						5	Arsenal	21	11	5	5	38	26	12	38
7						6	Tottenham	20	11	4	5	39	20	19	37
8		To date:	31/12/2017			7	Burnley	21	9	7	5	18	17	1	34
9						8	Leicester	21	7	6	8	31	32	-1	27
10						9	Everton	21	7	6	8	25	32	-7	27
11						10	Watford	21	7	4	10	30	37	-7	25
12						11	Huddersfield	21	6	6	9	18	32	-14	24
13						12	Brighton	21	5	7	9	15	25	-10	22
14						13	Southampton	21	4	8	9	20	30	-10	20
15						14	Bournemouth	21	5	5	11	20	32	-12	20
16						15	Stoke	21	5	5	11	23	46	-23	20
17						16	Newcastle	21	5	4	12	19	30	-11	19
18						17	Crystal Palace	21	4	7	10	18	32	-14	19
19						18	West Ham	20	4	6	10	22	38	-16	18
20						19	West Brom	21	2	10	9	15	28	-13	16
21						20	Swansea	21	4	4	13	13	32	-19	16
22															

Figure 16-13: Update League Table button with limited results

Figure 16-14 shows the code for the **UpdateLeagueTable_Click** method which includes:

- o Setting an error trap and turning off of state settings.
- o Declaring and setting of the **ThisWorkbook** and **ActiveSheet** references.
- o Clearing the contents of any existing table.
- o Opening of the scores.csv file by the **openCSV** function.
- o Declaring and setting **boDataFound** to use as a flag for testing if data exists.
- o Declaring and setting the **cnMatches** collection object for storing the match results.
- o Declaring and setting the **obDict** dictionary object for storing the teams.
- o Declaring the **vtArrLeague** array to hold the league table information.
- o Loading the data via the **loadData** sub-routine and closing the scores.csv file.
- o If data has been found, posting the results to the worksheet via the **postResults** sub-routine.
- o Resetting state settings.

```vba
UpdateLeagueTable                                              Click

    Private Sub updateLeagueTable_Click()
        On Error GoTo ErrProc
        turnOffStateSettings

        ' Declare and initialize this workbook
        ' this worksheet and clear old league table results.
        Dim wb As Workbook: Set wb = ThisWorkbook
        Dim ws As Worksheet: Set ws = wb.ActiveSheet
        ws.Range("F2:O21").ClearContents

        ' If able to open CSV continue.
        If openCSV(wb.Path & "\scores.csv") Then
            ' Declare and initialize data sets, data found check
            ' league table array, matches collection & dictionary of teams.
            Dim boDataFound As Boolean: boDataFound = False
            Dim vtArrLeague() As Variant
            Dim cnMatches As collection: Set cnMatches = New collection
            Dim obDict As Object: Set obDict = CreateObject("Scripting.Dictionary")

            ' Load data then close workbook.
            loadData cnMatches, obDict, vtArrLeague, _
                    ActiveWorkbook.Sheets(1), ws, boDataFound
            ActiveWorkbook.Close savechanges:=False

            ' If load found data then post results.
            If boDataFound Then postResults cnMatches, obDict, vtArrLeague, ws
        End If
        resetStateSettings
        Exit Sub
    ErrProc:
        MsgBox Str(Err.Number) + " - " + Err.Description
    End Sub
```

Figure 16-14: The UpdateLeagueTable_Click method code (DataImport2 worksheet code)

Note: In Figure 16-14, **Option Base 1** is used to set the array dimensions starting at 1 rather than the default 0 (zero) to avoid confusion between item numbers in the collection and the array. Also, ff the opening of the **scores** file is successful, the **obDict** object is set via late binding to the **Scripting.Dictionary** object type. For the sake of the examples and portability, this automatically creates a reference for this type of object without the requirement to set it via **Tools->References**.

The **openCSV** UDF in Figure 16-15 checks for the existence of the **scores.csv** file and then opens it as a new temporary workbook in a delimited format (standard for CSV files). The function returns a **Boolean** value for success or failure, which can then be used in the calling routine to either continue or exit the routine.

```
(General)                                    ▼   openCSV                                          ▼
    Private Function openCSV(stFileName As String) As Boolean
        On Error GoTo ErrProc

        ' Declare and set file system object to test if file exists.
        Dim obFileSys As Object: Set obFileSys = CreateObject("Scripting.FileSystemObject")

        ' If no file go to error handler.
        If Not obFileSys.fileexists(stFileName) Then GoTo ErrProc

        ' Open file and return true.
        Workbooks.OpenText fileName:=stFileName, DataType:=xlDelimited, Local:=True
        openCSV = True
        Exit Function
    ErrProc:
        ' Cannot open so return false and show message.
        openCSV = False
        MsgBox "Cannot open " + stFileName
    End Function
```

Figure 16-15: The openCSV UDF (DataImport2 worksheet code)

Figure 16-16 shows the class module declaration for **clsMatch**, the properties for each match used to create items in the matches collection. The properties comprise the match date with home and away teams plus the scores for each.

```
(General)                                    ▼   (Declarations)                                   ▼
    Option Explicit

    Public MatchDate As String
    Public HomeTeam As String
    Public AwayTeam As String
    Public HomeScore As String
    Public AwayScore As String
```

Figure 16-16: The clsMatch class module declarations

16 - CONNECTING TO EXTERNAL DATA

Shown in Figure 16-17, is the **loadData** sub-routine used in the creation of the matches collection.

The routine works as follows:
- o An error trap is set so that if no data is found the **boFound** flag is not updated.
- o A dictionary item pointer (**lnDictItems**) is declared and set to zero.
- o A temporary match class is declared using the **clsMatch** structure.
- o The **vtData** array is declared and set to the entire range of the first sheet of the temporary workbook.
- o Each item in the **vtData** array up to and including the **ToDate** is processed as follows:
  - o A temporary match object **clsMatchTemp** is created and set to the current **vtData** item.
  - o The **clsMatchTemp** item is added to the matches collection.
  - o The **creationDictionary** sub-routine is used to add new teams to the dictionary.
- o The **boFound** flag is updated to indicate data has been found.

```
(General)                                               loadData

    Private Sub loadData(cnMatch As collection, obDict As Object, _
            vtArrLeague As Variant, wsLoadSheet As Worksheet, _
            ws As Worksheet, boDataFound As Boolean)
        ' On error just report it.
        On Error GoTo ErrorProc

        ' Create and set dictionary items to zero.
        Dim lnDictItems As Long: lnDictItems = 0
        ' Declare temporary match class.
        Dim clsMatchTemp As clsMatch
        ' Load data to vtData from worksheet.
        Dim vtData As Variant: vtData = wsLoadSheet.Cells(1).CurrentRegion


        ' Create a match collection from loaded data.
        Dim lnItem As Long
        For lnItem = 1 To UBound(vtData)
            ' Use ToDate on worksheet to filter loaded data.
            If vtData(lnItem, 1) > ws.Range("ToDate") Then Exit For
            Set clsMatchTemp = New clsMatch
            With clsMatchTemp
                .MatchDate = vtData(lnItem, 1)
                .HomeTeam = vtData(lnItem, 2)
                .AwayTeam = vtData(lnItem, 3)
                .HomeScore = vtData(lnItem, 4)
                .AwayScore = vtData(lnItem, 5)
            End With
            ' Add match item to collection & home/away teams to dictionary.
            cnMatch.Add clsMatchTemp
            createDictionary obDict, clsMatchTemp, vtArrLeague, lnDictItems
        Next lnItem
        boDataFound = True
        Exit Sub
    ErrorProc:
        MsgBox "Data set empty ", vbExclamation
    End Sub
```

Figure 16-17: The loadData sub-routine (DataImport2 worksheet code)

Figure 16-18 shows the **createDictionary** sub-routine which:

- o Checks for the existence of the Home team in the dictionary and if not found:
- o Increments the dictionary item pointer (**lnDictItems**).
- o Adds the Home team to the dictionary.
- o Re-dimensions the **vtArrLeague** array to include and then adds the new team.
- o Repeats the same process as above for the Away team.

```
(General)                                    ▼   createDictionary                                       ▼

Private Sub createDictionary(obDict As Object, _
        cnMatch As clsMatch, vtArrLeague As Variant, lnDictItems As Long)
    ' Add new Home item if not already in dictionary keeping count of item total
    ' for use in adding to array.
    If Not obDict.exists(cnMatch.HomeTeam) Then
        lnDictItems = lnDictItems + 1
        obDict.Add cnMatch.HomeTeam, lnDictItems
        ReDim Preserve vtArrLeague(1 To 10, 1 To lnDictItems)
        vtArrLeague(2, lnDictItems) = cnMatch.HomeTeam
    End If
    ' Add new Away item if not already in dictionary keeping count of item total
    ' for use in adding to array.
    If Not obDict.exists(cnMatch.AwayTeam) Then
        lnDictItems = lnDictItems + 1
        obDict.Add cnMatch.AwayTeam, lnDictItems
        ReDim Preserve vtArrLeague(1 To 10, 1 To lnDictItems)
        vtArrLeague(2, lnDictItems) = cnMatch.AwayTeam
    End If
End Sub
```

Figure 16-18: The createDictionary sub-routine (DataImport2 worksheet code)

The **postResults** sub-routine in Figure 16-19, calculates the league table results based on the matches collection.

```
(General)                                    ▼  postResults                                    ▼

Private Sub postResults(cnMatches As collection, obDict As Object, _
    vtArrLeague() As Variant, ws As Worksheet)
    vtArrLeague = initLeague(vtArrLeague)
    Dim lnItem As Long, lnInnerItem As Long, lnHome As Long, lnAway As Long
    For lnItem = 1 To cnMatches.count
        ' Home and Away team location in dictionary.
        lnHome = obDict(cnMatches(lnItem).HomeTeam)
        lnAway = obDict(cnMatches(lnItem).AwayTeam)
        ' Matches played.
        vtArrLeague(3, lnHome) = vtArrLeague(3, lnHome) + 1
        vtArrLeague(3, lnAway) = vtArrLeague(3, lnAway) + 1
        ' Home win, Away win or Draw
        Select Case cnMatches(lnItem).HomeScore
            Case Is > cnMatches(lnItem).AwayScore ' Home win.
                vtArrLeague(4, lnHome) = vtArrLeague(4, lnHome) + 1
                vtArrLeague(6, lnAway) = vtArrLeague(6, lnAway) + 1
            Case Is < cnMatches(lnItem).AwayScore ' Away win.
                vtArrLeague(4, lnAway) = vtArrLeague(4, lnAway) + 1
                vtArrLeague(6, lnHome) = vtArrLeague(6, lnHome) + 1
            Case Else      ' Draw.
                vtArrLeague(5, lnAway) = vtArrLeague(5, lnAway) + 1
                vtArrLeague(5, lnHome) = vtArrLeague(5, lnHome) + 1
        End Select
        ' Goals for and against.
        vtArrLeague(7, lnHome) = vtArrLeague(7, lnHome) + Val(cnMatches(lnItem).HomeScore)
        vtArrLeague(8, lnHome) = vtArrLeague(8, lnHome) + Val(cnMatches(lnItem).AwayScore)
        vtArrLeague(7, lnAway) = vtArrLeague(7, lnAway) + Val(cnMatches(lnItem).AwayScore)
        vtArrLeague(8, lnAway) = vtArrLeague(8, lnAway) + Val(cnMatches(lnItem).HomeScore)
    Next lnItem
    ' Goal difference and points.
    For lnItem = 1 To UBound(vtArrLeague, 2)
        vtArrLeague(9, lnItem) = vtArrLeague(7, lnItem) - vtArrLeague(8, lnItem)
        vtArrLeague(10, lnItem) = vtArrLeague(4, lnItem) * 3 + vtArrLeague(5, lnItem)
    Next lnItem
    ' Sort by points, goal difference, then goals for high to low.
    Dim vtArrCols As Variant: vtArrCols = Array(7, 9, 10)
    reverseSort vtArrLeague, vtArrCols
    ' Save position in first column.
    For lnItem = 1 To UBound(vtArrLeague, 2)
        vtArrLeague(1, lnItem) = lnItem
    Next lnItem
    ' Copy transposed vtArrLeague array to worksheet & autofit columns.
    ws.Range("F2:O21").Value2 = Application.Transpose(vtArrLeague)
    ws.Range("F1:O21").Columns.AutoFit
End Sub
```

Figure 16-19: The postResults sub-routine (DataImport2 worksheet code)

The dictionary is used to return the row location of each team, both home and away, which is then used as the array index (subscript).

The goal difference and points columns are calculated separately as these are simple formulae based on the accumulated values.

The league table array can be initialized with zeroes (in case any values are not calculated) using the **initLeague** UDF (Figure 16-20).

```
(General)                                              initLeague

    Private Function initLeague(vtArrLeague() As Variant)
        Dim lnItem As Long, lnInnerItem As Long
        For lnItem = 1 To UBound(vtArrLeague, 2)
            For lnInnerItem = 3 To 10
                vtArrLeague(lnInnerItem, lnItem) = 0
            Next lnInnerItem
        Next lnItem
        ' Return league table with zeroes.
        initLeague = vtArrLeague
    End Function
```

Figure 16-20: The initLeague UDF (DataImport2 worksheet code)

This **reverseSort** sub-routine (Figure 16-21) sorts the final league table by multiple columns, as determined by the **vtArrCols** array. In the example, three columns are needed, goals for, goal difference and points (columns 7, 9 and 10 in the **vtArrLeague** array).

```
(General)                                              reverseSort

    ' Sort vtData array using multiple keys listed as column numbers
    ' from host array in vtArrCols array in minor to major order.

    Public Sub reverseSort(vtData() As Variant, vtArrCols As Variant)
        Dim lnItem As Long, lnInnerItem As Long, lnCol As Long
        For lnItem = 1 To UBound(vtData, 2) - 1
            For lnInnerItem = lnItem + 1 To UBound(vtData, 2)
                For lnCol = 1 To UBound(vtArrCols)
                    If vtData(vtArrCols(lnCol), lnInnerItem) > vtData(vtArrCols(lnCol), lnItem)
                        swapArrayRows vtData, UBound(vtData, 1), lnItem, lnInnerItem
                    End If
                Next lnCol
            Next lnInnerItem
        Next lnItem
    End Sub
```

Figure 16-21: The reverseSort sub-routine (Sorting module)

After sorting, the league position can be added for each team and then the final league table is transposed and added to the worksheet range. Finally, the autofit of the columns is applied to improve the look of the table.

Note: It is possible to create the league table and team names at the outset and then match home and away teams for the scores. An advantage of this approach is improved performance i.e. no requirement to create the dictionary from matches. The disadvantage is that, a typing error in a team name will mean that no results are collected for that team. In the previous example using Power Query, the team names were typed in on the worksheet, they were required to pre-exist for the data query to work correctly.

17

RESOLVING WORKBOOK CORRUPTIONS

17 - RESOLVING WORKBOOK CORRUPTIONS

There are a variety of methods which one can employ to clean up and/or resolve potential workbook corruption issues. The method to use will be determined by accessibility to the tools, different versions available and ability of the user.

Saving in a newer or different format

If a workbook was created in a previous version, it is quite possible that opening it in a newer version and then re-saving it either in the same format or a different format may make it usable again. Once a corruption has been removed, the new workbook may then be re-saved back in its original version (if required).

Note: When a workbook becomes unusable in a version of Excel but can be opened in a different version of Excel, this could be an indication that an update may be the cause of the issue.

Using a different environment to open the workbook

It may be possible to open the workbook in a different environment with the same version (perhaps an earlier release of the same version) of Excel, for example via an RDP connection to a server-based installation.

Note: When a workbook becomes unusable in the current environment but can be opened in a different environment, this may indicate a corruption within the current environment, such as an issue with the operating system or user profile.

Manually cleaning up a workbook containing macros

Sometimes cleaning up a workbook with issues may require the copying of individual worksheets to a new workbook, exporting modules and forms to separate files and then re-importing the modules and forms to the new workbook. VBA code may be written to automate some or all of these tasks.

At other times it might be a simple case of cleaning up the project only by exporting objects, saving as a format without a project and then re-importing and saving as a macro enabled workbook.

Note: Some code may be attached to worksheet controls or the **ThisWorkbook** object which is copied across as part of the object.

Instructions which may help clean up a workbook and the project manually are:

1. Head all modules **Option Explicit** (if not already) and then select **Debug->Compile VBAProject**, make any corrections if/as required.

2. Drag all normal and class modules and any forms into a new project.

3. Copy and save all code in the workbook and worksheet object modules (e.g. onto sheets in the workbook where the modules were dragged to).

4. Save the original workbook as an xlsx (if necessary first change the **IsAddin** property if it's an add-in). This will remove the VBAProject.

5. Drag all the modules and forms back and copy back any code to object modules.

6. Re-save as xlsm or xlam.

It is recommended that the **Debug->Compile VBAProject** is used again to check that there are still no errors.

Note: Sometimes a workbook containing macros may exhibit issues either in execution or apparent corruption. Cleaning up the workbook may resolve such issues.

As stated earlier, it is possible to partly or completely automate the process of copying worksheets and all project components from a workbook to a new workbook.

In some situations, it may be better to export components separately, to avoid the situation where a component which is causing an issue, prevents an automated routine from completing successfully.

Writing code to clean up the project

In the **ProjectExamples.xlsm** workbook (available to accompany this document) routines have been created to work with the project for automation of export, import and displaying information relating to the project.

For routines to function correctly the **Microsoft Visual Basic Applications Extensibility 5.3** library is required to be activated from the **Tools**->**References** menu option in the VBE.

The modules and routines available are:
- **ExportProjects**
    - exportChosenProject
    - exportVBComponents
    - getComponentExtension
    - getFragment
    - projectToExport
- **ExportWorkbook**
    - exportWorksheets
    - workbookToExport
- **ImportToProjects**
    - getFolder
    - importToProject
    - importVBComponents
- **MakeNewWorkbook**
    - makeNewWorkbookFromAnother
- **ProjectInformation**
    - listLibraryReferences
    - listVBComponents

The **makeNewWorkbookFromAnother** sub-routine as shown in Figure 17-1 attempts to completely automate the task of copying from one workbook to another all of the VB components. The routine prompts for which workbook to export from those currently open. Once a workbook is selected a project reference is set and a folder name created.

A reference to the folder is returned from the full path of the current workbook by using the **getFragment** function (Figure 17-2) from the **ExportProjects** module to return the part without the file extension.

Worksheets and VBE components are then copied from the current workbook to a new workbook. Finally, a reference is set to the newly created and active workbook project and the VB components are imported to this new workbook.

```
(General)                                              makeNewWorkbookFromAnother

Public Sub makeNewWorkbookFromAnother()
    ' Declare references for the workbook, from and to projects and folder name.
    Dim wb As Workbook
    Dim vbpFrom As VBProject, vbpTo As VBProject
    Dim stFolder As String

    ' For each workbook in application.
    For Each wb In Application.Workbooks
        ' Do we want to export this workbook and its components.
        If MsgBox("Export Workbook: " & wb.Name, vbYesNo) = vbYes Then
            ' set current project and folder location
            Set vbpFrom = wb.VBProject
            stFolder = getFragment(vbpFrom.Filename, ".", True) & "\"
            ' Export worksheets and components.
            exportWorksheets wb
            exportChosenProject vbpFrom, stFolder

            ' Set new project and import components.
            Set vbpTo = ActiveWorkbook.VBProject
            importVBComponents vbpTo, stFolder
        End If
    Next wb
End Sub
```

Figure 17-1: The makeNewWorkbookFromAnother sub-routine (MakeNewWorkbook module)

The **getFragment** function in Figure 17-2 takes the string to split, the separator to look for in the string and whether to return the left or right part of the string. For example, a full file path for a workbook would have a file extension, so the separator would be the "." (full stop) which can be used to return the file path without file extension or just the file extension.

```
(General)                                              getFragment

Function getFragment(stURI As String, stSeparator As String, boLeft As Boolean)
    ' Get fragment (without separator) left part if boLeft is True.
    ' else right part where separator is unique in stURI i.e. not / or \.

    If boLeft = True Then
        getFragment = Left$(stURI, InStr(stURI, stSeparator) - 1)
    Else
        getFragment = Right$(stURI, Len(stURI) - InStr(stURI, stSeparator))
    End If
End Function
```

Figure 17-2: The getFragment function (ExportProjects module)

17 - RESOLVING WORKBOOK CORRUPTIONS

The **exportWorksheets** sub-routine in Figure 17-3 copies worksheets from the current workbook to a new workbook and makes this the **ActiveWorkbook**.

```
(General)                                      ▼   exportWorksheets                        ▼
    ' Export worksheets to new workbook.
    Sub exportWorksheets(wb As Workbook)
        wb.Worksheets.Copy
    End Sub
```

Figure 17-3: The exportWorksheets sub-routine (ExportWorkbook module)

The **exportChosenProject** in Figure 17-4 is used to create the folder required (if it does not yet exist) with same name as the project and then the **exportVBComponents** sub-routine is executed (Figure 17-5).

```
(General)                                      ▼   exportChosenProject                     ▼
    ' Process selected project.

    Sub exportChosenProject(vbp As VBProject, stFolder As String)
        ' check if folder exists and create if it does not.
        Dim obFileSys As Object
        Set obFileSys = CreateObject("Scripting.FileSystemObject")
        If Not obFileSys.folderexists(stFolder) Then obFileSys.createfolder (stFolder)

        exportVBComponents vbp, stFolder      ' export objects to folder.
    End Sub
```

Figure 17-4: The exportChosenProject sub-routine (ExportProjects module)

To export each component, a file name is constructed using the folder and component name plus a correct file extension for the type of component (Figure 17-5).

```
(General)                                      ▼   exportVBComponents                      ▼
    ' Export all objects from the selected vb project.

    Private Sub exportVBComponents(vbp As VBProject, stFolder As String)
        Dim cp As VBComponent, stFile As String

        ' traverse components and export to folder.
        For Each cp In vbp.VBComponents
            stFile = stFolder & cp.Name & getComponentExtension(cp)
            cp.Export Filename:=stFile
        Next cp
    End Sub
```

Figure 17-5: The exportVBComponents routine (ExportProjects module)

The VB component file extension is determined by the type of component and this is returned from the **getComponentExtension** function (Figure 17-6).

```
(General)                                    ▼   getComponentExtension                         ▼

    ' Get file extension for component type.

    Private Function getComponentExtension(cp As VBComponent)
        Select Case cp.Type
            Case vbext_ct_MSForm
                getComponentExtension = ".frm"
            Case vbext_ct_Document, vbext_ct_ClassModule
                getComponentExtension = ".cls"
            Case Else
                getComponentExtension = ".bas"
        End Select
    End Function
```

Figure 17-6: The getComponentExtension function (ExportProjects module)

Once the export has finished the **importVBComponents** sub-routine (Figure 17-7) is executed which uses the reference to the new active workbook and the VB components are imported one by one from the export folder to complete the process.

```
(General)                                    ▼   importVBComponents                            ▼

    ' Import objects from folder.

    Sub importVBComponents(vbp As VBProject, stFolder As String)
        ' Declare and then set file system objects to folder.
        Dim obFileSys As Object, obFolder As Object
        Dim obFiles As Object, obFile As Object
        Set obFileSys = CreateObject("Scripting.FileSystemObject")
        Set obFolder = obFileSys.getFolder(stFolder)
        Set obFiles = obFolder.Files
        ' For each file in folder.
        For Each obFile In obFiles
            ' Import components from file path.
            vbp.VBComponents.Import obFile.Path
        Next obFile
    End Sub
```

Figure 17-7: The importVBComponents sub-routine (ImportToProjects module)

The **importVBComponents** sub-routine assume that all components in the folder are required which should normally be the case.

However, the routine could be amended to require confirmation on a component by component basis before importing.

Should the automated process fail, there are separate routines for each stage of the process.

To export just the VB components, the **projectToExport** sub-routine is available (Figure 17-8). Once a project is selected from those presented from the **VBProjects** collection, the **exportChosenProject** sub-routine (Figure 17-4) is executed to complete the task.

```
(General)                                    projectToExport

' Get the vb project to export objects from.

Public Sub projectToExport()
    ' Declare references to VBE, Project.
    Dim ed As VBE: Set ed = Application.VBE
    Dim vbp As VBProject
    Dim stFolder As String
    ' Traverse each project and prompt whether to export or not.
    For Each vbp In ed.VBProjects
        If MsgBox("Export Project: " & vbp.Name, vbYesNo) = vbYes Then
            stFolder = getFragment(vbp.Filename, ".", True) & "\"

            ' Export chosen project.
            exportChosenProject vbp, stFolder
        End If
    Next vbp
End Sub
```

Figure 17-8: The projectToExport sub-routine (ExportProjects module)

Similarly, the **workbookToExport** sub-routine (Figure 17-9) can be used to export a selected workbook to a new workbook using the **exportWorksheets** sub-routine (Figure 17-3). Each workbook in the **Workbooks** collection is presented within a Yes/No input message box and only selected workbooks call the **exportWorksheets** sub-routine.

```
(General)                                    exportWorksheets

' Prompt for which workbook to export and then export worksheets to a new one.

Public Sub workbookToExport()
    Dim wb As Workbook
    For Each wb In Application.Workbooks
        If MsgBox("Export Workbook: " & wb.Name, vbYesNo) = vbYes Then
            exportWorksheets wb
        End If
    Next wb
End Sub
```

Figure 17-9: The workBookToExport sub-routine (ExportWorkbook module)

The **importToProject** sub-routine (Figure 17-10) enables standalone importing of VB components to a selected project. It works as follows:

- o A reference is set to the VBE and used in traversing the **VBProjects** collection in the VBE.
- o A message box with Yes/No inputs is presented for each project.
- o For each project confirmed with a **Yes** input, the **getFolder** function is called to return the folder where the components for importing are stored.
- o If a valid folder name has been found the **importVBComponents** sub-routine is called to import the VB components to the selected project.

```vba
(General)                                          importToProject

' Get the vb project to import objects to and then get them from chosen folder.

Public Sub importToProject()
    ' Declare references to VBE & Project.
    Dim ed As VBE: Set ed = Application.VBE
    Dim vbp As VBProject
    Dim stFolder As String
    ' Traverse each project and prompt whether to import to or not.
    For Each vbp In ed.VBProjects
        If MsgBox("Import to Project: " & vbp.Name, vbYesNo) = vbYes Then
            stFolder = getFolder()                  ' get folder.
            ' Import objects to project from folder if it exists.
            If Not IsEmpty(stFolder) Then importVBComponents vbp, stFolder
        End If
    Next vbp
End Sub
```

Figure 17-10: The importToProject sub-routine (ImportToProjects module)

The **getFolder** function (Figure 17-11) is required so that the user can select the folder where the VB components to import are stored. The salient points are:

- o The **FileDialog** is set to return a folder from the picker to the **fd** reference.
- o If a folder has been selected in the file dialog, the file name is returned otherwise the **vbNullString** is returned.

```vba
(General)                                          getFolder

' Get folder to import from.

Private Function getFolder()
    ' Declare and set filedialog object for folder browse and selection.
    Dim fd As FileDialog
    Set fd = Application.FileDialog(msoFileDialogFolderPicker)
    With fd
        .AllowMultiSelect = False
        If .Show = -1 Then
            getFolder = .SelectedItems(1)
        Else
            getFolder = vbNullString
        End If
    End With
End Function
```

Figure 17-11: The getFolder function (ImportToProjects module)

To list all the VB components to the **Immediate Window** in all open projects the **listVBComponents** sub-routine (Figure 17-12) can be used. It works as follows:

- o For each project from the **VBProjects** collection in the VBE the project name is displayed in the **Immediate** Window.
- o Within the project each VB component in the **VBComponents** collection is identified by its type and this information is used to display the name and type to the **Immediate** Window.

```
(General)                                        listVBComponents

' Prints the VBE component information contained in each open project.

Public Sub listVBComponents()
    ' Declare rerences to the VBE, project, component and its type.
    Dim ed As VBE: Set ed = Application.VBE
    Dim vbp As VBProject, cp As VBComponent, stType As String

    ' Traverse each project from projects collection.
    For Each vbp In ed.VBProjects
        Debug.Print "Project Name: " & vbp.Name
        ' Traverse each component in this project.
        For Each cp In vbp.VBComponents
            ' For each component type store the type for later.
            Select Case cp.Type
                Case vbext_ct_Document
                    stType = "Sheet (Workbook)"
                Case vbext_ct_MSForm
                    stType = "Form"
                Case vbext_ct_StdModule
                    stType = "Standard Module"
                Case vbext_ct_ClassModule
                    stType = "Class Module"
            Case Else
                stType = "Unknown"
            End Select
            Debug.Print cp.Name & " [" & stType & "]"
        Next cp
        Debug.Print "----------------------------------------"
    Next vbp
End Sub
```

Figure 17-12: The listVBComponents sub-routine (ProjectInformation module)

Using third-party tools to clean up workbooks

There are a variety of third party clean up tools which automate the task of cleaning up the project.

Repairing a workbook

When opening a workbook via the **Open Dialog** *click* the dropdown arrow at the side of the **Open** button and then select the **Open and Repair** option from the dropdown menu. At the prompt choose to attempt a **Repair** of the workbook.

This option may prompt to **Update Links** and **Repair/Extract Data**.

A link for viewing a log file of the repair operation is available at the bottom of the completion dialog and a **Close** button for exiting.

Attempt to load the workbook in safe mode

A problematic workbook may load in Safe Mode which is possible simply by holding down the Ctrl (Control) key, then clicking the option to load Excel prior to attempting to open the workbook.

Re-engineering macro code

Sometimes recorded macro code may be the culprit of potential corruptions. Some features may require recoding to make sure that they execute as expected.

Conflicts with other software/features

There are many factors which may interfere with trouble free loading of workbooks.

It is always worth checking that there is enough memory, processing power and diskspace available by monitoring the loading of a workbook.

Anti-virus software, third party add-ins and drivers for both video and printers may also cause conflicts. Disabling, changing or removing software which may interfere, can resolve issues.

Various features may also cause issues such as hardware graphics acceleration and event handling. Turning off such features may resolve the issue.

In particular, the use of additional libraries may cause conflicts. Removing or including the same libraries may resolve the issue.

18

AN EXAMPLE APPLICATION

18 – AN EXAMPLE APPLICATION

The example application automates the calculation of road fuel scale charges for those in the UK using a business car for private purposes. The "calculator" works out how much Value Added Tax (VAT) is to be paid back to HM Revenue & Customs and displays the inclusive, VAT and exclusive elements of the charge.

The calculation is based on the CO_2 emission figures if available or the engine size where such figures are not available. The CO_2 figures in the published tables are banded in multiples of 5 starting at 120 (also used for emissions lower than the band) and ending at 225 (also used for emissions higher than the band). Where CO_2 emissions are not an exact multiple of 5 they are rounded down to the nearest multiple of 5.

In cases where engine size (cc) is used, the banding is currently:
- o 1400cc or less: use band 140
- o 1401cc to 2000cc: use band 175
- o 2001cc or above: use band 225

In the application a user can either manually input details for a single vehicle in the cells provided within the calculator or import a list of vehicles and batch process the calculation.

The results of a batch calculation can be:
- o Added to the original list as additional columns.
- o Used to create an entirely new list with columns made up from the calculator.
- o Used to create individual calculator workbooks for each vehicle.

The configuration for the import is handled by the filling in of a form including:
- o Loading the import workbook.
- o Indicating whether the import workbook has a header row.
- o Mapping import columns to required inputs for the calculator.
- o Choosing the type of batch process to execute.
- o Initiating the processing of the vehicles import list.

The separate import vehicles list workbook must contain some unique identifier column, which is mapped to the **ID** defined name within the calculator. The **ID** is used as a filename for individual workbooks. For a correct calculation, the calculator also requires the CO_2 column and engine size column where any CO_2 column cell is blank.

In this example application, a workbook named **ScaleCharges.xlsm** is used which contains:
- o Three worksheets (all protected by default):
  - o ScaleChargeImport.
  - o ScaleChargeCalculator.
  - o ScaleChargeRates.
- o The fmImportAndCalculate form and attached code. Requires the **Microsoft Forms 2.0 Object Library** to be added via **Tools**->**References** in the VBE.
- o The StateSettings module.
- o Additional code within the ScaleChargeStart worksheet object.

18 - AN EXAMPLE APPLICATION

Figure 18-1 shows the **ScaleChargeImport** worksheet which has a single command button which when *clicked* loads the **Import & Calculate** form for importing a vehicle list for batch processing.

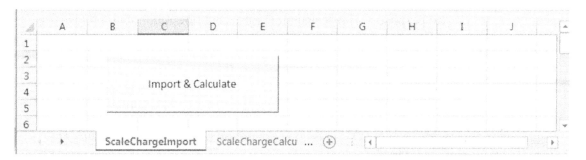

Figure 18-1: ScaleChargeImport worksheet command button

Figure 18-2 shows the **ScaleChargeCalculator** worksheet where values can be either manually input into the cells provided or imported from a separate vehicle list (an example in Figure 18-6).

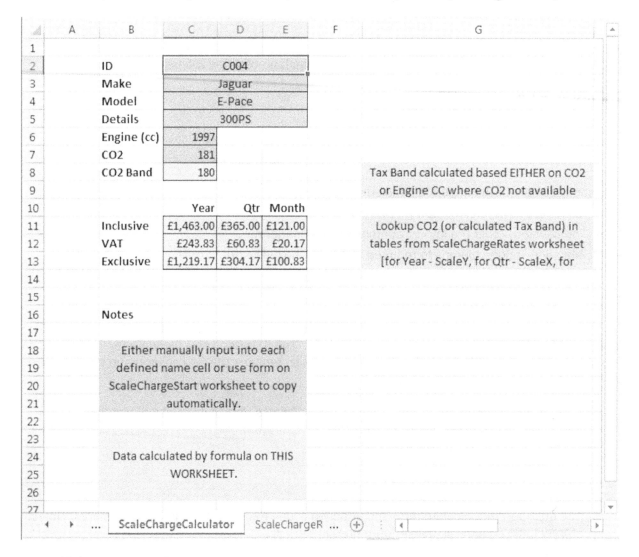

Figure 18-2: ScaleChargeCalculator worksheet

Figure 18-3 shows the **ScaleChargeRates** worksheet which contains the tables used for looking up the CO_2 band to retrieve the Inclusive, VAT and Exclusive amounts for year, quarter and month. Where the CO_2 figure is not available the engine size (cc) is used to initially retrieve the CO_2 band which can then be used for the lookup. The tables are valid for one year, so would require updating each year.

Note: This example application could be extended to take account of calculations for VAT quarters that cross over two different sets of tables.

Road fuel scale charges form 1 May 2018 to 30 Apr 2019

12 Month VAT Scale Charges (£)						Quarterly VAT Scale Charge (£)						Monthly VAT Scale Charge (£)						CO2 Figures not available	
Lookup	Band	Incl	VAT	Excl		Lookup	Band	Incl	VAT	Excl		Lookup	Band	Incl	VAT	Excl		CC	CO2 Band
0	120	562	93.67	468.33		0	120	140	23.33	116.67		0	120	46	7.67	38.33		0	140
120	120	562	93.67	468.33		120	120	140	23.33	116.67		120	120	46	7.67	38.33		1401	175
125	125	842	140.33	701.67		125	125	210	35.00	175.00		125	125	70	11.67	58.33		2001	225
130	130	900	150.00	750.00		130	130	224	37.33	186.67		130	130	74	12.33	61.67			
135	135	954	159.00	795.00		135	135	238	39.67	198.33		135	135	79	13.17	65.83			
140	140	1,013	168.83	844.17		140	140	252	42.00	210.00		140	140	84	14.00	70.00		Notes	
145	145	1,067	177.83	889.17		145	145	266	44.33	221.67		145	145	88	14.67	73.33			
150	150	1,125	187.50	937.50		150	150	280	46.67	233.33		150	150	93	15.50	77.50			
155	155	1,179	196.50	982.50		155	155	295	49.17	245.83		155	155	98	16.33	81.67		Where CO2 emission	
160	160	1,238	206.33	1,031.67		160	160	309	51.50	257.50		160	160	102	17.00	85.00		figure not a multiple of 5,	
165	165	1,292	215.33	1,076.67		165	165	323	53.83	269.17		165	165	107	17.83	89.17		rounded down to next	
170	170	1,350	225.00	1,125.00		170	170	336	56.00	280.00		170	170	111	18.50	92.50		multiple of 5	
175	175	1,404	234.00	1,170.00		175	175	351	58.50	292.50		175	175	116	19.33	96.67			
180	180	1,463	243.83	1,219.17		180	180	365	60.83	304.17		180	180	121	20.17	100.83			
185	185	1,517	252.83	1,264.17		185	185	379	63.17	315.83		185	185	125	20.83	104.17			
190	190	1,575	262.50	1,312.50		190	190	393	65.50	327.50		190	190	130	21.67	108.33			
195	195	1,630	271.67	1,358.33		195	195	407	67.83	339.17		195	195	135	22.50	112.50			
200	200	1,688	281.33	1,406.67		200	200	421	70.17	350.83		200	200	140	23.33	116.67			
205	205	1,742	290.33	1,451.67		205	205	436	72.67	363.33		205	205	145	24.17	120.83			
210	210	1,801	300.17	1,500.83		210	210	449	74.83	374.17		210	210	149	24.83	124.17			
215	215	1,855	309.17	1,545.83		215	215	463	77.17	385.83		215	215	154	25.67	128.33			
220	220	1,913	318.83	1,594.17		220	220	477	79.50	397.50		220	220	159	26.50	132.50			
225	225	1,967	327.83	1,639.17		225	225	491	81.83	409.17		225	225	163	27.17	135.83			

ScaleChargeRates

Figure 18-3: ScaleChargeCalculator worksheet

Clicking the **Import & Calculate** command button triggers the **ImportButton_Click** event handler which is shown in Figure 18-4. The sub-routine uses the **Show** method to display the **fmImportAndCalculate** form (Figure 18-5).

```
ImportButton                                    ▼   Click                          ▼

Option Explicit

' When user clicks import button run this routine.
' Shows form (see form code).

Private Sub ImportButton_Click()
    fmImportAndCalculate.Show
End Sub
```

Figure 18-4: The ImportButton_Click sub-routine (ScaleChargeImport worksheet code)

Figure 18-5 shows the form which is loaded when the **Import & Calculate** button on the **ScaleChargeImport** worksheet is *clicked*. The settings shown are the defaults, it is assumed that the import workbook will have a title row and the columns A to F will hold the corresponding columns required for the calculator. As indicated **ID** and **CO2** are required columns.

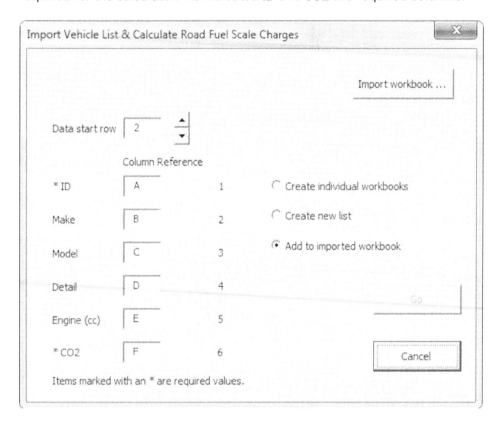

Figure 18-5: Import and calculate configuration form

On the form in Figure 18-5, *Clicking* the **Import workbook...** button displays the file dialog for selecting the vehicle list workbook to import. Once opened the import workbook can be viewed side by side with the form, so that the columns can be mapped to the applicable calculator cells.

The "Data start row" textbox value can be changed by the spinner button up and down options. By default, this is set to the value **2**.

Column references are input in their alphabetic form although their equivalent numeric value is also displayed alongside.

Choose one of the three methods of processing by *clicking* on the relevant option. By default, it is assumed that the scale charge calculation columns will be appended to the import worksheet data.

Click the **Go** button to initiate the batch calculation process which will unload the form on completion.

Click the **Cancel** button to unload the form.

Two example files are provided **Vehicle_List.xlsx** (with title row) and **Vehicle_List_NoHeader.xlsx** (without a title row) for import testing.

Figure 18-6 shows **Vehicle_List.xlsx** (with titles) which could be used for import, columns A to E corresponding to the form defaults but column G (CO2) would replace column F on the form.

	A	B	C	D	E	F	G	H
1	ID	Make	Model	Details	Engine (cc	Fuel	CO2	Tax
2		Alfa Romeo	Stelvio	all	1995	Petrol	161	I
3	C002	Aston Martin	DB6	classic		Petrol		
4	C003	Ford	Fiesta	classic	1100	Petrol		
5	C004	Jaguar	E-Pace	300PS	1997	Petrol	181	J
6	C005	Jaguar	F-Pace	250PS	1997	Petrol	170	I
7	C006	Lexus	RX450h	SE	3456	Hybrid	120	G
8	C007	Lexus	RX450h	non SE	3456	Hybrid	127	G
9	C008	Lexus	RX450h	L	3456	Hybrid	138	H
10	C009	Lexus	NX 300h	all	2494	Hybrid	135	H
11	C010	Land Rover	Discovery S	240PS	1997	Petrol	181	J

Cars

Figure 18-6: Example vehicle list workbook

Figure 18-7 shows the module level declarations including references to the calculator worksheet, its input cell range and their string references (**m_stArrCol** array), a new workbook and the import workbook. There are also constants for the 6 input cell columns and 10 extra columns (scale charges) added from the calculator.

(General) | cancelInput

```
' IMPORT VEHICLE LIST OR MANUALLY INPUT TO SCALE CHARGE CALCULATOR
'
' Author: Simon A.Towell
' Last Modified: 21 Sep 2018
' Copyright 2018, Simon A. Towell (all rigts reserved)
' Prerequisites:  Microsoft Forms 2.0 Object Library
'
' OPTIONS ARE:
'    1. Copy to/Save calculator to new individual workbooks for each vehicle in list.
'    2. Create new single workbook with vehicle list populated with new information.
'    3. Append new columns to imported workbook.
'
' Worksheets Used:
'    1. ScaleChargeImport - button to load fmImportAndCalculate form for import
'       and calculations.
'    2. ScaleChargeCalculator - calculates charges based on CO2 emissions
'       (or engine size if CO2 omitted).
'    3. ScaleChargeRates - holds current scale charge tables.
'
Option Explicit
Option Base 1
' References to calculator worksheet & input range so we can clear in one hit.
Private m_wsCalc As Worksheet, m_rgCalc As Range
' References to new workbook (required only for options 1 and 2).
Private m_wbNew As Workbook
' Reference to import workbook.
Private m_wbImport As Workbook
' Reference to column array used in dictionary creation and calculator input boxes.
Private Const mc_lnColumns As Long = 6
Private Const mc_lnExtraColumns As Long = 10
Private m_stArrCol(1 To mc_lnColumns) As String
```

Figure 18-7: Module level declarations (fmImportAndCalculate form code)

Figure 18-8 shows the code executed when the form initializes (the **UserForm_Initialize** event) as follows:

o The module level **m_stArrCol** array is set with string references to the defined names used in the calculator which are consistent throughout the application. Form text boxes use the same names but with a "tb" prefix and labels have the "lb" prefix. The additional numerical column label also has a suffix of "No" to distinguish it from the descriptive labels to the left of the column input text boxes.

o Text boxes for the required columns are set to defaults A to F (**mc_lnColumns** is set as a constant at module level with a value of 6) and labels are set to the equivalent numerical values (1 to 6) using the defined name string references with the addition of "tb" for text boxes and "lb" for labels (also suffix of "No" for numerical column references).

o The data start row textbox and controlling spin button are set to the default value of 2.

o The radio button for the default option is set to true (the append option).

o The module level worksheet reference (**m_wsCalc**) is set to the **ScaleChargeCalculator** worksheet.

o The defined name input cells on the calculator are joined together as a single range so that they can be cleared in one hit using the defined name range string references.

```
UserForm                                          ▼   Initialize                                              ▼

' Initialize form by creating array of labels which store actual column number
' rather than data input which is column ref in alphabetic format.

Private Sub UserForm_Initialize()
    ' Set array items to range names for input to calculator.
    ' Also use as label names by prefix/suffix to name eg. lb(name)No.
    m_stArrCol(1) = "ID"
    m_stArrCol(2) = "Make"
    m_stArrCol(3) = "Model"
    m_stArrCol(4) = "Details"
    m_stArrCol(5) = "Engine"
    m_stArrCol(6) = "CO2_Value"

    ' Assume form columns assumed by default to be A to F (1 to 6).
    Dim lnCount As Long
    For lnCount = 1 To mc_lnColumns
        Me("tb" & m_stArrCol(lnCount)).Value = Chr(64 + lnCount)
        Me("lb" & m_stArrCol(lnCount) & "No").Caption = lnCount
    Next lnCount

    ' Data start row default to 2 (spin button and displayed text box).
    Me.sbDataStartRow.Value = 2: Me.tbDataStartRow.Value = 2

    ' Set default option button rbAppend to true
    Me.rbAppend.Value = True

    ' Set references to calculator and range we need to reset after each new item.
    Set m_wsCalc = ThisWorkbook.Worksheets("ScaleChargeCalculator")
    Set m_rgCalc = m_wsCalc.Range(m_stArrCol(1))
    For lnCount = 2 To mc_lnColumns
        Set m_rgCalc = Union(m_rgCalc, m_wsCalc.Range(m_stArrCol(lnCount)))
    Next lnCount
End Sub
```

Figure 18-8: Form initialize event handler (fmImportAndCalculate form code)

Note: The **Me** reference is used to explicitly show the **form controls** used in the VBA code as opposed to objects and variables declared within the modules.

In Figure 18-9, the code for the **Import workbook...** button click event method
(**bnImportWorkbook_Click**) is shown and works as follows:

- o The open file dialog is presented (showing only files corresponding to the "*.xl*" wildcard string) and the opened workbook reference is stored to the **vtFileName** variant variable.
- o If the **vtFilename** value is not false, the **Go** button is **enabled**, the full path of the opened workbook is displayed (**lbFileName**), a reference to the open workbook is set (**m_wbImport**) and the data start row is set.
- o If no workbook was opened the **Go** button is **disabled** and the **lbFileName** reference (displayed as the full path on the form) is set the **vbNullString**.

```
bnImportWorkbook                                          ▼    Click                                          ▼

    ' Open workbook and set form controls when Import Button clicked.

    Private Sub bnImportWorkbook_Click()
        ' Declare and set file name via open file dialog.
        Dim vtFileName As Variant: vtFileName = Application.GetOpenFilename("Workbook, *.xl*")
        Select Case vtFileName
            Case Is <> False
                ' For a valid file name Go button is enabled,
                Me.bnGo.Enabled = True
                ' Set form label for file name & set reference to import workbook.
                Me.lbFileName.Caption = vtFileName
                Set m_wbImport = Workbooks.Open(vtFileName)
                ' Attempt to guess data start row and set.
                setDataStartRow m_wbImport.Worksheets(1)
            Case Else
                ' No file name returned so disable Go button & set label to null.
                Me.bnGo.Enabled = False
                Me.lbFileName.Caption = vbNullString
        End Select
    End Sub
```

Figure 18-9: Import Workbook button click event handler (fmImportAndCalculate form code)

In Figure 18-10, the spin button on the form (up and down arrow keys) controls the value of the data start row textbox (**tbDataStartRow**). They are always in sync.

The data start row can be changed to match the actual value on the import vehicle list manually.

```
sbDataStartRow                                          ▼    Change                                          ▼

    ' When spin button value changed data start row value displayed with new value.

    Private Sub sbDataStartRow_Change()
        Me.tbDataStartRow.Value = Me.sbDataStartRow.Value
    End Sub
```

Figure 18-10: Spin button change event handler (fmImportAndCalculate form code)

Note: An attempt to **guess** the data start row is made once the vehicle list to import is opened. The spin button and/or textbox should be used to override this guess, once it has been made.

In Figure 18-11, the **setDataStartRow** attempts to **guess** the data start row as follows:

- o Set references to a Boolean found flag (**boFound**), start row (**lnRow**), start column (**lnCol**), last column used on worksheet (**lnLastCol**) and the data type (**lnType**).

- o Check each of the used columns on a row by row basis (up to 3 rows) comparing the previous rows cell data type with the current one, ignoring empty and null cells and set the **boFound** flag to **true** if a difference is found.

- o Set the data start row either to the guessed row or to 1 if none found.

```
(General)                                              setDataStartRow

' Attempt to locate data start row.
' Set the boFound flag, start at the first row and column.
' Check column by column for each row (3 max).
' Use the variable type to determine if current and previous rows differ.
' When comparing ignore empty or null cell values.
' If a type difference is found, set the flag and set the data start row.
' Otherwise assume there are no titles and set as 1.

Private Sub setDataStartRow(ByVal ws As Worksheet)
    Dim boFound As Boolean: boFound = False
    Dim lnRow As Long: lnRow = 1
    Dim lnCol As Long: lnCol = 1
    Dim lnLastCol As Long: lnLastCol = ws.UsedRange.Columns.Count
    Dim lnType As Long
    Do Until lnCol > lnLastCol Or boFound
        lnType = VarType(ws.Cells(lnRow, lnCol).Value2)
        Do Until lnRow > 3 Or boFound
            lnRow = lnRow + 1
            Select Case VarType(ws.Cells(lnRow, lnCol).Value2)
                Case Is > 1
                    boFound = (lnType <> VarType(ws.Cells(lnRow, lnCol).Value2))
            End Select
        Loop
        lnCol = lnCol + 1
        If Not boFound Then lnRow = 1
    Loop
    If boFound Then
        Me.sbDataStartRow.Value = lnRow: Me.tbDataStartRow.Value = lnRow
    Else
        Me.sbDataStartRow.Value = 1: Me.tbDataStartRow.Value = 1
    End If
End Sub
```

Figure 18-11: The setDataStartRow sub-routine (fmImportAndCalculate form code)

The **Cancel** button when *clicked* unloads the form (referenced by **Me**), as shown in Figure 18-12.

```
bnCancel                                               Click

' Cancel button clicked so unload form.

Private Sub bnCancel_Click()
    Unload Me
End Sub
```

Figure 18-12: Cancel button click event handler (fmImportAndCalculate form code)

Each time a key is pressed within a calculator column textbox the corresponding **KeyPress** method is executed as shown in Figure 18-13. All methods execute the **allowedInput** sub-routine to validate the keyboard input so as to make sure that an alphabetic character has been pressed as follows:

- o   The **KeyAscii** argument is checked to make sure the value is either in the range 65 to 90 (upper case) or 97 to 122 (lower case).
- o   If an invalid key has been pressed the **KeyAscii** value is set to **0** (the null character) and a message box is displayed to indicate the error.

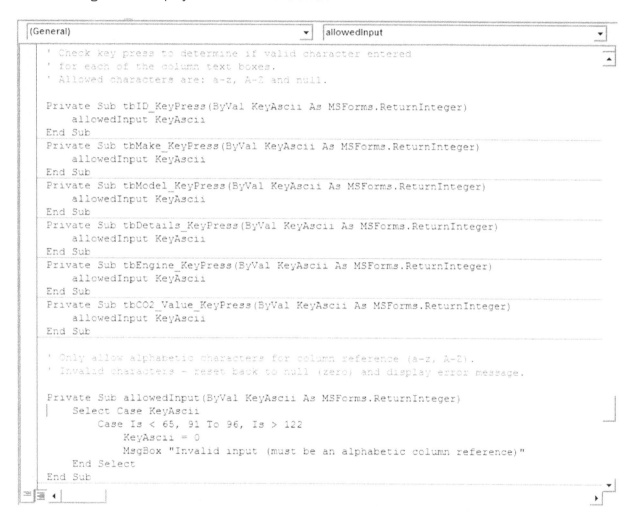

```
(General)                                          allowedInput

' Check key press to determine if valid character entered
' for each of the column text boxes.
' Allowed characters are: a-z, A-Z and null.

Private Sub tbID_KeyPress(ByVal KeyAscii As MSForms.ReturnInteger)
    allowedInput KeyAscii
End Sub
Private Sub tbMake_KeyPress(ByVal KeyAscii As MSForms.ReturnInteger)
    allowedInput KeyAscii
End Sub
Private Sub tbModel_KeyPress(ByVal KeyAscii As MSForms.ReturnInteger)
    allowedInput KeyAscii
End Sub
Private Sub tbDetails_KeyPress(ByVal KeyAscii As MSForms.ReturnInteger)
    allowedInput KeyAscii
End Sub
Private Sub tbEngine_KeyPress(ByVal KeyAscii As MSForms.ReturnInteger)
    allowedInput KeyAscii
End Sub
Private Sub tbCO2_Value_KeyPress(ByVal KeyAscii As MSForms.ReturnInteger)
    allowedInput KeyAscii
End Sub

' Only allow alphabetic characters for column reference (a-z, A-Z).
' Invalid characters - reset back to null (zero) and display error message.

Private Sub allowedInput(ByVal KeyAscii As MSForms.ReturnInteger)
    Select Case KeyAscii
        Case Is < 65, 91 To 96, Is > 122
            KeyAscii = 0
            MsgBox "Invalid input (must be an alphabetic column reference)"
    End Select
End Sub
```

Figure 18-13: KeyPress textbox control methods (fmImportAndCalculate form code)

Figure 18-14 shows the **BeforeUpdate** event methods for each textbox control and the **cancelInput** function. Every event method calls the **cancelInput** function which then returns a **Boolean** value to the **Cancel** parameter of the event method used to stop focus from being lost when an invalid column reference is input. Some column references are required inputs, so an argument is passed to this effect for each control and used when an attempt is made to bypass the input.

The **cancelInput** function returns the result of checking for a valid column reference and does not allow exit from the textbox if the result is **True** as follows:

- o The input column reference (alphabetic) is passed as a **String** argument to **stInput** and the required column flag (**boRequired**).
- o A temporary **Long** type variable (**lnTmp**) is declared and set to **0** (zero).
- o An error trap is set and an attempt made to store the numeric equivalent of the input alphabetic column reference.
- o The error trap is reset and the **Boolean** result of **lnTmp** equalling **0** (zero) is passed back.
- o Before returning the result, a message box indicating an invalid column location is displayed if the return value is **True**.

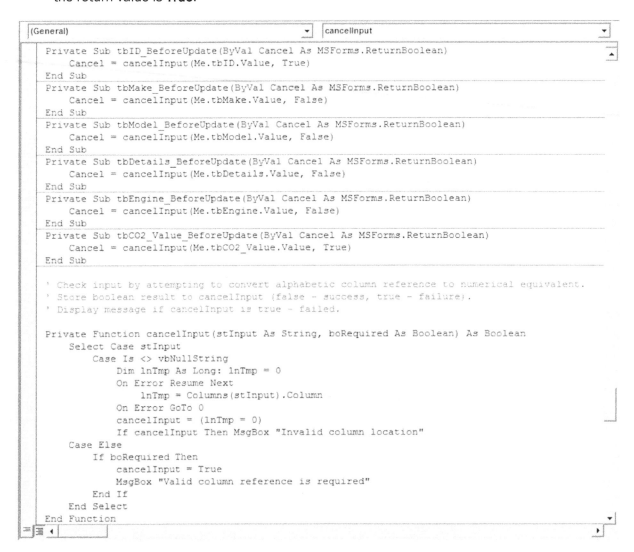

```
(General)                                              cancelInput

Private Sub tbID_BeforeUpdate(ByVal Cancel As MSForms.ReturnBoolean)
    Cancel = cancelInput(Me.tbID.Value, True)
End Sub
Private Sub tbMake_BeforeUpdate(ByVal Cancel As MSForms.ReturnBoolean)
    Cancel = cancelInput(Me.tbMake.Value, False)
End Sub
Private Sub tbModel_BeforeUpdate(ByVal Cancel As MSForms.ReturnBoolean)
    Cancel = cancelInput(Me.tbModel.Value, False)
End Sub
Private Sub tbDetails_BeforeUpdate(ByVal Cancel As MSForms.ReturnBoolean)
    Cancel = cancelInput(Me.tbDetails.Value, False)
End Sub
Private Sub tbEngine_BeforeUpdate(ByVal Cancel As MSForms.ReturnBoolean)
    Cancel = cancelInput(Me.tbEngine.Value, False)
End Sub
Private Sub tbCO2_Value_BeforeUpdate(ByVal Cancel As MSForms.ReturnBoolean)
    Cancel = cancelInput(Me.tbCO2_Value.Value, True)
End Sub

' Check input by attempting to convert alphabetic column reference to numerical equivalent.
' Store boolean result to cancelInput (false - success, true - failure).
' Display message if cancelInput is true - failed.

Private Function cancelInput(stInput As String, boRequired As Boolean) As Boolean
    Select Case stInput
        Case Is <> vbNullString
            Dim lnTmp As Long: lnTmp = 0
            On Error Resume Next
                lnTmp = Columns(stInput).Column
            On Error GoTo 0
            cancelInput = (lnTmp = 0)
            If cancelInput Then MsgBox "Invalid column location"
        Case Else
            If boRequired Then
                cancelInput = True
                MsgBox "Valid column reference is required"
            End If
    End Select
End Function
```

Figure 18-14: BeforeUpdate textbox control methods (fmImportAndCalculate form code)

When a valid input has been made into any of the column reference text boxes, the **AfterUpdate** event is trapped so that the input can be re-formatted into **Upper Case** and the value of the numerical equivalent column can be displayed alongside as a label caption.

Figure 18-15 shows the **AfterUpdate** methods for each textbox control and the **formatTextBox** sub-routine which formats each input accordingly. The salient points to note are:

- o The **formatTextBox** sub-routine is passed as arguments the actual name of each control as a string.
- o The string name is used with the **Me** statement to construct a reference to the textbox control and then its value is set to **Upper Case**.
- o The **Me** statement is used to construct a reference to the label caption which is changed to the equivalent numerical column reference where there is a non-null value.

```
tbID                                    ▼   AfterUpdate                              ▼

   ' Check value entered for each column and make upper case.
   ' Also convert to actual column number for lable caption or display error message.

   Private Sub tbID_AfterUpdate()
      formatTextBox "tb" & m_stArrCol(1), "lb" & m_stArrCol(1) & "No"
   End Sub
   Private Sub tbMake_AfterUpdate()
      formatTextBox "tb" & m_stArrCol(2), "lb" & m_stArrCol(2) & "No"
   End Sub
   Private Sub tbModel_AfterUpdate()
     formatTextBox "tb" & m_stArrCol(3), "lb" & m_stArrCol(3) & "No"
   End Sub
   Private Sub tbDetails_AfterUpdate()
      formatTextBox "tb" & m_stArrCol(4), "lb" & m_stArrCol(4) & "No"
   End Sub
   Private Sub tbEngine_AfterUpdate()
      formatTextBox "tb" & m_stArrCol(5), "lb" & m_stArrCol(5) & "No"
   End Sub
   Private Sub tbCO2_Value_AfterUpdate()
      formatTextBox "tb" & m_stArrCol(6), "lb" & m_stArrCol(6) & "No"
   End Sub


   ' Format text box input as upper case
   ' and label caption to show numeric column reference (or reset if blank).

   Private Sub formatTextBox(stTextbox As String, stCaption As String)
      Me(stTextbox).Value = UCase(Me(stTextbox).Value)
      If Me(stTextbox).Value <> vbNullString Then
         Me(stCaption).Caption = Columns(Me(stTextbox).Value).Column
      Else
         Me(stCaption).Caption = vbNullString
      End If
   End Sub
```

Figure 18-15: AfterUpdate textbox control methods (fmImportAndCalculate form code)

When configuring the elements on the form before clicking the **Go** button, the type of batch process required, needs to be selected. The default is to append to the vehicle import list.

Note: The **Go** button is only **enabled** after all required information has been configured on the form, including vehicle list to import and required column references.

---

18 - AN EXAMPLE APPLICATION

Figure 18-16 shows the code for the **Go** button click event method which works as follows:

- o The **columnsValid** function (Figure 18-17) is used to determine if all column references are unique and any required column references are not blank.
- o To improve performance various state setting values are recorded, then turned off in the **turnOffStateSettings** sub-routine (Figure 15-1).
- o The form is hidden during processing and calculations are set to automatic, so the scale charge calculator will function correctly.
- o The **calcScaleCharges** sub-routine is executed to batch process the vehicle import list.
- o On completion the form is unloaded and state settings are returned to their original settings in the **resetStateSettings** sub-routine (Figure 15-1).

```
bnGo                                          ▼   Click                                           ▼
' Go button clicked.
' Check via dictionary creation for unique column references,
' finish if this step fails.
' Turn off state settings to improve performance.
' If columns are unique, hide form, set calculation automatic for calculator to work,
' run CalcScaleCharge routine to do caclulation then unload form.
' Finally reset state settings.

Private Sub bnGo_Click()
    If columnsValid Then
        turnOffStateSettings
        Me.Hide
        Application.Calculation = xlCalculationAutomatic
        calcScaleCharges
        Unload Me
        resetStateSettings
    End If
End Sub
```

Figure 18-16: Go button click event method (fmImportAndCalculate form code)

The **columnsValid** function in Figure 18-17 determines if column references are unique and works as follows:

- A reference to the dictionary object **obDict** is created.
- The result is assumed **false** until determined otherwise i.e. we need to cancel the dictionary function and the batch processing will stop.
- The array of column reference labels (**m_stArrCol**) is traversed and for each item the numerical column value is checked to make sure that it is valid.
- Valid column references are checked for existence in the dictionary and if new added, otherwise there is a duplication and returns a failed result.
- Invalid column references are checked to make sure that they are not required references, if so a failed result is returned.

```
(General)                                        columnsValid

' Add column references to dictionary checking for blanks and duplicates.
' Assume all is OK to begin with, then traverse array of column references
' but if blank for required columns (1 - ID and 6 - CO2), show error
' and return result as failure.
' Convert each reference to a numeric value and then attempt to add to dictionary
' with any duplicates being detected, message displayed to indicate error
' and return result as failure.

Private Function columnsValid() As Boolean
    Dim lnCount As Long, lnCol As Long
    Dim obDict As Object: Set obDict = CreateObject("Scripting.Dictionary")
    columnsValid = True
    For lnCount = LBound(m_stArrCol) To UBound(m_stArrCol)
        lnCol = val(Me("lb" & m_stArrCol(lnCount) & "No").Caption)
        Select Case lnCol
            Case Is > 0
                Select Case obDict.exists(lnCol)
                    Case False
                        obDict.Add lnCol, m_stArrCol(lnCount)
                    Case Else
                        MsgBox "Duplicate column references not allowed."
                        columnsValid = False
                        Exit For
                End Select
            Case Else
                Select Case lnCount
                    Case 1, 6
                        columnsValid = False
                        MsgBox "Required inputs cannot be blank"
                        Exit For
                End Select
        End Select
    Next lnCount
End Function
```

Figure 18-17: The columnsValid function (fmImportAndCalculate form code)

Figure 18-18 shows the **calcScaleCharges** sub-routine which controls the batch processing of the imported vehicle list and calculates the scale charges for each item. The code works as follows:

- References are set to the import data worksheet (**ws**) and the vehicles array (**vtArrVehicles**).
- The import data is copied to the **vtArrVehicles** array, with references set to the data start (**lnDataStartRow**), last row (**lnLastRow**) and last column (**lnLastCol**).
- For a data start row of 1, an offset row (**lnOffsetRow**) is created for the additional of new titles where the new list option has been selected.
- An export array (**vtArrExport**) is created according to type of list process and if a new list reference a new workbook (**m_wbNew**) is added.
- The **vtArrVehicles** array is traversed for all items in the list and the scale charge calculator is populated (**populateCalculator** sub-routine)
- Using the calculator information list items are added via the **addItems** sub-routine.
- Post processing clears the calculator range (**m_rgCalc**) created earlier.
- Finally, if a new list has been created the **newListFinalize** sub-routine is called or if appending to the import list the **appendToListFinalize** sub-routine is called.

```
(General)                                    ▼    calcScaleCharges                        ▼

   Private Sub calcScaleCharges()
       Dim vtArrVehicles As Variant, lnLastCol As Long, ws As Worksheet, _
              lnLastRow As Long, lnDataStartRow As Long, lnOffsetRow As Long
       Set ws = m_wbImport.Worksheets(1)
       vtArrVehicles = ws.UsedRange
       lnLastRow = UBound(vtArrVehicles, 1)
       lnLastCol = UBound(vtArrVehicles, 2)
       lnDataStartRow = Me.tbDataStartRow.Value

       lnOffsetRow = 0
       If lnDataStartRow = 1 Then lnOffsetRow = 1

       If Me.rbNewList.Value Then
           ReDim vtArrExport(1 To lnLastRow + lnOffsetRow, 1 To mc_lnColumns + mc_lnExtraColumns)
       Else
           If Me.rbAppend.Value Then ReDim vtArrExport(1 To lnLastRow, 1 To mc_lnExtraColumns)
       End If

       If Me.rbNewList.Value Then Set m_wbNew = Workbooks.Add

       Dim lnRow As Long
       For lnRow = lnDataStartRow To lnLastRow
           populateCalculator vtArrVehicles, lnRow
           addItems vtArrExport, lnRow, lnOffsetRow
       Next lnRow

       m_rgCalc.Value2 = vbNullString

       If Me.rbNewList.Value Then
           newListFinalize vtArrExport, lnLastRow, lnOffsetRow
       Else
           If Me.rbAppend.Value Then appendToListFinalize vtArrExport, ws, lnLastCol, lnLastRow
       End If
   End Sub
```

Figure 18-18: The calcScaleCharges sub-routine (fmImportAndCalculate form code)

In Figure 18-19 the **populateCalculator** sub-routine fills in the input cells on the
ScaleChargeCalculator worksheet. The routine works as follows:

- o Declare counter and numerical column indicator.
- o Clear the current input cells, stored as a single range.
- o Traverse the array of defined name string references and use the numerical column label caption to store the column reference.
- o If the column reference is valid (greater than zero) use it to store the correct value from the import list array for the current row to the calculator input box.

```
(General)                                          populateCalculator

    Private Sub populateCalculator(vtArrVehicles As Variant, lnRow As Long)
        ' Declare counter and numeric column indicator, then clear calculator input cells.
        Dim lnCount As Long, lnCol As Long
        m_rgCalc.Value2 = vbNullString
        'Traverse calculator input cells.
        For lnCount = 1 To mc_lnColumns
            ' Make up and store the label caption (numerical column indicator).
            lnCol = val(Me("lb" & m_stArrCol(lnCount) & "No").Caption)
            ' Check that column is a number i.e. > 0.
            Select Case lnCol
                Case Is > 0
                    ' Copy vehicle list column item to calculator input cell.
                    m_wsCalc.Range(m_stArrCol(lnCount)).Value2 = vtArrVehicles(lnRow, lnCol)
            End Select
        Next lnCount
    End Sub
```

Figure 18-19: The populateCalculator sub-routine (fmImportAndCalculate form code)

In Figure 18-20 the **addItems** sub-routine calls the appropriate sub-routine based on which one (and only one) of the radio button selections has the value of **true** as follows:

- o Calls the **addNewWorkbook** sub-routine for creating individual workbooks for each item.
- o Calls the **addNewWorksheetItem** sub-routine for adding items to a new list.
- o Calls the **addVATItems** sub-routine for appending to the import list.

```
(General)                                          addItems

    ' Add items according to option selected on form.

    Private Sub addItems(vtArrExport As Variant, lnRow As Long, lnOffsetRow As Long)
        If Me.rbNewWorkbooks.Value Then
            ' Add new workbook, one for each item in list.
            addNewWorkbook
        Else
            If Me.rbNewList.Value Then
                ' Add item to new list.
                addNewWorksheetItem vtArrExport, lnRow + lnOffsetRow
            Else
                ' Append item to additional columns in imported list.
                addVATItems vtArrExport, lnRow, 0
            End If
        End If
    End Sub
```

Figure 18-20: The addItems sub-routine (fmImportAndCalculate form code)

In Figure 18-21 the **addNewWorkbook** sub-routine works as follows:

- o Sets a reference to (**m_wbNew**) and adds a new workbook.
- o Copies the calculator worksheet (**m_wsCalc**) as the first sheet in the new workbook.
- o Where the **ID** input cell is not empty (string reference to which is stored in **m_stArrCol(1)**) use it as the workbook name, then save and close it.

```
(General)                                        addNewWorkbook

  ' Add new workbook for an item on the list.
  ' Only save and close workbooks which have an ID (leave others open for saving later).

  Private Sub addNewWorkbook()
      ' Set reference to and add a new workbook.
      Set m_wbNew = Workbooks.Add

      ' Copy the calculator worksheet as the first sheet in the new workbook.
      m_wsCalc.Copy before:=m_wbNew.Sheets(1)

      ' Save and close with ID as workbook name if ID cell is NOT empty.
      If Not IsEmpty(Range(m_stArrCol(1)).Value2) Then
          m_wbNew.SaveAs m_wsCalc.Range(m_stArrCol(1))
          m_wbNew.Close
      End If
  End Sub
```

Figure 18-21: The addNewWorkbook sub-routine (fmImportAndCalculate form code)

Figure 18-22 shows the **addNewWorksheetItem** sub-routine which works as follows:

- o Traverse the calculator input cells and save each value to the corresponding location in the export array (**vtArrExport**).
- o Call the **addVATItems** sub-routine to add the extra scale charge VAT cells to the other columns in the export array.

```
(General)                                        addNewWorksheetItem

  ' Add item to worksheet of new workbook (option 2 - new list).

  Private Sub addNewWorksheetItem(vtArrExport As Variant, lnRow As Long)

      ' Declare counter and traverse calculator input cells.
      ' Copy each cell to new column entry in export array.
      Dim lnCount As Long
      For lnCount = 1 To mc_lnColumns
          vtArrExport(lnRow, lnCount) = m_wsCalc.Range(m_stArrCol(lnCount)).Value2
      Next lnCount

      ' Add VAT info columns (same as for imported list).
      addVATItems vtArrExport, lnRow, mc_lnColumns
  End Sub
```

Figure 18-22: The addNewWorksheetItem sub-routine (fmImportAndCalculate form code)

In Figure 18-23 the **addVATItems** is called both to add to the new list and for appending to the import list. Each value from the calculator VAT cells is added to the corresponding extra columns in the **vtArrExport** array.

```
(General)                                    ▼    addVATItems                              ▼

' Add calculator worksheet scale charge VAT cells to row of export array.
' (used by new list and imported list).

Private Sub addVATItems(vtArrExport As Variant, lnRow As Long, lnLastCol As Long)
    vtArrExport(lnRow, lnLastCol + 1) = m_wsCalc.Range("CO2_Band").Value2
    vtArrExport(lnRow, lnLastCol + 2) = m_wsCalc.Range("InclusiveY").Value2
    vtArrExport(lnRow, lnLastCol + 3) = m_wsCalc.Range("VATY").Value2
    vtArrExport(lnRow, lnLastCol + 4) = m_wsCalc.Range("ExclusiveY").Value2
    vtArrExport(lnRow, lnLastCol + 5) = m_wsCalc.Range("InclusiveQ").Value2
    vtArrExport(lnRow, lnLastCol + 6) = m_wsCalc.Range("VATQ").Value2
    vtArrExport(lnRow, lnLastCol + 7) = m_wsCalc.Range("ExclusiveQ").Value2
    vtArrExport(lnRow, lnLastCol + 8) = m_wsCalc.Range("InclusiveM").Value2
    vtArrExport(lnRow, lnLastCol + 9) = m_wsCalc.Range("VATM").Value2
    vtArrExport(lnRow, lnLastCol + 10) = m_wsCalc.Range("ExclusiveM").Value2
End Sub
```

Figure 18-23: The addVATtItems sub-routine (fmImportAndCalculate form code)

Figure 18-24 shows the **newListFinalize** sub-routine which:

- o Adds titles for the calculator input cells to the **vtArrExport** array.
- o Adds extra titles for the scale charges.
- o Formats the final worksheet.

```
(General)                                    ▼    newListFinalize                         ▼

' Finalize creation of new list.

Private Sub newListFinalize(vtArrExport As Variant, _
                lnLastRow As Long, lnOffsetRow As Long)

    ' Declare counter and traverse string reference array.
    Dim lnCount As Long
    For lnCount = 1 To mc_lnColumns
        ' Copy calculator input cell titles (stored in array) to
        ' row 1 of export array.
        vtArrExport(1, lnCount) = m_stArrCol(lnCount)
    Next lnCount

    ' Add additional titles from first scale charge VAT column title onwards..
    ' Note: Also used by append list so pass last column as argument.
    addExtraTitles vtArrExport, mc_lnColumns + 1

    ' Copy export array to worksheet, then make titles bold, format currency columns
    ' & autofit range.
    formatFinalWorksheet m_wbNew.Worksheets(1), vtArrExport, 1, _
        lnLastRow + lnOffsetRow, mc_lnColumns + mc_lnExtraColumns, mc_lnColumns + 2, True

End Sub
```

Figure 18-24: The newListFinalize sub-routine (fmImportAndCalculate form code)

The **appendToListFinalize** sub-routine shown in Figure 18-25 works as follows:

- o If there is header row the **addExtraTitles** sub-routine is called as extra titles are required.
- o An attempt is made to unprotect the worksheet, in case it is protected (possibly with a password).
- o If the attempt to unprotect is successful, the **formatFinalWorksheet** sub-routine is called to format the worksheet.
- o If it is not possible to unprotect the worksheet, an error message is displayed.

```
(General)                                          appendToListFinalize

' Finalize append to import list.

Private Sub appendToListFinalize(vtArrExport As Variant, ws As Worksheet, _
        lnLastCol As Long, lnLastRow As Long)

    ' Add extra titles to array which are appended so start at column 1.
    If Me.tbDataStartRow.Value > 1 Then addExtraTitles vtArrExport, 1

    ' Now Unprotect sheet just in case, copy export array and autofit extra columns.
    On Error Resume Next
        ws.Unprotect
    On Error GoTo 0
    If Not ws.ProtectContents Then
        ' Copy export data to worksheet, format currency columns.
        formatFinalWorksheet ws, vtArrExport, lnLastCol + 1, lnLastRow, _
                lnLastCol + mc_lnExtraColumns, lnLastCol + 2, Me.tbDataStartRow.Value > 1
    Else
        MsgBox "Worksheet you are trying to append to is password protected"
    End If
End Sub
```

Figure 18-25: The appendToListFinalize sub-routine (fmImportAndCalculate form code)

In Figure 18-26 the **addExtraTitles** sub-routine is called to add the titles for the scale charge additional columns to the **vtArrExport** array.

```
(General)                                          addExtraTitles

' Add additional column titles.

Private Sub addExtraTitles(vtArrExport As Variant, lnStartCol As Long)
    vtArrExport(1, lnStartCol) = "CO2_Band"
    vtArrExport(1, lnStartCol + 1) = "Inclusive Year"
    vtArrExport(1, lnStartCol + 2) = "VAT Year"
    vtArrExport(1, lnStartCol + 3) = "Exclusive Year"
    vtArrExport(1, lnStartCol + 4) = "Inclusive Qtr"
    vtArrExport(1, lnStartCol + 5) = "VAT Qtr"
    vtArrExport(1, lnStartCol + 6) = "Exclusive Qtr"
    vtArrExport(1, lnStartCol + 7) = "Inclusive Month"
    vtArrExport(1, lnStartCol + 8) = "VAT Month"
    vtArrExport(1, lnStartCol + 9) = "Exclusive Month"
End Sub
```

Figure 18-26: The addExtraTitles sub-routine (fmImportAndCalculate form code)

Figure 18-27 shows the **formatFinalWorksheet** sub-routine which works as follows:

- o The range specified on the new or existing worksheet (according to whether it is a new list or append to existing list option) is populated with the **vtArrExport** array contents.
- o If there is a header row, this is made bold.
- o The scale charge columns (excluding the CO_2 band) are formatted as the currency type.
- o The columns autofit option is called to improve the look of each column.

```
(General)                                    formatFinalWorksheet

' Format finalized worksheet.
' Copy export array to specified location on worksheet,
' make title bold (if there are any), format currency columns and then autofit columns.

Private Sub formatFinalWorksheet(ws As Worksheet, vtArrExport As Variant, _
            lnBegCol As Long, lnEndRow As Long, lnEndCol As Long, _
            lnCurrCol As Long, boBold As Boolean)

    ' Format finalized worksheet (new or appended list)
    With ws
        ' Copy final export array to new range on worksheet.
        ' Range will vary accordingly (new list starting at column 1)
        ' Append list will begin after existing columns.
        .Range(.Cells(1, lnBegCol), .Cells(lnEndRow, lnEndCol)).Value2 = vtArrExport

        ' If this worksheet has titles then make them bold.
        If boBold Then .Range(.Cells(1, lnBegCol), .Cells(1, lnEndCol)).Font.Bold = True

        ' For scale charge VAT columns make them currency format.
        .Columns(lnCurrCol).Resize(, mc_lnExtraColumns - 1).NumberFormat = "£#,##0.00"

        ' Autofit the used range.
        .UsedRange.Columns.AutoFit
    End With
End Sub
```

Figure 18-27: The formatFinalWorksheet sub-routine (fmImportAndCalculate form code)

APPENDICES

APPENDICES

File types, size and performance

Figure A-1 shows the **file types** and is arranged based on **version** and **ability** to embed VBA macros.

Version	Macros	File extensions
97-2003	allowed	xla, xlm, xls, xlt
2007-2016	allowed	xlam, xlsb, xlsm, xltm, xltx
2007-2016	disallowed	xlsx
any	dll style add-in	xll

Figure A-1: File types

There are now a wide variety of file formats compared to earlier versions.

One of the major changes in later versions was the creation of file types which cannot contain macros and those that can (see Figure A-2).

Format	Purpose
xlsb	Binary Workbook for 2007-2010
xlsm	Macro-Enabled Workbook for 2007-2016
xlam	XML based macro enabled Add-In format for 2007-2010
xltm	Macro-Enabled Template 2007-2016
xla	Add-In for 97-2003
xls	Workbooks 97-2003 & 5.0/95
xlt	Template Binary Format for 97-2003

Figure A-2: Macro capable file types

XLS Format

The XLS format is the same format as in earlier versions with a limit of 256 columns and 65,536 rows. When saving a workbook in XLS format, a compatibility check is performed. File size is similar to earlier versions although performance may be impaired.

XLSB Format

XLSB is the binary format structured as a compressed folder that contains a large number of binary files. It is much more compact than the XLS format, the amount of compression dependent on the contents of the workbook and may open and close faster. With larger workbooks this format can reduce the size substantially.

XLSX Format

The XLSX format (the default) is a compressed folder that contains a number of XML files (changing the file name extension to .zip, allows the opening of the folder and its contents to be examined). Typically, the XLSX format creates larger files than the XLSB format but they are still significantly smaller than the XLS files. Opening and saving times may be longer than for XLSB files.

Macro Enabled (XLS, XLM, XLSM)

Originally files with macros were indistinguishable from those without but in newer releases this feature was changed so that files are now saved to different file formats, those with macros and those without. If macros are added to an existing file type which does not support macros, the workbook has to be re-saved in a format that will allow macros. A message to this effect is displayed, detailing the options available.

Templates (XLT, XLTM, XLTX)

Templates can be created using any of the valid formats, the older XLT format, the newer XLTX (without macros) or XLTM (with macros). Rather than copy an existing workbook for a similar task a template can be created and then changed accordingly.

Add-Ins (XLA, XLAM)

An add-in can be created by simply changing a workbook's **IsAddin** property from **False** to **True** and then re-saving the file. This process works in reverse, so that an add-in can be loaded and then changed back a standard workbook via the **IsAddin** property.

Alternatively, a workbook can be saved as type **Excel Add-in**.

Note: By default, add-ins may be saved to the user's **AppData/Roaming/Microsoft/AddIns** folder. This should be changed to a more appropriate network folder if being made available to other users.

Abbreviations

Figure A-3 details the **abbreviations** used throughout the document.

Term	Details
ALT	Alt key (alt)
COM	Component Object Model
CTRL	Control key (ctrl)
CSV	Comma Separated Variable
END	End key
ENTER	Enter key (⏎)
F9	Function 9 key (Fn9)
F11	Function 11 key (Fn11)
IDE	Integrated Development Environment
SHIFT	Shift key (⇧)
UDF	User Defined Function
VB	Visual Basic
VBA	Visual Basic for Applications
VBE	Visual Basic Editor
VSTO	Visual Studio Tools for Office
XL	Microsoft Excel

Figure A-3: Abbreviations used in document

Application cursors and buttons

Application cursors change according to their current position and usage (Figure A-4).

Cursor Function	Image
Menu select mode	
Cells select mode	
Click and drag - shapes	
Auto fill – cells and positioning of shapes	
Resize column	
Resize row	
Text select	
Shape resize vertical	
Shape resize horizontal	
Shape resize diagonal (top right/bottom left)	
Shape resize diagonal (top left/bottom right)	
Close button	

Figure A-4: Application cursor types

VBA coding and naming conventions

Other the years many coding standards have developed with particular emphasis on the VBA language including the use of Hungarian Notation, the Reddick VBA Naming Conventions and Microsoft's own guides.

Throughout this document the author has used standards developed over his own forty years or more of programming in numerous languages, some of which coincide with those of others.

When declarations are made to VBA entities such as a variable or object there should always be a definitive syntax used to recognise the purpose of the entity.

For example, syntax such as the following could be used:
- o   Data type naming: **[scope][data type]DataNameOne**
- o   Procedural naming (camelCase): **proceduralNameOne**
- o   Module naming: **ModuleNameOne**

When naming a sub-routine or function using **camelCase** identifies user defined elements from VBA reserved words and thus easier to identify in code.

Within the VBA language there are different levels of **Scope**, the naming conventions used in this document are shown in Figure A-5.

Scope	Prefix	Purpose
Global	g_	Variable available everywhere in project
Module	m_	Variable available everywhere in module
Local		Only available at procedural level so no prefix required

Figure A-5: Scoping of variables

Data types are declared starting with the statement:
- o   Public – global level
- o   Private – module level
- o   Dim – procedural level

Constants are used for variables whose value does not change and scoped as in Figure A-6 and are declared with either **Public** or **Private** before the **Const** statement.

Scope	Prefix	Purpose
Global	gc_	Constant variable available everywhere in project
Module	mc_	Constant variable available everywhere in module

Figure A-5: Scoping of constant variables

Common primitive data types and their prefixes are shown in Figure A-6.

Data type	Prefix	Data type	Prefix
Boolean (true or false)	bo	Long (long integer)	ln
Byte	by	LongPtr (Long pointer)	lp
Currency	cu	Single (single precision)	si
Date	dt	String (text string)	st
Double (double precision)	db	Variant (default data type)	vt
Integer (short integer)	it		

Figure A-6: Common primitive data type prefixes

Note: Within the VBA language the use of the loop is common for traversing arrays or other types of item collection. With modern hardware the **Integer** data type is somewhat redundant in many scenarios. For flexibility, a larger range of values and consistency using the **Long** data type as a counter will cater for nearly all eventualities.

Form and worksheet control prefixes are shown in Figure A-7.

Control	Prefix	Control	Prefix
CheckBox	cb	MultiPage	mp
ComboBox	co	OptionButton	rb
CommandButton	bn	RefEdit	re
Form	fm	ScrollBar	sc
Frame	fr	SpinButton	sb
Image	im	TabStrip	ts
ImageList	il	TextBox	tb
Label	lb	ToggleButton	tg
ListBox	li	TreeView	tv

Figure A-7: Form and worksheet common control prefixes

Note: The **Me** reference is used with controls in the VBA code to more readily indicate their origin.

Prefixes used for common objects are shown in Figure A-8.

Objects	Prefix	Objects	Prefix
Application object	app	Name	nm
Code module	cm	Object (unknown type)	ob
VB component	cp	Reference	rf
VBE editor object	ed	Range object	rg
File dialog	fd	VBProject	vbp
Hyperlink	hl	Workbook object	wb
List object	lo	Worksheet object	ws

Figure A-8: Object prefixes

Miscellaneous prefixes are shown in Figure A-9.

Declartion	Prefix	Declartion	Prefix
Arrays (2nd prefix after data type)	Arr	Collection	cn
Class (user defined)	cls	Event handler (WithEvents)	eh

Figure A-9: Miscellaneous prefixes

Note: When defining UDFs for use as additional worksheet functions it is advisable to use a unique prefix to easily identify them. For example, a prefix such as "**uf**" (user function) or something to identify the company or group using them i.e. "**au**" for Audit Department. Using the same prefix will also keep them together in the intellisense list presented when typing the first few characters of a worksheet function.